Harrington on
Cash Games: Volume II

How to Play
No-Limit Hold 'em Cash Games

By
DAN HARRINGTON
1995 World Champion

BILL ROBERTIE

A product of
Two Plus Two Publishing LLC

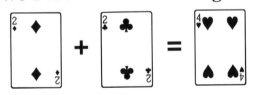

FIRST EDITION

Creel Printers, Inc.
Las Vegas, Nevada

Printed in the United States of America

Harrington on
Cash Games: Volume II
How to Play No-Limit Hold 'em Cash Games
COPYRIGHT © 2008 Two Plus Two Publishing LLC

For information contact: **Two Plus Two Publishing LLC**
32 Commerce Center Drive
Suite H-89
Henderson, NV 89014

ISBN: 1-880685-43-4
ISBN13: 978-1-880685-43-3

"Opportunity may knock, but it seldom nags."

— *David Mamet*

Table of Contents

i

About Dan Harrington

Dan Harrington began playing poker professionally in 1982. On the circuit he is known as "Action Dan," an ironic reference to his solid but effective style. He has won several major no-limit hold 'em tournaments including the European Poker Championships (1995), the $2,500 No-Limit Hold 'em event at the 1995 World Series of Poker, and the Four queens No-Limit Hold 'em Championship (1996).

Dan began his serious games-playing with chess, where he quickly became a master and one of the strongest players in the New England area. In 1972 he won the Massachusetts Chess Championship, ahead of most of the top players in the area. In 1976 he started playing backgammon, a game which he also quickly mastered. He was soon one of the top money players in the Boston area, and in 1981 he won the World Cup of Backgammon in Washington D.C., ahead of a field that included most of the world's top players.

He first played in the $10,000 No-Limit Hold 'em Championship Event of the World Series of Poker in 1987. He has played in the Championship a total of 15 times and has reached the final table in four of those tournaments, an amazing record. Besides winning the World Championship in 1995, he finished sixth in 1987, third in 2003, and fourth in 2004. In 2006 he finished second at the Doyle Brunson North American Championships at the Bellagio, while in 2007 he won the Legends of Poker Tournament at the Bicycle Club. He is widely recognized as one of the greatest and most respected no-limit hold 'em players, as well as a feared opponent in both no-limit and limit hold 'em side games. He lives in Santa Monica where he is a partner in Anchor Loans, a real estate business.

About Bill Robertie

Bill Robertie has spent his life playing and writing about chess, backgammon, and now poker. He began playing chess as a boy, inspired by Bobby Fischer's feats on the international chess scene. While attending Harvard as an undergraduate, he became a chess master and helped the Harvard chess team win several intercollegiate titles. After graduation he won a number of chess tournaments, including the United States Championship at speed chess in 1970. He also established a reputation at blindfold chess, giving exhibitions on as many as eight boards simultaneously.

In 1976 he switched from chess to backgammon, becoming one of the top players in the world. His major titles include the World Championship in Monte Carlo in 1983 and 1987, the Black & White Championship in Boston in 1979, the Las Vegas Tournaments in 1980 and 2001, the Bahamas Pro-Am in 1993, and the Istanbul World Open in 1994.

He has written several well-regarded backgammon books, the most noted of which are *Advanced Backgammon* (1991), a two-volume collection of 400 problems, and *Modern Backgammon* (2002), a new look at the underlying theory of the game. He has also written a set of three books for the beginning player: *Backgammon for Winners* (1994), *Backgammon for Serious Players* (1995), and *501 Essential Backgammon Problems* (1997).

From 1991 to 1998 he edited the magazine *Inside Backgammon* with Kent Goulding. He owns a publishing company, the Gammon Press (www.thegammonpress.com), and lives in Arlington, Massachusetts with his wife Patrice.

Part Six

Tight-Aggressive Turn Play

Tight-Aggressive Turn Play

Introduction

By the time you reach the turn, four of the five board cards have been dealt. Only one card remains to come. You know what you have, and it's pretty easy to calculate what you *could* have when the river card comes. If you have a made hand, you know just how much value you have, and you know exactly how many drawing cards can help you.

You also know a lot about the other hands. First of all, there probably aren't many players left at this point. Even if several players saw the flop, by now only one or perhaps two are left. You saw what they did preflop, and you saw what they did after the flop, so you should have been able to reduce their potential hands to a few key possibilities.

But the most important feature of turn play is that only one card remains to come. This feature has a number of important implications. Let's take a look at the main implications and see how they affect checking, betting, and calling on the turn.

Characteristics
of Play on the Turn

As just mentioned, the turn is different from the two previous rounds and thus requires a different set of strategies. So to start, let's understand what makes the turn unique.

Characteristic No. 1: An advantage is more significant. Being ahead on the turn is a much bigger advantage than being ahead on the flop. With only one card to come, any hand that trails on the turn has about half the chance of drawing out as the same hand on the flop. Here's a few common situations with the associated chances for the flop and the turn:

	After the Flop	After the Turn
Low pair versus high pair	10%	5%
Two overcards versus underpair	24%	13%
Two low cards versus two high cards	26%	14%
Flush draw versus high pair	38%	20%
Open-ended straight draw versus high pair	34%	18%

Characteristic No. 2: It's hard to get the pot odds to draw.
From the table above, it's obvious that getting the proper
expressed pot odds needed to draw at a hand on the turn is very
difficult. If you know you're trailing, almost any reasonably-sized
bet will price you out of the pot unless you believe you have
substantial implied odds.

**Characteristic No. 3: If on a draw, the texture of the board
determines your willingness to call a turn bet.** Since you need
implied odds to make draws playable, your willingness to call
with a draw depends on just how hidden the draw is. If you have

and the board is

the arrival of a fourth diamond on the river will probably freeze all
action.

But if your hand is

and the board is

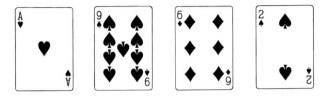

the arrival of a ten or five on the river usually won't be taken very seriously; your straight is too well concealed. If you're against a set of aces or nines, you may very well win his entire stack when you make your straight.

When you're drawing to a well-concealed straight, and you think your opponent is betting a made hand, you still need to pay attention to any flush draws, as they can limit your implied odds. In the previous example, for instance, your straight is much stronger if the flop was A♥9♠6♦ and the 2♠ came on the turn; in that case you won't be given credit for a flush draw. But if the flop was A♥9♠2♠ and the 6♦ came on the turn, your implied odds go down. If the T♠ hits on the river, your opponent may think you just hit a flush rather than a straight and refuse to pay you off!

Characteristic No. 4: Value bets have higher equity. Since your opponent has less chance to catch up when behind, it follows that value bets on the turn are inherently stronger than similar bets on the flop. That doesn't necessarily imply that you want to bet the turn with a strong hand. Depending on how you read the situation, you may want to check the turn and bet the river if you feel a river bet has a significantly better chance of being called.

Characteristic No. 5: Pot commitment starts to play a role. If you made large bets (approximately pot-sized) both preflop and on the flop, another large bet on the turn may commit you to the pot. This is especially true if either you or your main opponent in the hand started with a stack less than 100 big blinds.

Sample Hand

You're playing in a $5-$10 live game. Your stack is $800. You pick up

in first position and raise to $30. Player D in fourth position with a stack of $1,000 and Player F in sixth position with a stack of $1,200 both call your raise. The blinds fold. The pot is $105.

The flop is

You act first and bet $100, slightly less than the pot. Player D folds but Player F calls. The pot is now $305. Your stack now contains $670, and your opponent easily has you covered.

The turn is the 9♥. *Should you bet, and if so, how much?*

Whether to bet is very difficult and depends on what you know, if anything, about your opponent. Let's leave it aside for now and look at how big a bet should be.

If you make a pot-sized bet, you're now committing yourself to the pot. Let's take a look at the numbers. The pot is $305, so if you make a pot-sized bet of $300, the pot becomes $605 and your stack shrinks to $370. If your opponent now puts you all-in (by pushing $670 into the pot), the pot is $1,275 and you have to put in your last $370 to call. Your pot odds are 1,275-to-370, or just under 3.5-to-1. Can you fold an overpair getting 3.5-to-1?

Against an unknown opponent, the answer is "probably not." If you knew your opponent well and thought he couldn't make this move without a set or at least top two pair, then you could probably let the hand go.

You could give yourself more options by modifying your bet size. Suppose, for instance, you decide to bet half the pot rather than the whole pot on the turn. Now you're betting $150 and your stack still has $520 left. If your opponent now puts you all-in, the pot will be $1,125 and it will cost you $520 to call. Those are odds of 2.2-to-1, giving you an easier chance to walk away.

Should you bet at all? Given the strength of your hand, checking is probably a better option. The basic "small hand, small pot" rule applies here. Your hand is only an overpair, the pot is almost half your remaining stack, and if your opponent is trailing he has few outs. Simply checking the turn, keeping the pot small, and then betting the river when a blank comes is a more prudent choice.

Balancing Bet
Sizing and Pot Commitment

From our previous discussion, it's clear that turn bets involve a certain tension. If you have correctly analyzed the hand, you'd like to make a large value bet since your opponent, if behind, has little chance of catching up. But the larger the bet you make, the more likely you're committing yourself to the pot, which could be a disaster if you've misjudged the hand and you're actually behind.

The solution is to remember that you don't need to make a big bet to deny your opponent calling odds on the turn. Even when your opponent is drawing to a straight or flush, a modest bet is enough to make his call incorrect unless he has implied odds. You can also check the turn, since failing to bet when your opponent has few outs is not a big mistake.

Reasons for
Betting the Turn

Having looked at some general aspects of turn play, let's get more specific and consider some of the specific reasons for betting, checking, and bluffing. We'll start with the reasons for betting the turn.

Reason No. 1: Bet because you have a hand and you checked the flop. On some occasions you will flop a good hand (top pair or even better) but decline to bet on the flop. Perhaps you were out of position and wanted to give someone a chance to bet so you could raise, but no one bet. Or perhaps you acted before a preflop aggressor who you expected to make a continuation bet, but he didn't. Or perhaps you recognized that you have to check a few good hands so that your checked hands have a balanced mix of strong and weak hands, and this happened to be one of the hands you checked.

There are several reasons for sometimes not betting good hands on the flop. But what if you checked the flop and still have what looks like a good hand after the turn card arrives (or the turn card made you a hand)?

In this case, you will mostly, but not always, bet if you're first to act or the hand is checked to you. The reason is pretty simple: You probably have the best hand, and no one else has shown they have anything. In addition, the turn card will tend to put more draws on board, and you'd like to deny any possible draws a free card or proper drawing odds. (Of course, that's much easier to do on the turn since the draws have only one card left to make their hand.) Finally, if one of your opponents has a hand that's worse than yours but callable, you'd like to get some money in the pot. It's possible that your opponent is willing to call both a turn and river bet with his hand, in which case you'd like to get the ball rolling.

Assuming you checked the flop with a good hand and reach a situation where you could bet on the turn, how often should you do so? The best general answer is "Mostly, but not always." I bet about 75 to 80 percent of the time in this situation. You can't bet 100 percent of the time because you need to save a very few of your good or great hands and actually check them all the way to the river before you bet. In that way, your opponents will gradually understand that just because you've checked both the flop and the turn, it doesn't mean that you couldn't still be sitting there with a big hand.

For the vast majority of players, two consecutive checks (flop and turn) means "I have a weak hand, you can take the pot away if you want." You're going to have to check some hands you'd like to bet to avoid being one of those players.

Reason No. 2: Bet because you don't have a hand and you checked the flop. When everyone checks the flop, you have some good information that no one has much of a hand. In that case, you should be making some bets on the turn to steal the pot even if your own hand didn't improve.

Since you don't always bet the flop with your good hands, your bluffs on the turn are partly shielded by the good hands you're betting now (as described in Reason No. 1).

Reason No. 3: Bet as a double-barreled continuation/value bet. A few years ago, the idea of the continuation bet was not well-known outside of a circle of veteran players. Most players bet the flop when they hit it, and checked when they missed it. Now, the continuation bet is common currency among many players.

The continuation bet has itself spawned a counter-move, particularly among aggressive players in weaker cash games or tournaments. Since you can't tell if a flop bet represents real value or just a continuation bet bluff, just call all (most of) the bets when you have position. Then see if your opponent bets again on the turn. Since weak-tight players won't usually bet twice with a bluff, fold if they bet a second time, and bet if they check. Since they will mostly check (because most hands miss most flops, or because their original bet represented a weak hand like bottom pair), you'll win this maneuver most of the time.

This strategy, in turn, allows a counter-strategy. Fire a second barrel on the turn. This bet announces, "My hand was a big pair when I raised preflop, and my flop bet was for real, and I've still got that big hand and I'm coming after your whole stack, suckah!" Since many of the players who call your flop bet either have marginal hands (like second pair) or are calling to take the pot away on the turn, firing a second barrel when you miss the flop will take down most of those pots.

To make this play work, you will need to balance it by also firing a second barrel on the turn when you have a real hand and have bet on the flop. This is the double-barreled value bet.

These plays benefit strongly from some knowledge of your opponent. Ideally, you'd like to have seen him execute the flop call/turn bet maneuver on at least a couple of occasions in the past, so you know there's a chance he's not just calling with his good hands.

Reason No. 4: Bet because your opponent has a draw. If you have a good hand and there's a potential draw on board, there are actually three reasons to bet the turn.

The first is to deny the drawer the odds he needs to call. On the turn, that's not hard to do. By the turn you've seen six cards, leaving 46 in the deck. If he has a draw with 11 outs, his odds against making the draw are 35-to-11, or just over 3-to-1 against. If you bet half the pot, you're giving him just 3-to-1 to call, so you've succeeded in your purpose. If you bet the full pot, you're giving him only 2-to-1 odds to draw. (We'll ignore implied odds for the time being. He may have implied odds which make the draw worthwhile, but he can never be sure if he does or not.)

The second reason is the most basic of all: To just get your money in the pot while you're a favorite. If you have a made hand and he is drawing, you're a favorite. Consistently getting your money in when this is the case, is one of the keys to winning no-limit hold 'em.

The third reason is a crucial no-limit idea, and deserves its own section.

Reason No. 5: Bet before the 'Cooler' comes. The last reason for betting into a draw, and one of the most overlooked, is betting before the cooler card arrives.

The basic idea here is pretty simple. You have a very good hand. You already bet the flop. Your opponent has called. There is a potential draw on board.

You assume that your opponent called because he's drawing. But that's not the only, or most likely reason. He may have a medium strength hand that's not as good as yours. He thinks you may be bluffing, so he doesn't want to fold. But he also thinks you may have the draw, and be semi-bluffing.

Now what happens when a card comes that seems to fill the draw? You don't want to bet, because he'll raise if he hit the draw and fold otherwise. But he doesn't want to bet for the same reason. No one hit their draw, but the card froze all action. We call that card a 'cooler.' If you have a good hand but your opponent might or might not have a draw, the 'cooler' variation gives you another reason to bet the turn.

Reason No. 6: Bet to set up the all-in on the river. When you have a monster hand and think your opponent has a big hand, but not as good as yours, you may need to bet the turn to make sure you can get all-in on the river without a massive overbet of the pot. This can be a delicate process. You will have to show strength, but you don't want to show so much strength that your opponent suspects the worst and makes a great laydown. The deeper the stacks, the more carefully you have to calculate the hand to make sure all the money goes in.

Sample Hand

You're in a live game in Las Vegas. Blinds are $10 and $20. This hand, you're in the big blind. You're a loose-aggressive player, and the other players at the table, who are a mixture of loose and tight players, should be aware of that fact by now. You've had a good session, and after three hours your stack has tripled to about $6,200.

Player C, in third position, is a fine player. His style is mostly tight-aggressive, but he mixes in just enough deceptive hands to make himself very dangerous and very hard to read. His stack is $3,400.

You're not too sure about the small blind. You've never seen him before and he seems a little wacky.

The first two players fold. Player C calls $20. Everyone else folds to the small blind, who completes the bet for $10. The pot is $60. You have

and reasonably elect to check.

The flop is

giving you a straight. The small blind bets $60. Now comes your first big decision. How do you handle the straight?

Your first inclination should be to raise. There are three important reasons for raising here:

1. You have the second nuts (only seven-five beats you) and one player has already shown interest in the pot. The initial limper hasn't had a chance to act yet. It's reasonable to think that a raise may get called.

2. You're a loose-aggressive player which means you're betting and raising more than your fair share of weak hands. To achieve balance, you need to bet and raise a higher percentage of your strong hands than a tight player would.

3. There's a spade draw on board, and you have two opponents. You need to charge anyone who's drawing to a flush.

Those are all solid reasons. You raise to $200. The pot is now $320. Player C calls $200. The small blind folds. The pot is now $520.

So the small blind was just making a stab at the pot, but Player C has some real interest in the hand. Since he limped in relatively early position, we need to think a bit about what he might have. Here's a brief catalog of his possible holdings:

1. **An overpair:** Possible but not likely. The preflop limp was a trap, hoping to get raised. Post-flop, however, the overpair needs to be worried about all the flush and straight draws. With two limpers in the blinds, the low straight draws are more likely than in a normal hand. The overpair certainly wouldn't fold yet, but might have raised to define his situation a little better.

2. **A set:** Almost certainly not. The preflop limp with a low pair is fine. But the set has to raise post-flop with two players already betting and a dangerous, draw-heavy board.

3. **Two pair:** Fits in the same category as the overpair, possible but not likely. A tight but deceptive player could limp with the occasional four-three or six-four in early/middle position. Post-flop, the two pair might raise to see if they were against a made hand or a draw.

4. **Top pair:** Not likely. This requires an early limp with something like ace-six, seven-six, or eight-six, followed by a call of a bet and a raise. The only hand that makes sense is six-five, with top pair and a straight draw.

5. **A flush draw:** Possible. Perhaps he limped with something like A♠J♠ or K♠Q♠, and now has a flush draw with a couple of overcards that just might be good. That would justify the call.

6. **A straight draw:** Possible. He could have limped with ace-five suited, or six-five or five-four, then called the flop bet with a pair plus a straight draw or just the draw itself.

7. **A made straight:** It's just bad luck if he limped with seven-five and flopped the nut straight.

The most likely hands are the flush and straight draws, perhaps with a pair as well. The two pair and overpair hands are in a less likely category.

The turn card is the Q♣. No spade and no straight card leaves you in good shape. You should still have the best hand, and he should still be drawing.

You need to bet now because it may be your last chance to make money on the hand. If our analysis is correct and he's drawing to a flush, look what happens on the river. If the flush card hits, you're going to check, and he's going to bet if he hit the flush, and check otherwise. So you don't make any money.

But suppose our analysis is a little off, and he's been playing with a set or an overcard or two pair. Now he thinks that you may be the one drawing to the flush (or perhaps the straight). If the draw hits, he doesn't want to put any more money in the pot.

This is a common situation in no-limit hold 'em. The board is draw-heavy, and both sides can be in the position of fearing the other side is drawing. In that case, if you believe you are the favorite and the other side is drawing, you have to bet the turn because a 'cooler' card may come that freezes all action on the river.

In this case, you believe you have the best hand, and you think he may be drawing to beat you, so you have to bet. In fact, you bet $600. Player C calls. The pot becomes $1,720.

The river is the 7♠. That's the worst possible card that could hit. If he was drawing to a flush, he hit. If he had a five and was drawing to a straight, he also hit (although now you tie him with the same straight.) So you can't bet.

You check. He checks behind and shows 6♦4♦ for two pair. You take the pot.

He had two pair and thought you were possibly drawing at the flush. You though he was possibly drawing at the flush. If the cooler card hadn't come, you could have bet the river and might have won a little more money.

Beware the cooler! Bet the turn.

Bluffing on the Turn

Imagine the following hand. A couple of players limp from middle position, and you limp on the button with a hand like

The big blind hangs around.

The flop is nothing special,

The three players ahead of you all check. Should you bet to steal the pot, or not?

A lot of players bet here pretty routinely, counting on the fact that no one has shown strength yet, to take a pot that seems to be up for grabs. But I'm not excited about that play. It's an obvious play, and too vulnerable to someone who either slowplayed a reasonable hand, figuring someone would act behind him, or has a hand that he's happy to call a bet with, even though he doesn't really want to lead out. In my experience, trying to steal here is more or less just a break-even play.

The turn is a much better spot for stealing pots where the flop has missed everyone. Compared to the flop, two big things have happened: You've seen another round of action, and only one card remains to come, making most draws unplayable. Someone with a real hand mostly won't wait until the river to put in a bet. To have a chance of doing much more than pick up the blinds, he needs to start betting here. If no one acts in front of you on the turn, there's a very good chance you're not facing anything more than bottom pair or an underpair, a hand that can easily let the pot go.

Poker is fundamentally a game of patience and waiting for high-percentage situations, and this situation is a good example. Don't be in a hurry to bluff at pots on the flop; have the patience to wait a street, and you may be rewarded with a great situation rather than a marginal one.

Leverage on the Turn

All bluffs on the turn benefit from the idea of *leverage*, a concept first explained by Howard Lederer in his section of the *Full Tilt Poker Strategy Guide,* an outstanding book with much good advice. Although he defined the concept in the context of tournament play, it applies almost equally well to turn bets in cash games.

The idea is simple but powerful. When you bet on the turn, your opponent faces a dilemma; he doesn't really know what pot odds he's being offered. Although he might feel comfortable calling the turn bet, what if the turn bet is a prelude to a much larger bet on the river? Should the size of that potential river bet be factored into the calculations?

This leverage is especially potent if one of the players has reached the turn with a relatively small stack size.

Sample Hand

You're playing in a $5-$10 live game. The players are tight, smart, and aggressive. You've been whittled down to a stack of $660. In the next hand you're fourth to act.

Three players fold to you and you pick up

You reasonably raise to $30. The player in sixth position calls your $30. The hand folds to the big blind who calls $20. The pot is now $95, and you're in middle position after the flop.

The flop is

and you've hit top pair with a good kicker. The big blind checks and you bet $80. The player in sixth position folds, and the big blind calls. The pot is now $255. You have $550 left in your stack. The big blind has at least $1,500 left in his.

The turn is the A♣. The big blind fires out $150. *What do you do?*

The big blind is saying that the ace hit his hand. If he's telling the truth, you're beaten and you have only six outs on the river. If he's lying, you're a huge favorite, and it's even possible the big blind is drawing dead.

But here's the problem. The big blind knows if he's bluffing or not. If he's bluffing and you call, you probably won't win any more money on the river. But if he's not bluffing, he'll bet the rest of your stack, $400, on the river. You don't know if seeing your hand through to the end will cost you $150 or $550. He does know, and that's the essence of the leverage idea. His $150 is potentially a bet of your entire stack, and you have to call in a situation where he knows what's probably going to happen and you don't.

It's a tough situation with no purely correct answer. Against an "average" player, you would have to call this bet, and fold to a bet on the river despite the excellent pot odds. You would have to assume that you advertised your hand on the flop, and he wouldn't then make two bets on the turn and the river unless he had at least the ace. But of course, he probably knows that, and he would also know that a bluff on the river has a very high probability of success.

The leverage principle enhances the power of all turn bluffs. Pay careful attention to players who bet the turn aggressively, and try to find out how often they're bluffing. It's very useful knowledge.

Checking the Turn

Checking the turn is part of a complete no-limit strategy. You don't just check because your hand is poor and bet because you think you hold a powerhouse. You should check the turn for many strategic reasons. Let's examine some of them.

Reason No. 1: After a continuation bet. When you make a continuation bet after missing the flop, and you get called, you have a couple of choices on the turn. You can fire a second barrel and make another bet as we discussed previously. That's a high risk, high reward play. Or you can simply check, and give up on the hand. That minimizes your losses, but leaves you vulnerable to an aggressive player who is willing to call your flop bets and then try to take the pot away on the turn.

Reason No. 2: As a trap. One way to minimize your losses from checking on the turn with a continuation bet is to check the turn with some very strong hands. Now when an aggressive opponent calls the flop and tries to steal after you check the turn, you can respond with either a raise or a call. If you make both value bets and continuation bets on the flop, *trapping on the turn with a check is a vital move for your repertoire!* Otherwise, your continuation bets won't work frequently enough to be justified.

Reason No. 3: As a de-leveraging play. Earlier we discussed the power of *leverage*: making a bet on the turn which, if called, threatened your opponent with the possibility of calling an even bigger bet on the river. Since your opponent couldn't quantify his total risk on the hand, he was likely to fold a marginal hand rather than call the turn bet.

A leverage play is a great bluff. You know exactly what is happening. If your opponent calls your turn bet, you're not going to make that big bet on the river, or any other bet. Instead, you're going to concede the hand. But he can't know that, so his total risk may be his entire stack, and he's inclined to fold the hand.

Sometimes, however, your desire is exactly the opposite. You're sure you have the winning hand, and you think your opponent has enough value to put another bet in the pot, but probably not more than another bet. How do you get that last bet from him?

The answer may be a de-leveraging play. Instead of betting the turn, with its implied threat of a river bet to come, you check the turn and bet the river instead. Now your opponent can quantify his risk on the river; it's just the one bet he's facing. In that case, he may be willing to call, whereas he would have had to fold the turn bet. Plus, since you checked the turn, that may make him think your river bet is more likely to be a bluff. So he has even more incentive to call.

Reason No. 4: With a modest hand, but no draws for opponent. If you bet the flop with a marginal hand that nonetheless has some value (middle pair, bottom pair, or a pair in your hand below top pair), and got called, you will usually have to check the turn regardless of your position.

The operating principle here is "small hand, small pot." Your hope in betting the flop was that your opponent would fold, and when he doesn't, you've trapped yourself in a sense. Any more bets and the pot gets too big for your hand. Your goal is now to preserve what equity you have by seeing a cheap showdown. You might possibly call one more bet, but you'd like that bet to be on the river so you can see just how much money you'll need to commit. Betting on the turn defeats your own goal.

Note that this situation is fundamentally different from the case where you made a continuation bet on the flop with nothing. There you might consider firing again on the turn because it's your only chance to win the pot. If the hand goes to the showdown, you'll lose. But here you have a hand which might or might not win at showdown. Your goal is to get to that showdown as cheaply as possible, and see if you win it.

Reason No. 5: Bluff-catching hands. The last group of checking hands are the bluff-catchers. A bluff catcher is an unusual sort of hand. It's a hand with some value (usually a high-to-medium pair), with which you're willing to call a bet, but which you don't want to bet because, given how the hand has played up to that point, you will get a call from all the hands that beat you, but almost no hands that you can beat. In that case, you check the turn and hope to catch a bluff on the river.

Sample Hand

You're playing a live game, $5 and $10 blinds. You pick up

in second position. You've made a little money up to this point, and your stack has grown to $1,100. You raise to $30. You get a total of three callers, from positions 4, 5, and the button. The pot is $135.

The flop comes

There are no draws, so your top set looks pretty good. Players have been calling bets with marginal hands, so you decide to lead out and hope your move is interpreted by someone as a continuation bet.

You bet $70. The players in positions 4 and 5 fold, but the button calls $70. The pot is $275. Your stack is now $1,000, and as far as you can tell, the button has about $600 left.

The turn card is the 2♥. You assume the button has something, but probably not very much. If he thought you might be making a continuation bet, he might have called with middle pair or bottom pair, or something like a pair of nines. He likely doesn't have a queen because only one remains in the deck.

Suppose you make another half-pot bet, say $140. Now you've put the button in a very difficult position. Even if he thinks you're bluffing, will he really want to call? If he calls, the pot will be $555 and his stack will have shrunk to $460. You can easily put him all-in on the end and he'll need to invest his whole stack to see the hand through.

But if he has the kind of hand you think he does, he's not going to be interested to invest his whole stack just to see if you have a queen or not.

You need to lend him a hand here. Just check the turn, and give him a free pass to the river. Then bet your $140 or so. Now he knows the most he can lose, and you have shown weakness on the turn, so perhaps you're just trying to buy the pot on the end. He's much more likely to call this bet than the turn bet because you've de-leveraged the hand.

There's also a modest side bonus to this play. If he has a better hand than you suspect, he may take your turn check as weakness and bet, thus doing your job for you.

Handling Top Pair

The deeper you go into a hand, the better the holding you need to have in order to think you have the best hand. Preflop, a middle pair may well be best. On the flop, top pair top kicker will mostly be the best hand at the table. As you move from the flop to the turn, however, top pair needs to be reevaluated. The combination of the extra board card and the growing pot makes top pair an increasing vulnerable hand.

So how long should you stay with top pair, reasonable kicker? My rule of thumb is this:

> If you have shown consistent strength throughout the hand, and on the turn your opponent either bets into you or raises your bet, top pair is very unlikely to be good. Let the hand go.

Consistent strength refers to a scenario where you bet preflop, got called, and bet the flop and got called again. If your opponent now bets into you on the turn, or even worse, raises a bet by you, your top pair is in serious trouble.

Like all general rules in poker, you will have to violate this from time to time or risk being readable and easily exploited. But as a general rule, it's pretty useful. Except in a very weak game, strong betting action on the turn represents a hand better than top pair.

The Problems

Hand 6-1

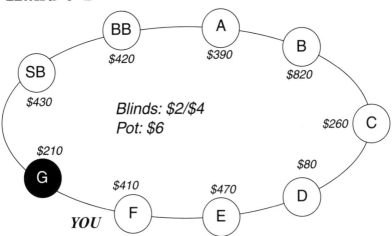

Blinds: $2/$4
Pot: $6

BB $420
A $390
B $820
SB $430
C $260
G $210
D $80
F $410
E $470

YOU

Situation: Medium stakes online game. You've been playing for about an hour. The table has been very tight for these stakes. Player G has only recently joined the table and bought in for a short stack.

Your hand: A♥9♣

Action to you: Players A through E fold.

Question: *Do you fold, call, or raise?*
> **Answer:** Ace-nine offsuit is strong enough to raise in the cutoff seat by anyone's estimation. A normal raise of three big blinds is perfectly appropriate.

Action: You raise to $12. Player G calls $12. The blinds fold. The pot is now $30.

Flop: J♣T♣3♣

Question: *What do you do?*

    Answer: You weren't happy that the button called, as you're out of position in the hand. The flop wasn't bad, however, since you now have a flush draw and an overcard.

    Flops with three of a suit are generally good bluffing flops. Well more than half the time your opponent won't have a club, and without a club it's very difficult to keep calling bets. In a sense, a flop like this minimizes his edge in position since you get to bet at the flop first. While I don't mind bluffing at these flops, here your bet has some value since you hold a moderately high club. I like betting at this flop 60 to 70 percent of the time, and checking the rest. If you check and he bets, you'll certainly call with your nine of clubs.

Action: You bet $16. Player G calls. The pot is now $62.

Turn: Q♣

Question: *What do you do?*

    Answer: The arrival of the Q♣ gives you a flush but creates some interesting problems.

    You made your bet and he called. With that board, it's hard for him to call with nothing. It's also hard for him to call without a club unless he has something reasonably good. Let's review the hands he might have before the turn card arrived.

1.   **A made flush with the A♣, or K♣:** An unlikely hand which, however, fits the betting perfectly. The call on the flop is just a trap.

2.   **A made flush with low cards:** The button might have called preflop with something like the 7♣6♣. The hand

makes a flush on the flop, but faces danger if you have a higher club. Many players would raise (on the flop) to guard against that situation.

3. **A set:** Very unlikely. If he flopped a set then he doesn't have a club, so his tendency would be to raise your bet on the flop. A raise either gets more money in the pot or protects his hand if you're on a draw (as you are). If he raises and gets reraised, you've announced that you've made your flush, and he can decide if he believes you or not.

4. **A high pair:** Also unlikely since he called your preflop raise with the blinds left to act. The normal play with a high pair would be to reraise and attempt to isolate you.

5. **A low pair (nines or below) without a club:** This hand would have called preflop, but has to fold on the flop with three clubs and two overcards on board.

6. **A low pair (nines or below) with a club:** This hand would have called preflop, and would probably be willing to call a flop bet as well. He may have the best hand, and if he doesn't, the club or spiking a set may give him outs.

7. **Two high cards above a jack with a club:** A hand like ace-queen, with either being a club, is good enough to call both bets (except we now know he can't have the Q♣).

8. **Two high cards above a jack, but no club:** This hand folds on the flop.

9.   **Two high cards, including a jack or ten, with a club:**
This is a very strong hand. It's easily worth a call
although many players would raise.

10.   **Two high cards, including a jack or ten, no club.**
Preflop, this hand easily calls a raise from a stealing
position. Post-flop, the absence of a club makes the call
much tougher, but many players would stay and see the
turn.

That's a lot of potential hands to be facing. We can
eliminate some of the non-club hands which would probably
have folded post-flop, but that still leaves us facing a lot of
different situations after the flop action.

The turn card, in some respects simplifies the decision-
making tremendously. The arrival of a club on the turn has
collapsed the range of possible hands that Player G would
still play. We've made our flush, and he has one of four
possible hands to continue:

1.   A better flush, with either the A♣ or the K♣. (If he has
both, he has a royal flush!)

2.   A worse flush.

3.   A draw to a full house or quads.

4.   None of the above, but something else like top pair.

Considering these possible hands, should we bet the
turn? Note that this question is not a simple matter of trying
to decide whether we're currently ahead or behind in the
hand. In fact, we're behind in the first case, and ahead in the
other three. What we really want to know is the following:

1.   If we're ahead, will he call a bet now and also a bet on the river?

2.   If we're ahead, will he call now but fold a bet on the river?

3.   If we're ahead, will he fold now but call a bet on the river?

Ignoring the first case, where we're losing to a better flush and we clearly don't want to bet, here's how the other hands break down.

If he has a weak flush, he will probably call a river bet if the turn is checked. Our check on the turn might indicate weakness, and if we check the turn and bet the river, he'll have the security of knowing that no further bets are possible, and therefore he can estimate his downside precisely. If we bet the turn, however, he has a problem. We bet the flop with three clubs showing, and now we're betting the turn with four clubs showing. That's hard to do with no clubs, so it's likely we have a club, and if we do, it's probably better than his low club. With no way of knowing how much we'll bet on the river, his more prudent course is to just fold the turn.

The something else like top pair are similar to weak flushes, but he's even less likely to call on the turn. He might, however, call a small bet on the river after a check on the turn.

If we knew he had a draw to a full house or quads, we'd want to bet the turn to charge him for drawing. But these hands are very unlikely, and when they do occur, they're big underdogs to hit. For example, suppose he has a set of jacks. Now he has ten outs on the river: three queens, three tens, three treys, and the last jack to make quads. That's ten outs in 46 cards, making him a 3.6-to-1 underdog. But a set doesn't square with his betting. He called preflop rather than raising, and he called on the flop, again passing up a raise. That's possible, but not likely.

If he has two pair rather than a set, you have even less need to bet. If he holds queen-jack, for instance, his only outs are the two remaining queens and the two remaining jacks, for a total of four outs. He's more than a 10-to-1 underdog! If you knew what he had, you'd make a small bet to force him to lay down the hand, but the hit is so unlikely that the bet wouldn't gain much. (In fact, it would be wrong if you can get him to call a river bet by checking.)

Lastly, if he has a better flush, you definitely don't want to bet. The more you bet, the more you lose. You also don't want to call a bet if you check.

Looking at all four cases together, you'll do better checking the turn than betting. When you're behind, you have only one out (the 8♣), and you can't make your opponent lay the hand down. When you're ahead, your opponent is more likely to call a river bet because his loss is defined, whereas a turn bet contains the threat of an even bigger bet on the river, which your opponent may not be able to call.

A further advantage of checking the turn is that it enables your opponent to bet with hands that might have folded to your bet. He might, for instance, decide to bluff a weak hand believing the check signified weakness. He might also bet a weak club now believing his low club flush to be best. Of course, he'll also bet if he has one of the high clubs that will beat you.

You will, of course, be calling his turn bets in any case. If he does have one of the high clubs, he's going to win a lot of money.

If you check the turn and he checks behind you, go ahead and bet the river.

Note that if you believed your opponent had a drawing hand with many outs, this advice wouldn't apply. Here, only sets or two pair are drawing hands, and not only are those hands very unlikely from the betting, but they contain relatively few outs.

Action: You bet $35. Player G folds. You win the pot.

Many players are lured into betting the turn here because they believe they have a strong hand. "I've got the third nuts. Only the A♣ or the K♣ can beat me. Why shouldn't I bet with such a good hand?"

But in fact you don't really have a strong hand at all. With four clubs on board, a flush just serves the function of top pair in a normal hand. If your opponent doesn't at least have a flush, he can't put any serious money in the pot. So what flush can he have? The Q♣, J♣, T♣, 9♣ and 3♣ are all accounted for, leaving just eight clubs. You can beat six of those eight clubs, and you lose to two of them. That sounds all right, but any good player holding the 5♣, 4♣, and 2♣ is seriously thinking of mucking them to a solid bet. Only a player with the A♣ or the K♣ is eager to play, and those are the very cards that beat you.

Don't be eager to get all your money in with a middling flush and four of a suit on board. If your betting hasn't chased your opponent away, your hand is very vulnerable.

Hand 6-2

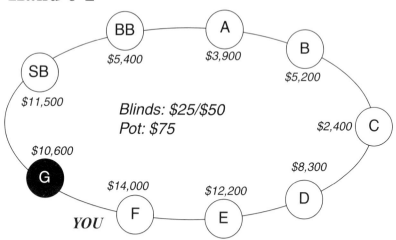

Situation: High stakes live game. You've been playing for a few hours. Most of the players at the table are good, appropriately loose preflop and appropriately aggressive post-flop. Player E is typical of the group. You've made some nice moves at the table and are probably perceived by most as a good player who likes to trap.

Your hand: 7♥7♦

Action to you: Players A through D fold. Player E raises to $200.

Question: *Do you fold, call, or raise?*
> **Answer:** I would never fold a medium pair in this situation. It's mostly a calling hand with an occasional raise thrown in for variety. I'd call 85 percent of the time, raise 15 percent.

Action: You call $200. The button and the blinds fold. The pot is now $475.

Flop: 9♠7♣3♥

Action: Player E bets $350. The pot is now $825.

Question: *What do you do?*

Answer: You've flopped middle set and your opponent, who bet preflop, is still betting. It's not a flop that should offer a lot of draws to a player who led preflop with several players left to act, although at a table like this, one can never be sure. So raising to deny drawing odds is not a priority here.

Since draws are unlikely, we can break your opponent's hands down into two categories:

1.   He has something (overpair like queens, jacks, or tens, or top pair).

2.   He has nothing (a pair under nines, or nothing at all).

It's possible he has a set of nines, of course, but that's so unlikely at this point that we'll ignore it in figuring out our best play. In the event he has a set of nines, you'll lose most or all of your stack. That's poker.

So we have two possible hand types on his part (something or nothing) and two possible plays (call or raise) on our part. Let's analyze the four possibilities and see if any play stands out.

1.   **He has nothing and we raise:** He may believe we're fooling around, but he doesn't have any weapons for fighting. If he really has nothing, he's going to fold. If he has a pair below nines, it's probably also below sevens, so he's looking at two overcards, plus the chance we had a pair to start. Perhaps he could call our raise with a pair of eights, but basically he's done with the hand and we win the current pot.

2. **He has nothing and we call:** This variation offers us some chance of making money. In our best case, he has a couple of overcards like ace-jack. Now he has six "outs" on the turn, where he can hit a card that will still leave him second-best, but he won't know that. In that case, he'll probably check and wait for us to bet, and call us when we do. Whether he'll call another bet on the river is impossible to say.

    If he has a pair below sevens, he has no "outs," although in this case he'd believe that if he makes a set, it would be best, and he would probably lose a fair portion of his stack. Otherwise, he's unlikely to stand another bet. Another possibility is that he has a hand like ace-eight or ace-six, where he has only three "outs" which will let him call another bet.

    If we quickly try to average these variations, we can probably say that about 10 percent of the time we can pick up another average-sized bet on the turn by calling now. This creates a pot of $1,175. A normal bet on the turn would be $600 to $700, so a good estimate would be that calling now might earn another $60 to $70 on average.

3. **He has something and we raise:** This is a very good variation for us. Assume he has an overpair, say jacks. Let's assume we put in $1,100, calling his $350 and raising another $750. He won't like the raise, but he'll at least call that bet with his overpair. The pot becomes $2,675. When a blank comes on the turn, he'll most likely check. If we bet at this point, say $1,200, will he call?

    The best guess we can make is that he'll call this bet some percentage of the time, perhaps about one-third. Assume that he won't call again on the river unless he substantially improves his hand, which rarely happens. In that case, we can estimate our profit in this variation as his call on the flop ($750) plus one-third of our bet on the turn ($400), or about $1,150 overall. That's a hefty profit.

4. **He has something and we call:** Our call makes the pot $1,175. Since he also sees that the board is relatively draw-free, we appear to have called with something like top pair, weak kicker or middle pair, or just a pair below nines. His hand still looks good.

 If a blank comes on the turn, he might or might not bet. To keep the calculations simple, let's assume that if he bets, we raise and take the pot, while if he checks, we bet and he calls, but he won't call a further bet on the river without improving. In either case, we pick up another bet, probably worth about $700 given the current pot size.

 In both these last two cases we've assumed that he doesn't improve to beat our set. We've made this assumption just to keep the logic simple and to avoid getting bogged down in complex "what if" scenarios. Our answers obviously aren't exact, but we're just looking for a quick path to a solution, and since a pair is a big underdog to improve and beat a set, that's a pretty good approach. In trying to reason out poker problems at the table, pretty good is usually good enough. Now let's take a look at the breakdown of our little matrix of possibilities:

	We Call	We Raise
He Has Nothing	+$70	$0
He Has Something	+$700	+$1,150

If having something and having nothing were equally likely scenarios, then raising would clearly be better because of the big gain when he has something. But the two scenarios aren't equally likely. There are far more non-paired hands than paired hands, and most hands miss most flops. Since continuation bets are common for a player out of position even when the flop is missed, we have to assume that he's more likely to have nothing than something.

Even if he's more likely to have nothing than something, however, the gain from raising when he has something is so great that it dwarfs the gain from calling when he has nothing. We gain $70 by calling when he has nothing, but we gain $450 by raising when he has something. Having nothing would need to be almost seven times more likely than having something for the calling play to be correct. That's a stretch, so raising is better.

Action: You raise to $1,100. He calls the extra $750. The pot is now $2,675. His stack is now $10,900. You have him covered.

Turn: K♦

Action: He checks.

Question: *What do you do?*

Answer: With your opponent's call of your raise, you need to reevaluate just what hands he might be holding. An overpair is still a strong possibility of course, as is something like ace-nine, giving him top pair, top kicker. The other top pairs are also possible. King-nine suited or queen-nine suited might have opened the betting preflop, and called with top pair, fairly good kicker.

A set of nines, which seemed very unlikely at first, is much more possible now. The longer the betting continues, the more likely this hand becomes. It's still not nearly likely enough to stop you from pushing the action.

The flop action also forces us to pay attention to two other hands that we didn't really consider before: ten-eight and eight-six, suited or unsuited. Both these hands now have open-ended straight draws which could account for the bet on the flop (which was a semi-bluff), followed by the call, with good implied odds for the draw. As play develops, hands which were very unlikely at first become more and more plausible based on the betting, so you have to be prepared to consider them anew.

You're still well ahead of all his holdings except nines and kings. You want to charge him for the draw, if that's what he has, but not bet so much that the overpairs and top pairs are forced out. Also remember that since you have a genuinely big hand and he seems willing to play, you need to keep building the pot. Your goal now should be to get his whole stack.

A bet of about half the pot seems like the right amount. It's enough money to charge the draws while still offering tempting odds to the pairs.

Action: You bet $1,400. He raises to $5,500. The pot is now $9,575, and it costs you $4,100 to call. His stack is $5,400.

Question: *What do you do?*
   Answer: Folding your set on this board isn't really an option. If he started with a pair of nines or kings, you'll just have to pay him off.

   Every now and then you'll see a player who lays down in this situation and his opponent shows him the higher set. He'll then brag about his great play for the next couple of years, explaining that such moves are the essence of winning poker. Don't believe it. For every such laydown he'll have three or four laydowns to someone on a bluff or a semi-bluff, or someone who just thought his pocket aces or two pair were still good.

Should you just call? Calling brings the pot to $13,675. If you call and your opponent pushes all-in on the river, will you fold? In that case the pot would be about $19,000 and you'd have to call $5,400, so you'd be getting close to 4-to-1 on your money with a set. Can't fold that.

If you can't fold on the river, and the pot is already larger than the stacks, you need to push in now. You rate to be getting your money in as a favorite, and you're denying your opponent the option of folding on the river when a card comes that's potentially too scary for him.

Action: You push all-in. He folds his hand.

Unexpected, but such things happen. He was bluffing, and his bet of half his stack on the turn was designed to make you think he had a very big hand. Unfortunately for him, you had the hand he was representing, so his play didn't work.

Hand 6-3

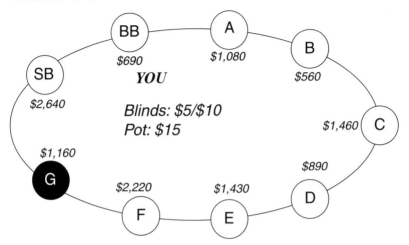

Situation: Medium stakes online game. The small blind is very loose, and will raise almost every pot preflop if he's first to act. Post-flop, he's a little more circumspect. Player A is moderately active preflop; when he plays from early position, he usually has strong cards. He likes to have a good hand to bet after the flop.

Your hand: 7♦3♦

Action to you: Player A limps for $10. Players B through G all fold. The small blind calls $5.

Question: *Do you check or raise?*
    Answer: Check, obviously. You're going to need a pretty good flop to continue against these two.

Action: You check. The pot is $30.

Flop: Q♦9♥5♦

Action: The small blind checks.

Question: *What do you do?*
  Answer: You have a draw to a low flush. There are arguments for betting, but I would usually check.

Action: You check. Player A checks also. The pot remains at $30.

Turn: A♦

Action: The small blind checks.

Question: *What do you do?*
  Answer: You hit your small flush, which should give you the best hand, but there's some danger of a fourth diamond on the river and someone with a single diamond in their hand could beat you.
  Whether you check or bet depends on the rank of the diamond that hit and what you know about Player A. You know that he likes to play high cards in early position, and the diamond that hit the board was an ace. Consequently, there's a pretty reasonable chance that either

1. Player A had an ace in his hand, hit it, and will now bet to claim the pot, or

2. Player A doesn't have an ace but thinks that both of you may believe he has one, and thus he can represent an ace and claim the pot.

  Either way, there is a way above average chance that Player A will bet after you check. If he actually has a good ace, he will probably call your check-raise. If he doesn't have an ace, he'll fold to your check-raise, but, in that case, he would probably have folded to your bet as well. So checking and raising is the better play.

I'd make the same play (checking with the intention of check-raising) if the K♦ had hit, for the same reason. I'd also try a check-raise if the J♦ or T♦ came because those cards connect with the board, allowing Player A to represent a straight or flush with a bluff.

If any lower diamond had appeared, I'd bet. Now the board doesn't have any scare cards, so there's more of a chance that Player A will just check if he has nothing or if he has a single diamond. In that case, I need to make a bet large enough to prevent anyone with a higher diamond from drawing. A bet of two-thirds of the pot would be about right.

Action: You check. Player A bets $30. The small blind folds.

Question: *What do you do?*
Answer: You need to raise, but you want to size your raise correctly. Right now the most likely case is that Player A has an ace but not a diamond, so you'd like to bet enough so that, if he has something like ace-king or ace-jack with no diamond, he's still comfortable calling your bet. At the same time, if he has a diamond, you want to deny him correct drawing odds. When you call, the pot will be $90, so a raise of another $60 should do the trick. He'll then see a pot of $150 and he'll need to put in $60 to call. So he'll be getting exactly 2.5-to-1 odds, not enough if he has a diamond draw, but tempting if he has just made a good pair of aces, in which case he may think you have a weaker ace.

Action: You raise to $90. Player A calls $60. The pot is now $210.

River: 7♠

Question: *What do you do?*

> **Answer:** No diamond arrived, so your flush is probably good. You should bet a solid amount, around 80 to 90 percent of the pot. You may get called if he has an ace and doesn't really think you have the flush.

Action: You bet $180. Player A folds.

Hand 6-4

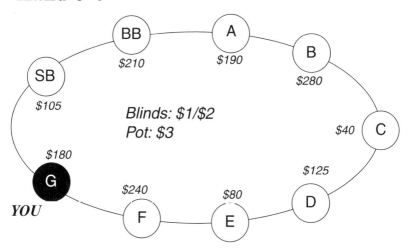

Situation: Medium stakes online game. You haven't been at the table long, but it seems to be tight.

Your hand: Q♥9♣

Action to you: Player A folds. Player B calls $2. Players C and D fold. Player E calls $2. Player F folds.

Question: *Do you fold, call, or raise?*

> **Answer:** You have position and your hand isn't terrible with a medium-sized double gapper. Of course, there's no harm in

folding, but since no one has shown any strength, I would be inclined to play this on the button.

Action: You call $2. The small blind calls $1 and the big blind checks. The pot is $10 and you act last after five players.

Flop: K♣7♥7♦

Action: All four players check.

Question: *What do you do?*

 Answer: No one showed great strength before the flop and no one has shown any interest on the flop. We have nothing, but should we try to steal?

 A loose-aggressive player would probably bet. It's not a bad play, but I wouldn't do it. With four opponents, it's my opinion you're about as likely to pick up the pot as to run into a raise from someone who hit a seven or a king and is laying low. Without knowing a lot about the specific players at the table, I don't think betting here is a money-making play.

 My plan with hands like this, where my only edge is position, is to get a little more information than I currently have before making a move. By checking and waiting for the turn, I'll actually pick up five more pieces of information: the turn card, plus the actions of my four opponents.

Action: You check. The pot remains at $10.

Turn: 6♦

Action: The blinds check. Player B bets $2. Player E calls $2.

Question: *What do you do?*

 Answer: Raise. You've just seen a lot a favorable information. The blinds checked for a second time, so it's clear they don't have much interest in the pot. Player B made a small bet, and Player D only called the small bet. Player D's call doesn't show much strength. If he only called a $2 bet, will he call a big raise? Probably not.

What about Player B's small bet? To interpret this bet properly, you need to factor in the level of the game. In a relatively small-stake game, these little bets on the flop or the turn tend to mean one of two things:

1. "I have a mediocre hand, but I want to see the next card, so please don't raise me."

2. "I have a draw, and I want to see the next card real cheap, so let's all be friends and by the way please don't raise me."

Either way, the right response is a big raise. Since no one else has shown any strength, this is now a situation where you have an excellent chance to take down a pot with a move. Make a big raise, something like 80 to 100 percent of the pot.

Action: You raise to $14. The blinds fold. Player B folds after some thought. Player E quickly folds.

The deep think indicates Player B did have some kind of draw and thought you might be bluffing.

What do very small bets mean in a high-stakes game? They're unusual because experienced players are wary of giving really good odds to call. A small bet might mean a good player is being tricky with a big hand, or, at the next level, it might mean some ultra-tricky deception designed to win the pot with no hand.

Hand 6-5

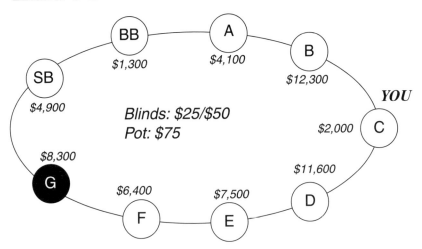

Situation: High stakes live game. You bought in for $5,000 and have taken some hits. You're at a casino you've never played before, and the players seem aggressive, tough, and tricky. You think you might be in over your head, but you decide to play a few more hands.

Your hand: T♣8♣

Action to you: Players A and B fold.

Question: *Do you fold, call, or raise?*

   Answer: You have a medium one-gap hand in relatively early position. You need to play a hand like this once in a great while for the metagame. How often? I would say at least 5 percent of the time, but certainly no more than 10 percent. I would raise rather than limp with the hand, which enables you to represent an ace-king type hand on a strong flop, while trapping when you actually hit something.

   Limping with hands like this in early position is especially dangerous because, in essence, you are accurately representing a weak hand. If you get raised you can get out since you're almost certainly beaten, but you may be letting people with queen-jack type hands chase you away. If you raise and get reraised, you can be pretty certain you were forced out by a strong hand.

Action: You in fact call $50. Player D raises to $250. Player E folds. Player F calls $250. Player G, on the button, calls $250. The blinds fold. The pot is $875 and it costs you $200 to call.

Question: *What do you do?*
   Answer: You're getting almost 4.5-to-1 odds, but you have a bad hand in bad position, and no idea what you're up against. You'll need to hit a great flop to continue. Fold.

Action: You in fact call $200. The pot is now $1,075, and you'll be first to act with three opponents.

Flop: K♦Q♦7♠

Question: *What do you do?*
   Answer: Check. You missed the flop, and it's a dangerous one, likely to hit one or two of your opponents. Betting here is just silly.

Action: You check. Everyone checks behind you.

Turn: Q♠

Question: *What do you do?*
   Answer: Continue to check. You're at an aggressive table, but no one made a stab at the flop after a lot of preflop betting. That should make you very suspicious. Even though you're down for the session, this isn't the time to make your money back.

If you acted last, and everyone checked again, you could venture a bet. A lot of information is then available to you, and it starts to get implausible that someone had a king or a queen but checked two streets.

Action: You bet $500, attempting to steal. Player D raises to $4,000. The other two players fold. The pot now contains $5,575, and it costs you $3,500 to call.

Question: *What do you do?*
    Answer: Fold, of course. You tried to steal and got caught. No sense losing the rest of your chips on this hand.

Action: You fold.

Hand 6-6

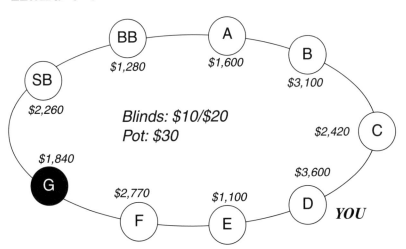

Blinds: $10/$20
Pot: $30

BB $1,280
A $1,600
B $3,100
SB $2,260
C $2,420
G $1,840
D $3,600 *YOU*
F $2,770
E $1,100

Situation: Medium stakes live game. You've almost doubled your initial buy-in after a few hours. Player B is loose-aggressive and tricky. Player G is tight and solid. Your table image is loose and aggressive. You've played a lot of pots and pushed them hard.

50 Par Six: Tight-Aggressive Turn Play

Your hand: A♦8♥

Action to you: Player A folds. Player B raises to $80. Player C folds.

Question: *Do you fold, call, or raise?*
> **Answer:** Against a tight player, you should certainly fold. A solid raise from a tight player in second position will almost always mean a hand better than ace-eight offsuit. However, even against a loose player I would fold. Not only are too many players still left to act behind you, but ace-eight offsuit isn't a solid raising hand in this position when first to act.

Action: You call $80. Players E and F fold. Player G calls $80. The blinds fold. The pot is $270. You're second to act among three players.

Flop: J♥8♦5♣

Action: Player B checks.

Question: *What do you do?*
> **Answer:** First, you need to interpret Player B's check. He raised preflop from early position, indicating strength, and got two callers, one of whom is known to be tight. Now he checks.
>
> Your best guess should be that he doesn't want to automatically bet into two players, and is waiting for someone to act first. In this situation, you really don't know anything about his hand yet.
>
> So what to do? You have middle pair with top kicker. The board is pretty free of draws. Your hand is probably a slight favorite to be best here. You could bet or you could just check. I have a slight preference for checking and getting a little more information before acting with a marginal hand,

but betting 70 percent of the pot or so is certainly an acceptable play.

Action: You actually bet $250. Player G folds. Player B calls $250. The pot is now $770.

Turn: 6♦

Action: Player B checks.

Question: *What do you do?*

Answer: Now you have to check. Betting is a serious mistake. To see why, ask yourself what hand Player B might have. You made a big bet on the flop, showing some strength, and you got called anyway. A drawing hand is very unlikely, since Player B would have to have exactly ten-nine or seven-six. He called out of position, and then he checked the turn, so it's very unlikely that he's running some sort of elaborate bluff. The hand that best fits his play is top pair with a medium-strength kicker, or possibly middle pair, in which case he has a weaker kicker than yours. If he had a pair all along, it's more likely that he either has a set or a pair higher than yours than he is to have a lower pair.

In short, there's not much he can reasonably have that you can beat. Take the free card and check. Another big bet here is very expensive, and you have no good reason to think it will work.

Action: You actually bet $700. Player B thinks awhile and moves in pushing $2,800 into the pot. It's a $2,100 raise to you and the pot is $4,270.

Question: *What do you do?*

    Answer: You can't call an all-in bet with middle pair unless you seriously think he may be bluffing. He probably hit a set and was trapping. Let it go.

Action: You fold.

    The turn bet with a relatively weak hand was the big error. Your opponent gave you the chance to see the river for free with position, and you should have taken it. Once you bet with middle pair and get called, your goal is to see the hand down cheaply.

Hand 6-7

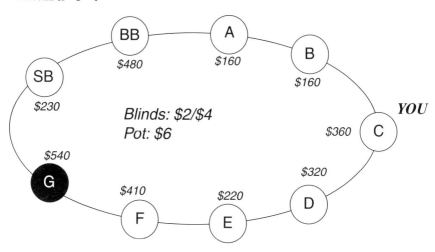

Situation: Medium stakes online game. There are no obvious loose players at the table. Most players bought in for less than the maximum and have played cautiously.

Your hand: A♦8♣

Action to you: Player A calls $4. Player B folds.

Question: *Do you fold, call, or raise?*

 Answer: This hand should just be folded. Ace-eight offsuit isn't a strong hand in third position even without a limper already in the pot. I might occasionally call after a limper with ace-eight suited, but it would be a play made solely for variety and deception, not because I had any confidence in the hand.

Action: You raise to $20. Player D folds. Player E calls $20. Player F, the button, and the blinds fold. Player A calls $16. The pot is $66.

Flop: A♠J♣4♦

Action: Player A checks.

Question: *What do you do?*

 Answer: You made a big raise with your medium ace but got two callers from this tight table. An ace came on the flop, which might be good news, and now the first player has checked.

 A bet here is very reasonable. Your hand may be best, and the bet may win the pot. There are no draws available except a possible inside straight draw if someone was holding king-queen or king-ten. It's unlikely anyone with those hands will call a bet with the ace showing.

 If someone else does have an ace, they'll probably call at least one bet. A jack might or might not call, probably depending on its kicker.

Action: You bet $32. Player E calls $32. Player A folds. The pot is now $130.

Turn: 3♣

Question: *What do you do?*

   Answer: You're in a similar position to the last problem although your hand is relatively better. Your opponent's call indicates he has an ace or a jack. You're beating the jacks, and you're beating some of the aces (the less likely ones, unfortunately) and losing to the others.

   However you stand relative to player E, the situation isn't likely to change on the last card. If he's beating you with a better ace, you only have three outs (the last three eights), so you're about 8 percent, counting ties, to improve to a winning hand. If you're ahead of him, the relative situation is reversed. If he has a worse ace, you're about 92 percent to win, and if he has something like jack-ten, he has five outs and you're about 89 percent to win.

   Pot commitment is starting to become an issue. You have about $300 left in your stack, and the pot is already $130. That's a big enough pot for a hand with top pair, modest kicker. Just check and see if you can check the hand down.

Action: You actually bet $60. Player E folds.

   Most likely he had a jack of some sort and decided your bets were for real. You're glad to win the pot, but you probably would have won anyway with less risk by checking.

Hand 6-8

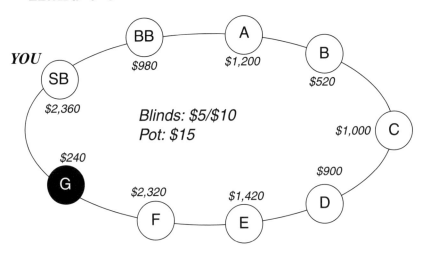

Situation: Medium stakes online game. You're a tight player who's had a good run of luck. The big blind has only played about 10 hands.

Your hand: J♣T♣

Action to you: Players A through G fold.

Question: *Do you fold, call, or raise?*
>   **Answer:** Jack-ten suited is certainly a good enough hand to play in a blind against blind situation. Since you'll be out of position after the flop, and since the big blind doesn't know anything about you yet, I prefer a raise to a fold.

Action: You raise to $30. The big blind calls $20. The pot is $60.

Flop: 8♠6♦3♣

Question: *You act first. What do you do?*
    Answer: You showed strength before the flop, so there's no harm in being the aggressor and making a continuation bet. Let's find out.

Action: You bet $35. The big blind calls $35. The pot is now $130.

Turn: K♠

Question: *What do you do?*
    Answer: You still don't have anything, but your opponent has only called your bets, rather than raised, so he may not have anything either. The K♠ is a potential scare card if it missed him. Your opponent hasn't been at the table long enough to draw any conclusions about your style, so he can't assume your bets are bluffs.
    Having said all that, you still have a real choice here. You can check and fold if he bets. Or, you can make a second continuation bet and see if it works. A second bet shows real strength, and a lot of players who know they have to stand up to one continuation bet will fold when the second barrel is fired. This is as good a time as any to see where the big blind stands, particularly since your jack-high probably won't win any showdowns.

Action: You bet $80. The big blind folds.

Two continuation bets are much more likely to work than one, especially when the turn is an overcard. Of course, the risk is also higher.

Hand 6-9

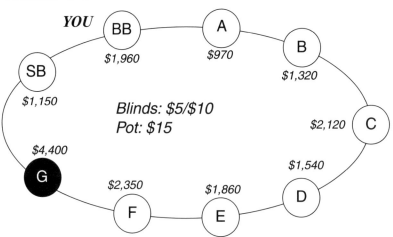

Situation: Medium stakes live game. You've been playing a while and the game has been loose and wild. Players have been opening with a lot of different hands and seeing raises with all sorts of cards. There's been a lot of semi-bluffing with drawing hands. You've played tight and solid and have done well.

Your hand: A♦5♦

Action to you: Player A folds. Player B calls $10. Players C and D fold. Player E calls $10. Player F folds. Player G, the button, raises to $60. The small blind folds. The pot is $95.

Question: *Do you fold, call, or raise?*

> **Answer:** Ace-small suited is not a powerhouse hand, but if things go right it could develop into a big hand, which might get paid at this table. Since players have tended to call, you might get four-way action for another $50. So calling is reasonable. I'd call 50 percent of the time and fold the other 50 percent. Raising is definitely too speculative. As yet you have no idea what you're up against.

Action: You call $50. Player B calls $50. Player E calls $50. The pot is $245. You're first to act among four players.

Flop: A♠A♣5♠

Question: *What do you do?*
> **Answer:** Very nice. You have the best possible full house, so your focus has shifted to maximizing your winnings on the hand. This situation is more favorable for making money than most full house flops because although there aren't many aces and fives left in the deck, flush and straight draws are both possible. With three loose opponents, you can be pretty sure that someone will take the lead in the betting. A check looks like the best choice, although betting into this crowd isn't a bad alternative. I would probably bet 30 percent of the time and check 70 percent in this situation.

Action: You check. Player B checks. Player E checks. Player G bets $120. The pot is $365.

Question: *What do you do?*
> **Answer:** As in most cases where you make a huge hand on the flop, you have a choice.

1. Assume that nobody at the table has much and try to pick up an extra bet along the way.

2. Assume that Player G is betting with the case ace or a flush draw in which event you can raise, get called, and perhaps double your stack.

In deep stack no-limit cash games, the payoff from making the second choice is so huge that it dwarfs the more frequent small wins from assuming that nobody has much. So raise and keep the ball rolling.

Action: You raise to $500. Players B and E fold. Player G calls $380. The pot is $1,365. You have $1,400 left in your stack. Player G has you covered.

Turn: 3♠

Question: *What do you do?*

    Answer: That's an incredibly perfect card for you. If you've read the situation right, Player G has probably just made a flush. If you're right, a bet will get called, but how much should you bet?

    The answer is — push all-in. Too many cards can come on the river that will cool the action. Suppose Player G was playing with two medium spades — say the T♠9♠. If the last ace or either of the last two fives arrive, he may well decide that you do have the full house, and lay his hand down. If a fourth spade arrives, he'll be afraid that you have something like an ace and the K♠, or maybe an ace and the Q♠, and now you've made a flush that beats his.

    If you bet all-in now, he'll probably think that you have a big hand plus a draw to beat him, and he'll call. If you wait or make a smaller bet, he might be able to get away on the river.

Action: You move all-in for $1,400. Player G calls. The river is the K♣, and he turns over the T♠8♠. You double up.

Hand 6-10

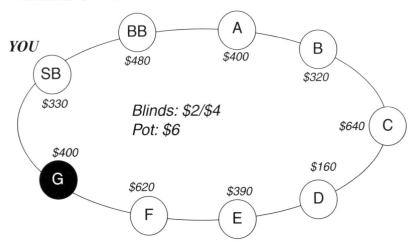

Situation: Medium stakes online game. The game is fairly tight. Player D is especially tight and somewhat passive.

Your hand: 5♣5♠

Action to you: Players A, B, and C fold. Player D raises to $8. Players E, F, and G fold.

Question: *Do you fold, call, or raise?*
  Answer: You hate to fold pairs in cash games because the set potential is so powerful. This situation is less favorable than most; you only have one opponent so far, he's tight and passive, and his stack is only 20 times the size of the bet you're calling. (You wish he had a larger stack for better implied odds.)

  Still, his passiveness gives you some extra ways to win. You may be able to take down some pots with your unimproved pair if he shows weakness. Calling is reasonable.

Action: You call $6. The big blind folds. The pot is $20.

Flop: J♠6♦5♦

Question: *What do you do?*
    Answer: You've hit bottom set, which on this board is very likely to be the best hand. Two draws are possible. The small straight draw is unlikely against a tight player who raised from middle position. The flush draw is possible, but not a serious worry right now.
    Your opponent took the lead in the betting, so it makes sense to let him continue betting. You should check.

Action: You check. Player D bets $10.

Question: *What do you do?*
    Answer: Should you raise or just call? Let's give him four possible hands and see how a tight player might respond in each case.

1.   **He has top pair or an overpair:** If he has one of these hands, he'll call your raise. He may not bet again, however, and when you bet again, he'll have a tough choice. If you just call, however, he'll believe he has the best hand and probably call another bet. Edge to calling.

2.   **He has a pair under top pair**. As an example, let's say he has the 9♣9♥. He might fold immediately since your check-raise probably means you have a jack. If he called this bet, he would likely fold to a second bet unless he hit one of his two outs. Edge to calling.

3.   **He has two overcards**. A tight player would likely fold two overcards to a raise. Since he has no outs and you might win another bet if one of his overcards hit — edge to calling.

4.   **He has a flush draw**. A tight player might fold to a raise as he couldn't be sure what his implied odds looked like when the obvious flush card hit. He might also call. Edge to raising.

As you might expect, calling is a better choice.

Action: You call $10. The pot is $40.

Turn: 9♣

Question: *What do you do?*
   Answer: Check. Tight players tend to keep betting when they have something and there are some obvious (if unlikely) draws on board. Give him a chance to bet.
   If you bet first, he'll decide you probably don't have a draw, and he'll have to worry about calling this bet and then calling an even bigger bet on the turn. Instead, he'll lay down all but his very best hands.
   You're not in a favorable situation for winning his whole stack, but give yourself the best chance to win one more good-sized bet. De-leverage the hand by checking now and betting on the river.

Action: You check. He checks behind you. The pot remains at $40.

River: K♣

Question: *What do you do?*
   Answer: That's a good card for you since it might have hit him if he was playing ace-king or king-queen. You've shown an appropriate amount of weakness, and you should be able to make a good-sized bet and get it called.

Action: You bet $30. He calls $30 and shows A♥K♦. Your set beats his pair of kings.

Hand 6-11

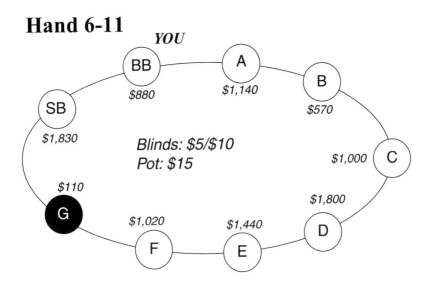

YOU

BB $880

A $1,140

B $570

SB $1,830

C $1,000

Blinds: $5/$10
Pot: $15

$110

G

F $1,020

E $1,440

D $1,800

Situation: Medium stakes online game. Player F has played a tight game so far. Player G and the small blind are loose and very aggressive.

Your hand: A♣9♣

Action to you: Players A through E fold. Player F raises to $30. Player G and the small blind fold. The pot is $45.

Question: *Do you fold, call, or raise?*
    Answer: Ace-nine suited is good enough to call a raise from a player in the cutoff seat. Since he's tight, however, you think he's probably still raising with good cards, so this is only a marginal call. You'll have to be careful if an ace comes.

Action: You call $20. The pot is $65.

Flop: Q♣J♦2♥

Question: *Do you check or bet?*
> **Answer:** You check. You missed the flop and your opponent, who has position, may have a good hand. The queen and the jack are particularly bad cards since, if he was playing two high cards, he probably hit his hand. If he was playing any pair, of course, you're still behind.

Action: You check. He checks behind you.

Turn: A♦

Question: *Do you bet or check?*
> **Answer:** The arrival of the ace presents us with a very interesting problem. At first glance, everything seems to have gone well for us. Our opponent didn't bet, possibly indicating weakness, and then we hit our ace. Surely we must bet now, right?
>
> Not so fast. We actually don't have such a good hand after all. In fact, we just have a bluff-catcher, and we should check. Let's see why.
>
> Remember what can happen when we make a bet. There are four possibilities:

1. When better hands than ours call (or raise), we lose money.

2. When better hands fold, we gain money.

3. When weaker hands call, we gain money.

4. When weaker hands fold, we gain a little money by eliminating the chance they can draw out. We gain less

on a turn bet than a flop bet because there is only one more card to come. Exactly how much we gain depends on how many outs they have, but it probably isn't much.

The important possibilities are the second and third ones. Can we get better hands to fold, and can we get weaker hands to call? Let's see what happens in this hand.

Will any better hands fold? Almost certainly not. The better aces are AK, AQ, AJ, and AT. All of those hands will call a bet. Other better hands are two pairs and sets, and they're certainly at least calling.

Will any weaker hands call? Now we have to think about just what weaker hands he might have given his style and the way the hand has played out so far.

1. Could he have a single queen or a single jack? Probably not since he didn't bet the flop. If his hand were king-queen, for instance, that flop would have looked pretty good, and he likely would have bet it after our check. The same holds for hands like king-jack and jack-ten.

2. Could he have two high cards without a queen or a jack? Maybe, but unfortunately all those hands (ace-king, ace-ten, king-ten) now beat us.

3. Could he have a pair? No. Aces beats us. Kings would have bet the flop. Queens and jacks beat us. And all the lower pairs will fold with three higher cards on board.

4. Could he have Ace-x? All the aces down to ace-nine either beat or tie us, as does ace-deuce. So we're looking at ace-eight through ace-trey. While we're beating all these hands, we have to look at how the hand has played out and see if any of them are a realistic possibility at this point. Would he have raised preflop with these

hands facing two loose aggressive players on the button and in the small blind? Possibly, and more likely for the higher aces. Would he have checked these hands on the flop? Probably not. After our check, he usually would have made a continuation bet to take down the pot right away. Would he call now if we bet? Maybe with one of the high kickers. Our bet on the turn has signaled that we liked the turn card, so he would probably fold the low aces.

In short, the only weaker candidate hands that might call are the low aces. The problem here is that those hands require a whole series of somewhat unusual plays to have happened for us to make money. They had to raise preflop, despite the presence of two loose-aggressive players behind them, then they had to check the flop after our check, although a continuation bet would be natural, and finally they have to call the turn, although we show strength when the ace hits. That long and unlikely sequence means this is an unlikely variation.

In short, a bet here might win a pot that we rate to win anyway, but it doesn't rate to make us any money. We should check.

Action: You check. Player F checks. The pot remains at $65.

River: K♠

Question: *Do you bet or check?*
  Answer: Now any ten will make a straight and beat us, so check.

Action: You check. Player F checks. He shows a pair of sevens and you take the pot.

Hand 6-12

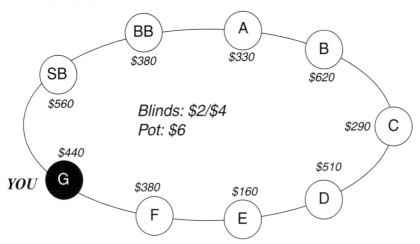

Situation: Medium stakes online game. The big blind is a tight player but hard to chase away when he has a hand. The small blind is also tight.

Your hand: K♦2♦

Action to you: Players A through F fold.

Question: *Do you fold, call, or raise?*
    Answer: You don't have much of a hand, but a king is worth something, as are two suited cards. You're entitled to try some steals from the button, and this is as good a time as any with two tight players behind you.

Action: You raise to $12. The small blind folds. The big blind calls. The pot is now $26.

Flop: T♣6♥2♣

Action: The big blind checks.

Question: *What do you do?*

Answer: Check. You have position, and a hand which you're content to check down. If your opponent called in the big blind with a pair, it's better than yours, and on this flop, he'll suspect that you're bluffing.

Why not make a continuation bet? It's not a bad play, and it might even work. But the problem is that the flop doesn't back up your story. If you made a legitimate raise preflop, then this flop probably missed your hand.

Use your position and try to keep the pot small. If he called you with two high cards, he actually doesn't have that many outs against your pair.

Action: You check behind him. The pot remains at $26.

Turn: 3♦

Action: He bets $44.

Question: *What do you do?*

Answer: This bet is pretty easy to read, but that knowledge doesn't do you much good. Generally, a big overbet on the turn means "I have a hand and I really don't want you to draw out on me so please go away." It's likely that the big blind called with a pair like nines, eights, or sevens, and is afraid that you're hanging around with some kind of draw, perhaps a flush or two overcards. He's tired of waiting and wants to win the pot right now.

There's one other possibility, which is that the bet is a plain bluff. In that case, the bet has the strength of *leverage*; if you call the bet, you might have to call another bet for all your chips on the river.

The prudent course is just to fold. You're probably beaten, and even if you're not, you won't be able to tell where you stand unless you hit your hand again on the river. Let it go.

Action: You fold.

Hand 6-13

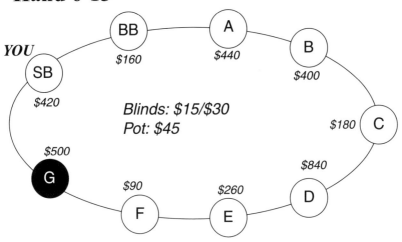

Blinds: $15/$30
Pot: $45

Situation: Medium stakes online game. The table has played tight so far.

Your hand: 7♦5♦

Action to you: Player A calls $4. Players B through F fold. Player G calls $4. The pot is now $14.

Question: *Do you fold, call, or raise?*
 Answer: Your cards are almost connected and suited, and the pot is offering you 7-to-1 odds. I would play more or less any suited or closely connected cards in this spot, or hands with an ace or a king. The hands which should be quickly thrown away are the queen-four or jack-trey type hands where you're

essentially playing with just one card and no chance of making a straight.

Action: You call $2. The big blind checks. The pot is $16, and you'll be first to act out of four players.

Flop: Q♥8♦2♦

Question: *What do you do?*
> **Answer:** Check. You have a diamond draw, but it's a low draw and you have three opponents, so you can't be sure the draw is any good. A semi-bluff is possible and wouldn't be the worst play in the world, but I like to save my semi-bluffs for situations where I know I'm drawing to the nuts.

Action: You check. The other three players check behind you. The pot remains at $16.

Turn: 7♠

Question: *What do you do?*
> **Answer:** Now you definitely want to bet. It's a bet buttressed by three considerations, none of which on its own is good enough to move, but all of which taken together form a compelling argument.

1. It's partly a value bet because you have a pair, although it's only third pair. Still, it may be the best hand out there right now.

2. It's partly a semi-bluff because although only one card remains to come, you can make a diamond flush with any of nine diamonds, and trips with either of the last two sevens. It's also possible that the three remaining fives would give you a winner.

3. It's partly a leveraged bluff based on the weakness shown so far by everyone, and the implicit threat that you might make a bigger bet on the end.

I would make a relatively large bet, almost the size of the pot. About $15 seems right.

Action: You actually check again. The other three players also check.

River: 9♣

Question: *What do you do now?*
   Answer: You've missed your chance. Your draws didn't come in and you're stuck with a pair of sevens and three overcards on board. Just check and hope you win the showdown.
   It's just possible that a bet might chase away someone with a pair of eights. But it might not, and given the weakness shown on the flop and the turn, a bet certainly won't chase away anyone with a pair of nines or queens.

Action: You check. The big blind bets $12. Players A and G fold. The pot is $28.

Question: *What do you do?*
   Answer: If the bet had come from the button after three checks you could call since the bet might be a bluff and your hand is strong enough to be a bluff-catcher. However, this bet came from the big blind who still had three live players left to act behind him. Since it's not an especially large bet, he's anticipating a call, so fold.

Action: You actually call. The big blind shows J♥T♣ for a straight, and takes the pot.

Part Seven

Tight-Aggressive River Play

Tight-Aggressive River Play

Introduction

In deep stack no limit hold 'em, the river is the most important street. Why is the river so important? There are basically three reasons.

The first reason is that bets on the river are much, much larger than bets on the early streets. If you're playing $5 and $10 blinds, the first raise preflop might be $30. Even if you make a horrible preflop raise, say with 7♥2♦ in first position, the actual cost of that error might be no more than $10 or so, on average. But a bet on the river could be several hundred dollars, so the cost of a big mistake on the river is much, much greater than the cost of a mistake on an early street.

The second reason is that by the time you reach the river, all the cards have been dealt. Having the best hand no longer means you're 60, 70, or 80 percent to win; it means you're 100 percent to win as long as you see the hand through to the end.

The third reason is that more information is available to you on the river than on any other street. You've seen the preflop action, the flop, the betting on the flop, the turn, the betting on the turn, and the river card. If you have position on the river, you've even seen your opponent's action on the river. That's a lot of information. The more skilled you are, the more you can put that information to good use.

Deep-Stack Cash Games Versus Tournament Play

We can now start to see clearly why deep stack cash games favor the skillful player more than tournaments. In tournaments, an unskilled player only has to survive the first couple of blind levels, where the stacks are truly deep, before the skill gap between him and some of the other players is reduced. After that, the blinds start getting large relative to the stacks, and many hands end with an all-in move from a short stack, eliminating all further play and reducing the hand to a simple pot-odds proposition.

In deep stack cash games, on the other hand, the hand progresses from street to street, with all-in moves being very rare. At each street, the amount of information available to each player increases along with the size of the pot and the cost of a mistake. As a result, the skillful player's edge against a beginner grows with the duration of the hand.

It's not at all unusual to see relatively inexperienced players place well or even win a major tournament, then move to the cash game tables to show the so-called "pros" just how the game should be played. Such adventures often don't end well.

Betting the River: Where Do You Stand?

By the time a hand reaches the river, generating simple rules of thumb to govern betting, checking, and calling is more difficult. (Not that it's easy on earlier streets.) By this time you've seen the entire hand play out, and the hand tells a sort of story. It's a story with three parts:

1. The hand you actually have.

2. The set of hands your opponent might have, as described by his actions.

3. The set of hands you might have, as a reasonable player might interpret your actions.

Every story is a little different, and every story is affected by its context, the set of information that you know about your opponent, and the set of information that he might reasonably know about you. The best way to learn how to interpret these stories is by example (coupled with lots of practice), and that's why we've included so many sample hands at the end of this chapter.

Although the stories are all different, there are certain common situations that occur on the river. Let's start by considering your hand only. You could find yourself with the absolute nuts, or nothing at all, or several situations in between. To simplify, we'll group your hand into one of five categories:

1. You have the nuts.
2. You have a very strong hand, but not the nuts.

3. You have a good hand given the board and the betting action.
4. You have a hand with some value.
5. You have zilch.

Let's take a look at the issues with each possible type of hand and get an idea of just what our goals should be.

You Have the Nuts

When you actually have the nuts, you're in a very enviable situation. You don't have to worry about winning the hand, you just have to worry about winning the most money.

How do we win the most money? Let's start with a basic principle of playing the nuts, which comes as a shock to most players:

> If you don't know anything about your opponents, and they don't know anything about you, and your only concern is maximizing the amount you win this hand, in general, you want to push all-in when you have the nuts.

The alert reader will notice that we put a lot of qualifications on that apparently bold statement, and we'll explain why in a bit. But first, let's explain the basic idea that pushing all-in is the right play when you have the nuts.

To see what's going on more clearly, let's imagine a typical river situation. The pot is $500. Our stack is $2,000, and so is our opponent's. We hit the nuts on the river, but our opponent has showed some strength throughout the hand.

We don't know what our opponent has. He's a tricky player, and he may have been betting a strong hand, or he may have been bluffing. We believe that his *river profile* (the likelihood that he can take various actions on the river) looks something like this:

1. 20 percent of the time he thinks he has a great hand and will call a bet of any size.

2. 30 percent of the time he thinks he has a very good hand and will call anything up to a pot-sized bet, but an overbet will scare him away.

3. 20 percent of the time he has a pretty good hand and will call a bet up to 70 percent of the pot, but fold otherwise.

4. 30 percent of the time he was either bluffing or has a hand of marginal value. He'll fold to a bet of any size.

Against this river profile, what happens if we make bets of various sizes? Let's see.

- If we bet half the pot ($250), he'll call 70 percent of the time. We make $175.

- If we bet the pot ($500), he'll call 50 percent of the time. We make $250.

- If we push all-in ($2,000), he'll call only 20 percent of the time. We make $400.

Of those three bets, pushing all-in is completely dominant against this river profile. In fact, as long as we believe he has a 20 percent chance of calling a huge all-in, he'd have to be almost 100 percent to call a pot-sized bet for the pot bet to be the better play. You'll almost never see a profile like that (100 percent to call a pot-sized bet or less, 20 percent to call an all-in) in practice.

We used an example where the ratio between the stacks and the pot was actually pretty large (4-to-1). As the stacks get closer in size to the pot, the ratio between the likelihood of calling the all-in and the likelihood of calling the pot bet get closer and closer, obviously. If the pot is $500 and your stack is $700, how often will you call a $500 bet, but fold a $700 bet? Clearly, those two probabilities will be about the same. However, as the stacks get very large relative to the pot, even a small chance of having the all-in bet called causes it to dominate the pot-sized bet.

So how should we play in practice? Even if we're convinced that an all-in move with the nuts is theoretically correct in the absence of any other factors, in the real world we do have many other considerations. The most important real-world consideration is our need to disguise exactly what our bets mean. Just as we varied our hands and bets preflop and on the flop, we also need to vary our river bets among our possible situations. We can't allow our opponents to deduce that all-in means the nuts while a pot-sized bet or smaller means something less than the nuts.

In practice, I'd use a distribution that looks as follows:

● **You have the nuts and are first to act.**

1. Push all-in 40 percent
2. Bet the pot 20 percent
3. Bet three-fourths of the pot 15 percent
4. Bet half the pot 10 percent
5. Bet one-third of the pot 10 percent
6. Check 5 percent

That distribution accomplishes all your goals with a nut hand. You're making the "best" play, which is pushing all-in more than any other. But you're distributing your nut hands among all the other possible river bets you might make so that each bet on the river, when you're first to act, carries the threat of a nut hand behind it.

Suppose your opponent acts first. He can either bet or check, and each one will have its own possible distribution. Here are my recommendations.

- **You have the nuts, your opponent acts first and bets the pot.**

    1. Raise all-in 70 percent
    2. Raise the pot 30 percent

Your task is easier here because you have to raise, and your opponent has already shown strength by betting, so you can dispense with small raises and just go for the throat.

- **You have the nuts, your opponent acts first and checks.**

    1. Push all-in 20 percent
    2. Bet the pot 20 percent
    3. Bet three-quarters of the pot 20 percent
    4. Bet half the pot 30 percent
    5. Bet one-third of the pot 10 percent

Once our opponent acts first and doesn't bet, we now have a strong indication that he's weak and probably can't call a big bet. So we'll scale our betting down in the hopes of capturing some extra profit from the hand. Note that, compared to acting first, checking disappears entirely as an option.

You Have a Very
Strong Hand, But Not the Nuts

Suppose you have a hand which is very, very good, but not the absolute nuts. How should you play that hand on the river? To handle these situations, I ask myself a simple question. If I were to make a good-sized bet, let's say a bet the size of the pot, and my opponent then puts me all-in, could I get away from the hand given how the hand has been played so far? If the answer is "No, I'd have to call that bet," then I'll simply treat the hand as though I had the nuts and play accordingly. If, given what I knew about my opponent, I actually would fold my hand to a big bet, then I'd play more cautiously, as in the next sub-chapter.

In the real world, you will mostly go all the way with these hands. As a rule, there will always be enough holdings you can beat that could have been played the same way to compel you to get all your money in.

Note, by the way, that many all-in confrontations between strong hands occur on the turn rather than the river. The underlying reason was discussed in the turn section. If you have a very strong hand by the turn, you're concerned that the river card might be a 'cooler' that freezes betting action on the last street. If both sides have big hands, this consideration pushes both players to get the money in before the river card arrives.

You Have a Good Hand Given the Board and the Betting Action

In this sub-chapter we're referring to hands that are not the nuts, or the second or third nuts, but hands that are nonetheless 'pretty good,' much better than hands that merely have some value as bluff catchers.

Exactly what constitutes a 'pretty good' hand depends on the cards outstanding and how the hand has been played. If the board has paired, for instance, quads are the nuts and full houses are possible, so flushes and straights might qualify as pretty good hands. When the board has no pair and no more than two cards of any suit, the top straight is the nuts and trips or two pair probably constitute a pretty good hand.

Identifying pretty good hands is important. One of the most expensive errors made by beginner or intermediate-level cash game players is the failure to bet good hands on the river. Why is betting the river so crucial? Because if you think you have the best hand and you're right, you're 100 percent to win. Your opponent can't outflop you and he can't draw out. Your bet, if called, represents pure profit.

To see just how profitable a good river bet can be, consider these two scenarios.

Scenario No. 1: You're in game with blinds of $5 and $10. A player in early position, who has allowed his stack to shrink to $100, raises to $30. Everyone folds around to you on the button, and you look down and find aces. You raise to $100, to put the original raiser all-in. The blinds duly fold and the original raiser calls and turns over a pair of tens. How do you feel?

If you're like most people, you feel great. But now let's see just how good a situation you really have. Before the flop, your aces are about 80 percent to hold up against his underpair. That means 80 percent of the time you'll make a profit on the hand equivalent to his stack ($100) and the blinds ($15). That's $92.

$$\$92 = (0.8)(\$115)$$

But 20 percent of the time you'll lose, and your loss is the $100 you put in the pot. That's equivalent to -$20.

$$-\$20 = (0.2)(-\$100)$$

Your expectation from this wonderful preflop situation is just +$72.

$$\$72 = \$92 - \$20$$

Scenario 2: You're still in the same game with blinds of $5 and $10. You have a pair and raise to $30 preflop. You get two callers, so the pot is $105. On the flop you hit a set. You slowplay, one player bets $80, the other player folds, and you call. The pot is now $265. On the turn you bet $120 and your opponent calls. The pot is now $505. The river comes and you have second set. You believe your hand is best. You bet $500.

Compare this to the previous scenario. If you've analyzed the hand correctly, your $500 river bet is pure profit when it's called. (The rest of the pot doesn't count because you're going to win it in any event.) Your net expectation is $500 which dwarfs the expected profit from the previous preflop scenario — one of the most favorable preflop scenarios possible.

Players who are reluctant to bet on the river are often paralyzed by the sheer number of possible threats that a board can represent. If the board is paired, any hand up to quads is possible. If the board has three of a suit, flushes are possible. Even without a pair or flush, it's a rare board where straights aren't possible. (It can happen, however; A-J-9-6-2, no more than two of a suit, is an example of a board where top set is the nuts.)

With all the threats that are possible, even on a modest board, a lot of players will have trouble betting something like top two pair or a low set on the river. The trick is to analyze hands step by step as you move through the streets, remembering that players usually have solid reasons for the bets or calls they're making.

When analyzing a hand on the river, I like to remember the difference between criminal law and civil law. In a criminal trial, the prosecution is required to prove its case *beyond a reasonable doubt*. In a civil trial, the burden for the plaintiff is lighter: it's only necessary to demonstrate that a *preponderance of the evidence* favors the plaintiff's case.

Thinking about the river is like that. You don't want to put yourself in the position of requiring evidence beyond a reasonable doubt that your hand is best; you'll never achieve that degree of certainty because you can always decide that your opponent has been trapping and tricking and weaving and bobbing and could now hold almost any legal hand. Instead, you want to establish a preponderance of evidence that you have the best hand. This basically means using the techniques of hand analysis that we discussed early to narrow your opponent's possibilities down to a few key hands.

One last point. Deciding that you probably have the best hand on the river gives you a reason to make a bet; either the initial bet, if you're first to act, or a bet in response to his check, if you're last to act. If he acts first and bets, your calculations have to change since his river bet becomes a big piece of evidence that his hand may be better than you think.

Remember the principle we elaborated on page 105 in "Hand Analysis: Weighing the Evidence" in "Part Two: The Elements of No-Limit Hold 'em Cash Games" of *Harrington on Cash Games: Volume I.* Your confidence in the information content of a bet is roughly proportional to its size. You should have the least confidence in deductions based on preflop bets since they're very small bets, and the most confidence in deductions based on late street bets since those bets are relatively large.

Sample Hand

You're in a $5-$10 live game. It's a tough game with a lot of sharp, experienced players. Your stack is $1,500. Player B, in second position, limps for $10. Player C, in third position, also limps for $10. Both these players have seemed tight and a little passive. You're in fourth position and you look down to see

You've been playing tight up to now, so you figure a raise should get some respect. You raise to $50. The players in fifth and sixth position fold. Player G, on the button with a stack of about $2,200, raises to $150. The small blind, with the biggest stack at the table, calls $145. The big blind folds, as do Players B and C.

Your pair of eights have shrunk a little bit, but the pot now contains $380 and it costs you $100 to call, so you're getting almost 4-to-1 odds. You figure that given the action you've seen so far, hitting your eight could win someone's whole stack, so your implied odds are huge. You decide to call, putting in $100 more. The pot is now $480. You're in middle position.

The flop is

You didn't hit your set. The big blind checks. You check. The button checks. After the preflop action, you're suspicious that someone is slowplaying a monster, waiting for someone else to take the lead in the betting.

The turn is the K♣. It's now hard to believe that someone doesn't have at least two high pair. Once again, the big blind checks. You check. The button checks.

The river is the 8♥, finally giving you a set. The big blind bets $200. *What do you do?*

Your first problem is to determine just how good your hand really is. Do you have a pretty good hand, a hand with some value, or a hand that's close to the nuts?

No flushes are possible, and the only possible straight is incredibly unlikely given the preflop action. (Who's going to put in the second raise, or call two raises, with jack-ten?) So the winning hand is probably going to be a set, and you have fourth set. Is that close to the nuts?

The answer, unfortunately, is "probably not." What hands, after all, were responsible for all that preflop action? You raised two limpers, and the button then put in the second raise. That should mean a big pair or an ace-king. Then the big blind just called that raise although you were still active in the hand. That indicates another big pair and probably not an ace-king. You then called for set value.

The flop put an ace and a queen on board, and everyone checked. That actually makes sense. Someone with a set of aces might be trapping, someone with a pair of kings would be afraid of the ace after all the preflop action, and someone with a pair of queens would be worried they might not have the best set.

The turn put a king on board. Again everyone checked. This most likely means that no one has a set of aces. But if someone just hit a set of kings, they wouldn't necessarily know that fact yet, especially if they were first to act. (Remember, from their point of view, you might be lying in wait with any of these pairs.) Once everyone checks, it's likely that no one has a set of aces, and if anyone has a set of kings, it's the big blind.

On the river, you hit your set and the big blind bets. You're getting 3.4-to-1, but it's actually a very tough call. (Give yourself many demerits if you actually thought about raising.) The big blind probably has a set of kings, and there's a decent chance the button has a set of queens. Your set of eights, in this situation is just a hand with some value. The 3.4-to-1 odds look good, but you can't be sure that another raise isn't coming from behind you. At a loose table I would most likely call here, but at this tight, tough table I'd regrettably let this go.

You fold. The button calls. The big blind shows a set of kings and the button mucks his hand.

You Have a
Hand with Some Value

When you have some value in your hand, you'd like to see the showdown as cheaply as possible. Your ideal situation is to be in position so that you can check after your opponent checks, and see if your hand is good.

If you're in position and your opponent bets, you have a trickier problem. If he makes a small bet that gives you pot odds of 4-to-1 or 5-to-1, you'll frequently make what's called a *crying call*. You don't really think your hand is good, but the pot odds are so favorable you have to see. As long as you can win one hand in five or one hand in six, you'll show a profit with these calls.

If he makes a large bet, you'll need to decide if he's bluffing. In no-limit hold 'em, everyone has to bluff on the river sometimes so that players will call with their merely good hands. Since they have to bluff sometimes, you need to call sometimes. (If you only call with big hands, your opponents will pick up on this and bluff you unmercifully.)

You could, if you wanted, stagger your calls at random. That's usually not an ideal solution, but it's better than always folding. A better way, however, is to review the hand and see if your opponent's betting fits the hand that he's representing. If there's a good fit, let the hand go. Save your calls for the hands where there are obvious discrepancies between the betting history and the hand that's being represented. You won't win all these because your opponents will sometimes trick you. But your calls will have a higher batting average than if you just call randomly.

Another way to protect a hand with some value is through what's called a *blocking bet*. Suppose you have a hand of moderate value where you don't mind calling a small bet but you'd rather not have to call a big bet. If you act first, you can bet with the idea of preempting your opponent and setting the betting level for the river. Your opponent, who might have bet a larger amount had you checked, may decide that he doesn't want to open up the betting again and just call, either out of fear or laziness. If he does elect to raise, he's given you more information than a simple bet on his part would have provided, and you can fold more easily. Since a blocking bet looks much like a suck bet, he may even decide that your bet represents great strength and fold a better hand.

Sample Hand

You're in a $25-$50 live game. Your stack is $9,500. Player G, a loose-aggressive player on the button, limps for $50. The small blind, a tight player with flashes of wildness, raises to $200. You're in the big blind with

and you elect to call $200. (I would have folded, but I have my tight "Action Dan" image to maintain.) Player G calls $150. The pot is now $675, and you have middle position after the flop which is:

That's a good flop for you, giving you an open-ended straight draw. The small blind bets $350. Although there's a possible flush draw on board, you decide your open-ended straight draw against two players is worth a call, so you put in $350. Player G calls as well. Player G's call makes the threat of a flush draw a little more real. The pot is now $1,725.

The turn is the Q♦. You make a pair of queens, but a third diamond arrives on board. The nut straight now becomes the ace-high straight, which you can't make. The small blind checks. You check. Player G bets $900. The small blind folds. You call $900, which is a mistake. You're against a player who's betting into a very dangerous board, and who may now have a hand that beats what you're drawing to. This was a good point to fold and cut your losses. The pot is now $3,525. You have $8,050 left in your stack. Player G has about twice as much.

The river is the 8♥. You now have a queen-high straight, which on this board counts as a very middling hand. You act first. *What do you do?*

You have a low straight which might be best, but might not. Better straights are possible, as are flushes and even straight flushes. You'd like to see the showdown, but you don't want to call a pot-sized bet.

A reasonable solution is to stick in a blocking bet of about one-third of the pot. The play has two advantages:

1. If your opponent has been playing with a single high diamond or a set, the bet may win the pot by making him go away. Otherwise, a check lets him bluff at the pot, (but he probably

won't bluff a set), a bluff which would be hard for you to call.

2.   A number of the hands which beat you may not raise your bet. If your opponent has a better straight or a flush with two low cards, he'll think there's a reasonable chance he's beaten and just call.

You actually bet $1,000. Your opponent moves all-in. You fold, and he shows 9♦8♦ for a straight flush.

You Have Zilch

When you reach the river with nothing, your standard play will obviously be to check and fold to a bet. But you can't do that all the time because your opponents will know that a check from you on the river means weakness, and a bet means strength. Because of the size of river bets, it's much, much worse for your opponent to be able to read you on the river. So if you're used to diversifying your play preflop and on the flop, remember that maintaining a balanced approach on the river is even more important.

When you bluff on the river, you want to bluff with your weakest hands in accordance with the First Principle of Poker. Use hands like jack-high, ten-high, or worse. They can't win the pot any other way, and since they're worthless, you can easily fold if you get raised. Bluffing with middling-strength value hands like middle pair is a waste because those hands might actually win the pot in a showdown, and if you bluff and get chased off the hand by a bigger bluff, you've lost a lot of equity.

Even though you need to bluff on the river, you don't need to bluff a lot. Instead, you want to pick your spots carefully so your chance of success is highest and your bluffs remain profitable. Here are a few guidelines.

- Don't bluff a calling station. Hopefully, this is obvious.

- Don't bluff someone who's shown a lot of strength in the hand. If someone has a very good hand, they might be afraid you have them beaten, but they'll call anyway to find out.

- Don't bluff if your story is inconsistent. In particular, if you're representing a made hand, make sure that your action on the turn was the action you would have taken with the hand you're representing.

- Bluff players who've shown weakness somewhere along the way.

- Bluff when a plausible scare card arrives on the river. Good scare cards are cards that make a low pair on the board, or cards that seem to fill in a straight. The story you're trying to tell is that you had a mediocre hand with some outs, and now you hit the jackpot on the river.

- Bluff when you've been drawing with low cards and you missed your draw, but it's very possible that he missed his draw too. If you're right, you'll lose the showdown, but a bluff will win the whole pot. The corollary to this idea is not to bluff if you have a high card in your hand, as that will win a showdown between two missed draws.

Sample Hand

You're playing at a $5-$10 live table with a stack of $1,400. The table is a mixture of loose and tight players. You're on the button with

The first four players fold. The player in fifth position, a tight player with about $1,800 in front of him, bets $30. The cutoff seat folds, and you call $30. The blinds fold, so the pot is now $75.

The flop is

giving you a flush draw plus an overcard. Your opponent bets $55. You call. The pot is now $185.

The turn is the 6♣ which doesn't help you. Your opponent bets again, this time $150. Given what you know about this player, you think he has at least top pair. Your pot odds are $335-to-$150, or 2.2-to-1. If you have 12 outs as you suspect, the chances of drawing out on the river are 34-to-12 against, or 2.8-to-1. You can't be sure exactly what your implied odds are on the river, but you figure there must be some chance he'll call an additional bet, and most of your draws are to the nuts, so you call the $150. The pot is now $485.

The river card is the 2♠, missing all your draws. Your opponent checks. You doubt that your ace-high will be enough to win the pot. *Should you bet to try and steal it?*

No. This is a very poor spot to try and bluff. Your calls on the flop and turn with two hearts on board will be interpreted correctly by most players as draws to a flush which you just missed when a spade arrived on the river. Your bet is trying to say that you really had a set all along. But if you had a set, you could have raised on either street. The fact that you didn't might mean you were setting an elaborate trap, but most players will go for the simple and obvious explanation and call you. Don't waste your money. Just check. Furthermore, you have ace-high which will occasionally win.

You check and your opponent shows

for a pair of kings.

Bet Sizing on the River

Once you've decided to bet on the river, you have to decide how much to bet. Properly sizing a river bet isn't a simple matter. Intelligent sizing depends on a number of factors. Here's a brief list:

1. How good is your hand?
2. How big is the pot and the stacks?
3. How much strength has your opponent shown?
4. What do you know about your opponent?

How Good is Your Hand?

In general, the closer your hand is to being the nuts, the more you want to bet. In the extreme case where you have the nuts, the "optimal" bet is generally all-in, although practical considerations require that you frequently bet lesser amounts so that your opponents can't pull too much information from your bets.

As your hand gets further and further from the nuts, you'll bet, on average, less and less, while still varying your bets to confuse your opponents. The extreme case on the other end is a hand that has value only as a bluff catcher; you'll very rarely bet the hand, and you're looking to call a modest bet.

Your outright bluffs will be judged somewhat differently. When you bluff, your bluff bet needs to be sized according to the hand you're representing. Before you bluff, make sure that the hand you're trying to represent squares with the bets and calls you've made, then bet accordingly.

How Big Are
the Pot and the Stacks?

The ratio between the pot and the remaining stacks is the major factor in determining whether you can make bets of various sizes or whether an all-in move is the only reasonable bet left. Let's look at a couple of examples of pots and stacks and see what happens when we try to make moderate-sized bets.

Example No. 1: The remaining stacks are twice the size of the pot. Suppose the pot is $500 and each player has a $1000 stack left. Imagine that we act first and we're considering making a $350 bet, 70 percent of the current pot. If we make that bet, the pot becomes $850 and our stack shrinks to $650.

Now suppose our opponent decides to raise us. How big a raise can he make? If he moves in with his whole stack, the first $350 just calls our bet, and the last $650 is his raise. At that point the pot is $1,850 and it costs us just $650 to call, so we're almost getting 3-to-1 odds.

Unless our bet was a bluff, there will not be many legitimate hands where we're happy to make an initial bet of 70 percent of the pot and then fold our hand to a raise where we're getting 3-to-1 on our remaining money. So we can say that with stacks of twice the pot, a reasonable bet on the river will leave us pot-committed.

Example No. 2: Suppose we increase the stacks to four times the size of the current pot? Let's rerun our previous example with a $500 pot but $2,000 stacks, and see what happens. Now our initial $350 bet leaves us with a pot of $850 and a stack of $1,650. If our opponent wants to raise, he can put in $350 to call, creating a pot of $1,200, then make a three-quarter-pot raise by raising another $900. That creates a pot of $2,100 requiring us to put in $900 of our last $1,650 to call. Could we walk away from that bet getting

2.3-to-1 odds? I think we could if our original bet had been made with a somewhat marginal hand.

Conclusion: With stacks of twice the pot, any reasonable-sized bet that's not a bluff leaves us pot-committed. When the stacks reach four times the pot, we can make a bet and still walk away if we think our opponent's raise represents a premium hand. In between is our gray area where any decision will be a judgment call.

How Much Strength Has Your Opponent Shown?

If he's acted weak throughout the hand, checking when possible and calling when necessary, aim for bet sizes at the low end of your range. If he's acted strong, leading off with a bet or putting in a raise somewhere along the line, then skew your bets to the high side of your range. (Assuming you want to bet at all.)

What Do You Know About Your Opponent?

Some players are calling stations. They're terrified of being bluffed out of a hand, or they're just curious about what you have, or some combination of the two. If your opponent acts like a calling station, and you think you have the better hand, just bet the amount of his stack. There's an excellent chance he'll call you for the entire amount, solving all your problems.

If he's not a calling station, and you think you have the best hand and you want him to call a bet, you have to use some useful rules of thumb and a little amateur psychology.

- **Don't bet more chips than he has.** If your stack is much bigger than his, don't say, "I'm all-in" and push your whole stack into the middle of the table. Instead, try to estimate what he has and bet about that amount or a little less. A gesture like that seems less intimidating and is more likely to be called.

- **Remember you're not in a tournament.** In tournament play, you push all-in not only to win all his chips, but also to eliminate him from the tournament. Once he's eliminated, you automatically move up a notch on the pay ladder. But in cash games, you can't eliminate somebody even if you win all his chips because he can just buy back. As a result, there's nothing magical about pushing all-in. If you think a bet for 75 or 80 percent of his chips is more likely to be called, by all means bet the smaller amount.

- **If you're sure he won't call a large bet, then 30 to 50 percent of the pot is probably the optimal bet size.** With these bets, you're offering odds of anywhere from 5-to-1 to 3-to-1. Those are hard bets to fold when he holds a hand with some value and there's a chance you're bluffing.

Calling Bets on the River

In this section, we're going to consider one particular scenario. You have a hand on the river of middling strength: perhaps two pair, or an overpair, or maybe top pair with a good kicker. (Note that these would all be considered strong hands on the flop. By the time we get to the river, however, their stock has sold off a bit.) You don't have the nuts, but your hand is a lot better than nothing.

If your opponent is first to act, he bets. If you were first to act, you checked, and your opponent now bets. You're probably getting pretty reasonable odds on this bet; if he bets the pot, you're getting 2-to-1 on your call. If he bet half the pot, you're getting 3-to-1. Do you call or not?

By eliminating your very good and very bad hands, we've made the problem difficult. Obviously if you had a big hand you would raise, and if you had nothing you'd fold, except for once in a while when you would make a bluff raise for balance. But with a middling strength hand you have a tough problem.

First note that you must call some of these river bets when you don't have a massive hand. There are three main reasons:

1. Some river bets will be bluffs from hands that can't win a showdown.

2. Some river bets will be mistakes from middling hands worse than yours that should have checked to call a bluff, but elected to bet instead.

3. You have to call some hands to establish that you can't be pushed out of a pot on the river when you don't have a premium hand.

Given that you have to make some calls on the river, how can you tell when your opponent has a genuinely premium hand, and you should fold? While there are no certain indicators, here are some clues that will tend to point to a really strong holding on his part.

- **Your opponent's bets tell a consistent story.** If your opponent has had a strong hand from the beginning, it's unlikely that he waited until the river to try and make some money with the hand. Check out his preflop, flop, and turn action to see if they show consistent strength.

- **Your opponent bet the turn.** As we saw in the chapter on turn play, there are a lot of compelling reasons for betting the turn with a strong hand. One key reason is to build the pot in preparation for a big bet on the river. Another is to get a bet down before a 'cooler' card arrives on the river and freezes all action. While there are also some good reasons for not betting the turn, the presence of a substantial turn bet is the best single indicator that your opponent had a good hand prior to the river.

- **A danger card came on the river.** If your opponent has been calling bets prior to the river, with some obvious draws on board, then a river card arrives which seems to fill one of the draws and your opponent then takes the lead in the betting, the implication is that they hit their draw. On the other hand, if they've been calling bets and an irrelevant card comes on the river, and then they bet, the implication is they missed their draw and they're making a final stab to win the pot. (But be aware that if you take this too far you will be exploited.)

Since you're going to call some bets on the river but not all, use these guidelines to weed out the situations that most likely represent a strong hand, and focus instead on spreading your calls among the more ambiguous cases. Note in passing that the third clue is mutually exclusive with the first two; it covers the case where your opponent made his strong hand on the river, while the first two address the case where he's had a big hand throughout.

A slightly different case occurs with the so-called "suck bet" on the river. This is a small bet with a big hand which looks like a blocking bet. The pot odds are so good that you can't really fail to call with a hand of some value. The downside is that it costs you a little money to see his hand. The upside is that he sells his hand at a really cheap price, so you perhaps lose a lot less than you might have lost.

Sample Hand No. 1

At a $10-$20 live table your stack is $2,200. The table has been generally tight. You're in fifth position with

Four players in front of you fold and you raise to $60. Everyone folds around to the big blind who calls another $40. The pot is now $130. The big blind is a tight, unimaginative player with a starting stack of $1,800.

The flop comes

You have top pair, top kicker. There is a possibility of a club flush draw and a small possibility of a straight draw. The big blind checks and you bet $100. He calls and the pot is $330.

The turn is the T♦. Your opponent's call on the flop indicates he has something. He might have a jack with a weaker kicker, a seven for middle pair, or a flush draw. He could conceivably have trips and be slowplaying his hand. On this board, two pair seems very unlikely, as does a straight draw. An overpair is also unlikely since he didn't raise preflop.

He checks again. Since you're still beating almost all the hands he might have, and since you don't want to let him draw at a flush for free, you bet $220. He calls again. The pot is now $770. His remaining stack is $1,420, and you have him covered.

The river is the 4♣. Your opponent bets $400. *What do you do?*

For an average, somewhat tight player, your opponent's bets are consistent with the story that he had a club flush draw, called through the hand, and bet the flush on the river when he was first to act. If he had low clubs he wasn't getting the expressed odds he needed to call on the turn, but if he had something like A♣Q♣ he was all right, with a flush draw, an inside straight draw, and two overcards.

Rather than try to answer the very difficult question "Is this opponent, in this hand, bluffing or telling the truth?" Replace it with a better question. "Given that I'm going to call sometimes on the river with middling hands, and fold sometimes on the river with those same hands, is this hand a candidate for the calling group or the folding group?" Seen in that light, this hand belongs in the folding group. Your opponent's story is consistent and he could easily have the hand he's representing. Does he actually have it? That's a pretty imponderable question. But certainly situations will come along in the future where the argument for calling is more compelling that it is here. So let this one go.

Sample Hand No. 2

At a $10-$20 live table, your stack is $2,900. The table has been generally loose-aggressive. You're in fourth position with 9♦9♣. The three players in front of you fold and you raise to $80. Everyone folds around to the big blind who calls another $60. The pot is now $170. The big blind is a loose-aggressive player with a starting stack of $3,200.

The flop is K♥J♠4♥. You didn't make a set and you don't like the two overcards to your nines. However, if your opponent called with a small pair he doesn't like this flop either. Possible flush and straight draws are now floating around.

The big blind checks. You bet $100. The big blind calls. The pot is now $370. Your initial reaction is that his call indicates he has a pair of jacks or he's drawing to either the flush or the straight on board. Since he didn't raise, it's a little less likely he hit the king.

The turn is the K♦. If your previous assessment was correct, this card didn't help him. He checks. You check as well.

The river is the 5♦. The big blind bets $300. *Should you call?*

You don't exactly have a powerhouse hand, with third pair. But now let's ask what your opponent might have. He called preflop, checked and called on the flop, and checked the turn. The board had both flush and straight possibilities throughout. Did he have a king in his hand? If so he might have raised on the flop, and certainly should have bet the turn to shut out the draws. Does he have a jack? He might still have bet the turn since the arrival of a king lessens the chance you have one. Does he have a big pocket pair like aces or queens? Then he might have raised preflop. Does he have a pair of fives in the hole? Wouldn't he have folded on the flop in that case?

The big blind's story isn't consistent. Of course, he might have a king in his hand and just decided to check down to the river. But it's more likely he had a draw, didn't get there, and is now trying to steal the pot. You don't know that's the case, but remember our point from the last sample hand. You're going to call with some middling hands and fold others. This looks like one of the situations where you want to call.

You call. He shows Q♥T♥ for a busted straight draw and you take the pot.

Sample Hand No. 3

At a $2-$5 live table. Your stack is $470. You've just sat down a few hands ago and you don't yet know much. In first position, you pick up T♠T♣. You make a mini-raise to $10. Everyone folds around to the blinds who call for $8 and $5 respectively. The pot is now $30.

The flop is 4♣4♦3♦. Both blinds check. With a solid overpair and a flop that would probably have missed your opponents, you bet $15. The small blind folds but the big blind calls. The pot is now $60. You think your opponent most likely has a diamond draw, a pair lower than yours, or even a straight draw. Since he was the big blind and got to see the flop at a cheap price, it's also possible that the flop hit him in some way.

The turn card is the J♣. It's an overcard to your tens, but it's not a diamond or a card that could help a straight. The big blind checks. You figure the pot is large enough right now for your modest hand, so you check as well.

The river card is the 3♣. The big blind bets $20. *What do you do?*

Your opponent made a small bet of one-third the pot. It could be a blocking bet with a modest hand, or a suck bet with a big hand.

Unfortunately, the only "modest" hand you can beat right now is a pair below your pair: a pair of nines through fives, or a pair of deuces. Could he have one of those hands? The answer is a tentative "yes." They actually match the betting pretty well.

● The call preflop makes sense with a medium-to-low pair.

● The check-call on the flop makes sense. Although he has an overpair, it's not high, so he doesn't feel like raising since you've shown strength.

● The check on the turn makes sense. He's out of position, and not interested in leading into you.

● The bet on the river makes sense. It's a blocking bet. He's hoping you have something like ace-king, and you won't raise if he takes the lead, but you might make a big bet if he checks, a bet he won't want to call.

So the idea that he has a lower pair which you can beat matches the betting pretty well.

Unfortunately, if he hit the board at all, he's got you. If he did hit the board, it's most likely he has a trey or a jack in his hand, rather than a four. (If he had made three fours on the flop, he might have slowplayed that street, but he almost certainly would have bet the turn with two flush draws on board.) Either a trey or a jack, however, do make sense given how the hand was played. If that's the case, he thinks he has the best hand and he's just made a suck bet to try and squeeze a little money out of you.

Should you call? I would say yes. You're getting 4-to-1 odds on the bet and the hands you beat are not inconsistent with the play so far. You're probably going to lose, but 4-to-1 odds are great odds, and I wouldn't turn them down here.

You call $20 and he shows you 3♠2♠ for a winning full house.

The Problems

Hand 7-1

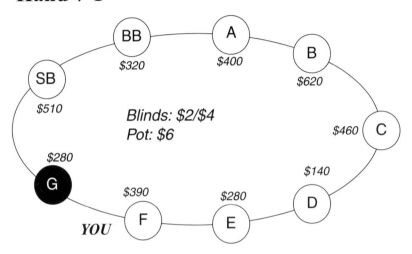

Situation: Medium stakes online game. The game is fairly tight. Player G has been loose and aggressive. He's made some moves, but so far they haven't worked well.

Your hand: Q♣Q♦

Action to you: Players A through E fold.

Question: *Do you call, or raise?*

    Answer: There's no reason not to raise. With a loose-aggressive player next to act, you might just call with the hope of being raised, but queens are not a hand where you want to let a bunch of people into the pot cheaply. If an ace comes on the flop, you'll have trouble making any money.

Action: You raise to $12. Player G raises to $24. The blinds fold. The pot is now $42.

Question: *Do you fold, call, or raise?*

    Answer: Raise. The only hands that beat you are aces and kings. Since you raised from the cutoff seat, your opponent probably interpreted your raise as a steal attempt and wants to know that you're serious about the pot. He could have made his raise with a lot of hands, so there's no reason yet to assume you're beaten.

    At the same time, queens aren't a hand for slowplaying. You'd like to win the pot right now, if you can. So stick in a big raise, at least tripling his amount.

Action: You reraise to $80. Player G calls $56 more. The pot is $178.

Flop: K♣T♣4♣

Question: *What do you do?*

    Answer: That's not a bad flop. Three clubs arrived, and you have the Q♣, so if a fourth club appears you will have the second nut flush. You also gain a little because, if our opponent holds an ace, the arrival of the A♣ will not beat you. So there are only three aces that are bothersome on the turn or the river.

    With a high pair and the Q♣, you have a good hand. Since he's already shown some interest in the hand, check to let him bet.

Action: You check. He bets $72.

Question: *What do you do?*

    Answer: You certainly aren't folding since your hand may be best right now, and if it isn't, you have many outs. So call.

Action: You call $72. The pot becomes $322. Your stack is now $238 while Player G's is $128.

Turn: T♦

Question: *What do you do?*
 Answer: The ten is a good card because it's unlikely that it made your opponent the leader. If he played preflop with king-ten, he was already beating us. But would he have raised, then called a reraise preflop with ace-ten, jack-ten, or worse? Probably not. So the turn is probably a neutral card.
 A neutral card on the turn is good for the player that's already in the lead. If that's you, fine, and if it's him, your position hasn't gotten worse. However, you're probably still in the lead, but have no reason to bet, and the pot is certainly big enough for your hand. So you check.

Action: You check. He checks behind you. The pot remains $322.

River: 3♣

Question: *What did his check on the turn tell you, and what do you do now?*
 Answer: His check on the turn told us he didn't have much of a hand. If he had a big hand, and the pot was $322 and his remaining stack was just $128, he would have pushed all-in before a cooler card could arrive which would prevent us from calling on the river.
 As it happens, that information doesn't help us much here because a fourth club arrived and we now have the second nut flush. But now we have to decide how best to play the hand. We have two choices:

1. Check, hoping to induce a bluff.

2. Bet, hoping to get a call if he has a club.

It's actually not clear at first which of these two possibilities has a higher profit potential. Let's see if we can break the problem down a little more.

Let's start by breaking his hand down into three categories and see how each of these categories might behave on the river.

1. **He has one club in his hand:** (He doesn't have two or he would have pushed in on the turn fearing the arrival of a fourth club on the river.)

2. **He has a hand, something like a pair of jacks or a pair of nines:** He can't have a pair of aces or a king, or a ten because again he would have pushed in on the turn.

3. **He has nothing and thinks he can only win by bluffing.**

How often does he have a hand in each category? Let's try to use some common sense to assign probabilities.

We'll start by figuring out how often he might have exactly one club. A priori, the chance that he had no clubs is about 56 percent.

$$.56 = \left(\frac{39}{52}\right)\left(\frac{38}{51}\right)$$

The a priori chance that he had exactly two clubs is about 6 percent.

$$.06 = \left(\frac{13}{52}\right)\left(\frac{12}{51}\right)$$

So by subtraction, the chance that he had exactly one club is approximately 38 percent.

$$.38 = 1.00 - .56 - .06$$

These are the approximate probabilities that he had no clubs, one club, or two clubs by dealing cards from a full deck. Now we need to adjust these numbers based on what we know.

First, we know that three clubs appeared on the flop. That means the chance that he had a club is reduced by some amount since we can account for the location of three other clubs. (Actually, it reduces the probability from 38 to about 33 percent.)

Second, we know that after the three cards appeared, Player G bet, then stopped betting on the turn. This information doesn't really tell us much. We could argue that he might be more likely to bet with a club in his hand, but three of a suit constitutes a good bluffing flop which could account for his action.

Let's estimate the chance that he has one club as the same as his a priori chance, about 33 percent. That takes care of Category No. 1, and leaves us 67 percent to divide among Categories Nos. 2 and 3.

Given the amount of betting that occurred in the hand, it's more likely that he has something than nothing, so we want the probability that he has something to be bigger than the probability that he has nothing. But Player G is a loose-aggressive player, so we can't make it too much bigger. Let's assign 40 percent to Category No. 2 (something), and the last 27 percent to Category No. 3 (nothing). That assignment leaves us with this breakdown.

- Category No. 1: He has a club = 33 percent

- Category No. 2: He has a hand without a club = 40 percent

- Category No. 3: He doesn't have a hand = 27 percent

Now, within each category, we have to estimate how he's likely to respond to either a check or a bet on our part.

One note before we continue. We're going to ignore the variation where the single club he holds is the A♣. If he holds that card, all the money will go in on the end and he'll win no matter whether we start with a check or a bet. So we'll consider only what happens in the other variations.

- **Category No. 1: He has a club but it's not the A♣.** If we bet, he'll call. Our bet gives him 3.5-to-1, and we'll make the fairly safe assumption that he can't lay down a flush in this case. If we check, he might check behind us if he has a low club, or he might push all-in, and we'll call. With four clubs showing, he won't be particularly eager to bet a low club. Let's estimate that he checks 60 percent and bets 40 percent.

- **Category No. 2: He has a hand but no club.** If we check, he'll check behind us with four clubs out there and see if what he has is any good. If we bet, he'll fold.

- **Category No. 3: He doesn't have a hand.** If we bet, he folds. If we check, he'll feel he can't win a showdown, but might be able to push us out with a bluff representing a club. How often he'll bluff in this case is very player-specific and all we can do is hazard a rough guess. Let's say he'll bluff 25 percent of the time and check the rest.

Now we just have to do the calculations, tabulate the results, and see if betting wins more money than checking and letting him try to bluff. We'll start by figuring out our profit if we bet. Remember, when the money goes in, our profit is just the rest of his stack, $128. If the money doesn't go in, our profit is zero since we're winning the existing pot ($322) whether the last of the money goes in or not.

1. **If we bet:**

    - 33 percent of the time we're in Category No. 1: He has a club but not the A♣, and he calls our bet. We win $128. Our weighted profit is $42.24.

    $$\$42.24 = (.33)(\$128)$$

    - 40 percent of the time we're in Category No. 2: He has a hand but no club, and he folds. Our weighted profit is $0.00.

    $$\$0.00 = (.40)(\$0)$$

    - 27 percent of the time we're in Category No. 3: He doesn't have a hand, and he folds. Our weighted profit is again $0.

    So our total weighted profit from betting is just $42.24 from Category No. 1 hands.

2. **If we check:**

    - 33 percent of the time we're in Category No. 1: He has a club but not the A♣, where he checks 60 percent of the time and bets 40 percent. We make nothing when he checks, but when he bets we make $16.90.

    $$\$16.90 = (.33)(.40)(\$128)$$

- 40 percent of the time we're in Category No. 2: He has a hand but not a club, and he checks behind us, and our profit is $0 again.

- 27 percent of the time we're in Category No. 3: He doesn't have a hand, where he checks 75 percent of the time and bets 25 percent. So our weighted profit is $8.64.

$$\$8.64 = (.27)(.25)(\$128)$$

So our total weighted profit from checking is just $16.90 plus $8.64, or $25.54.

The lesson from this analysis is fairly simple even though working through the mathematics took some patience. *If your hand is close to the nuts, checking to induce a bluff on the river is a common but very overrated strategy.*

When it works, it looks brilliant and you feel like you won some free money. The problem is that you never really know what he has, and even when you get to the river, his hand distribution will still be large enough that he'll have a reasonable probability of a hand he thinks is good enough to call you.

One last point before we leave this problem. Checking in this situation will always result in showing the hand down. (Either he checks and you show the hand, or he bets and you call.) Betting, on the other hand, mostly results in your winning the pot without a showdown. If you're going to adopt a mixed strategy of mostly betting strong hands but occasionally checking, you should choose as your checking hands those hands which you want to show to the table, while betting hands where you prefer the table not see your hole cards.

For example, let's say you're known as a tight player, but occasionally mix in suited connectors and other unusual hands among your starting cards. When you make a big hand on the river and you're in a bet-or-check situation similar to this example, you should tend to bet the hands that started as weak preflop hands while checking the hands that started as premium pairs or ace, good kicker hands. In that way, you help preserve the tight image you're trying to cultivate. Of course, if you're trying to cultivate a loose image, you should do the reverse.

Action: You bet $128. He folds.

Hand 7-2

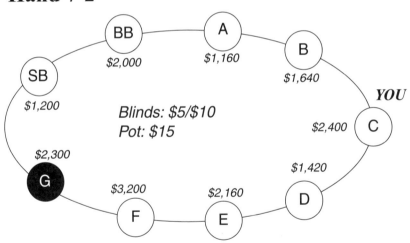

Blinds: $5/$10
Pot: $15

BB $2,000
A $1,160
B $1,640
SB $1,200
YOU
C $2,400
G $2,300
D $1,420
F $3,200
E $2,160

Situation: Medium stakes live game. The players have mostly bought in for big amounts and the table has been loose. Player F, in the cutoff seat, has been aggressive but hasn't ever been seen bluffing on the river.

Your hand: T♥T♦

Action to you: Players A and B fold.

Question: *Do you call or raise?*
> **Answer:** I would mostly raise with this hand in third position, but occasionally, I would call and play the tens as a low pair for trapping value.

Action: You raise to $35. Players D and E fold. Player F calls $35. The button and the small blind fold. The big blind calls $25. The pot is $110.

Flop: 8♥8♠3♥

Action: The big blind checks.

Question: *What do you do?*
> **Answer:** It's a reasonably safe flop, you have an overpair, and you were the initial aggressor, so a bet is in order. You also need to charge anyone who has a heart draw. With your overpair, you're actually making a value bet, so anything up to the size of the pot is reasonable.

Action: You bet $100. Player F raises to $300. The big blind folds. The pot is now $510.

Question: *What do you do?*
> **Answer:** Your hand is too good to fold to what may be a bluff or a semi-bluff. Call, but proceed cautiously on the turn.

Action: You call $200. The pot is now $710.

Turn: J♣

Question: *What do you do?*

    Answer: You don't like seeing an overcard to your tens. You're out of position and your opponent has taken the lead, so check to him and see what he wants to do.

Action: You check. Player F checks behind you. The pot remains $710.

River: 2♥

Question: *What do you do?*

    Answer: An interesting situation has arisen. The third flush card hit, but of course there's no guarantee your opponent was drawing to the flush. He may think you were drawing to the flush. Meanwhile, your tens never improved, but are still a reasonably good hand. One overcard appeared, but your opponent made his raise before the jack arrived, and checked afterward.

    You have two choices.

1.   **You can treat your hand as essentially a bluff-catcher and check.** If your opponent bets a reasonable amount (anything up to the size of the pot), you can call figuring that he might be betting a pair lower than yours or a bluff, and the pot odds (2-to-1 or better) will justify a call in such a murky situation.

2.   **You can bet, let's say $500 (70 percent of the pot).** Your opponent will either fold, call, or raise. If he raises, he'll probably put you all-in. At that point you will decide that he's unlikely to be bluffing because of the possibility you actually have an eight or a flush and fold. While he may bluff occasionally, you don't think he'll bluff often enough to justify the odds you'll get from the pot.

So we know our two choices. Now let's see what hands we might be facing. Player F's possible hands fall into these groups:

- A flush,
- Three eights,
- A pair better than ours,
- A pair worse than ours, and
- Nothing — A potential bluffing hand.

Hands in the top three groups beat yours, and hands in the bottom two groups lose. Here's a good rule of thumb for these situations: *Betting on the end with a medium-strength hand when your opponent can plausibly hold any of a wide range of hands, some better and some worse, is usually a mistake.* Instead, you should check. If he checks behind you, show the hand down and see who wins. If he bets, call with reasonably good pot odds (2-to-1 or better is a good guideline) and fold with poor odds.

Action: You check. Player F checks behind you and shows the 9♣9♦. You win the pot.

Hand 7-3

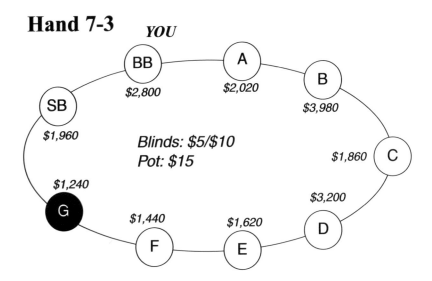

Situation: Medium stakes live game. The game is mostly loose, and the typical buy-in has been 200 big blinds. Player C has been loose and aggressive. Player D is one of the two tight players at the table, mostly playing solid values. Player G is a little wild and might be on the edge of steaming. He's lost a couple of big hands lately. You like to play a lot of hands and see a lot of pots. You're tricky and trappy.

Your hand: 6♦4♦

Action to you: Players A and B fold. Player C calls $10. Player D raises to $50. Players E and F fold. Player G calls $50. The small blind folds. The pot is now $125.

Question: *Do you fold, call, or raise?*
    Answer: I don't have any trouble playing six-four suited occasionally in a multiway pot. It's far down on my list of playable hands, but it certainly has surprise value, especially when flopping two pair or a straight draw. (When you flop a

flush draw you always have to be worried about a higher flush.)

The problem here is twofold. First, if you call you're going to be out of position after the flop, which cuts down the profit potential of a marginal hand substantially. Second, you don't know what's happening with Player C. He limped in early position at a loose-aggressive table. Early limps often get raised at such a table, and perhaps that's just what he was expecting. If he responds to your call with a big raise, you're going to have to fold.

Remember that a hand like six-four suited is not a hand you have to play. It's one of many hands that you want to play once in a while for balance and deception. Since you're only playing these hands occasionally, you can wait for situations where conditions are very favorable. Here they're not, so just fold.

Action: You actually call for $40 more. Player C calls $40. The pot is now $205, and you'll be first to act in a four-way pot.

Flop: T♦8♦5♣

Question: *What do you do?*

   Answer: That's a pretty good flop. You've got a flush draw and an inside straight draw. The flush draw could be vulnerable to a better flush draw, and the seven that you need for your inside straight could conceivably give someone a higher straight, but you're still in the hand, so count your blessings.

   With three aggressive players behind you, one of whom showed strength preflop, you can't really take any action. Just check and see what happens.

Action: You check. Player C checks. Player D bets $150. Player G folds. The pot is now $355, and it costs you $150 to call.

Question: *What do you do?*

Answer: Your hand has enough outs so that you're not going to fold. The real question is — do you want to raise? A semi-bluff is reasonable at first glance. You've got 13 outs, which is normally good enough to execute the play. But you do have a few problems.

- You may be against two players rather than just one which reduces the folding equity. When you execute a semi-bluff against a single player, you can usually get the folding equity you need. Against two players, that's more difficult.

- Your flush draw isn't to the nuts. In fact, it's not particularly strong. The odds are that neither opponent is drawing to the diamond flush; but when you're up against a better draw, it's a disaster (although if he doesn't have a pair it isn't as bad as it looks).

- You're out of position. If you make a semi-bluff raise and get a call, you'll have to act first on the turn. If you don't hit the draw, will you bet again, or check to get a free card? If you check and your opponent bets, will you call? Ideally, you'd like to be in position for a semi-bluff to have maximum effectiveness. That way, your opponent has to act first on the turn, and if he checks, you know you can see the second card for free.

Remember that big-stack poker is a game of patience. You don't have to make a big play in every marginal situation that comes along, just as a good hitter in baseball doesn't have to swing at balls outside the strike zone. Wait for good solid situations before making big plays. In this case, your choice is between a very marginal raise and a very solid call. Take the call.

Action: You call $150. Player C calls $150. The pot is now $655.

Turn: 6♠

Question: *What do you do?*
> **Answer:** You missed your draws but picked up a pair of sixes. Assuming Player D is betting a big pair, you've potentially at least two and perhaps five more outs.
>
> You should check. Your 15 (and perhaps 18) potential outs probably makes you better than a 2-to-1 underdog in the pot. Any reasonable bet from either opponent should give you those odds or better. With a check, you might even get to see the river card for free. A bet, on the other hand, opens the possibility of being raised off the hand.

Action: You check. Player C checks. Player D bets $400. The pot is now $1,055, and it costs you $400 to call.

Question: *What do you do?*
> **Answer:** The 2.5-to-1 pot odds make this an easy call despite the small possibility that Player C may stick in a raise.

Action: You call $400. Player C also calls $400. The pot is now $1,855.

Player C's action is starting to concern us. He limped and called preflop, checked and called on the flop, and checked and called again on the turn. Player D has bet consistently on each street. The most obvious read is that Player D has a high pair and Player C is on a draw of some sort.

If C has a draw, what draw is it? He could have been playing a straight draw if his hole cards were jack-nine, nine-seven, or seven-six, although the latter is less likely since two sixes are now accounted for. He could have a nut flush draw with A♦X♦, or simply a good flush draw with any two high diamonds.

Of these two possibilities, the flush draw is more likely. Since Player D seems to be betting a high pair, a flush draw containing the ace would probably have 12 outs: nine flush cards plus three ways to pair the ace. A flush draw headed by the king or the queen is less certain to have 12 outs, but might still be playable.

The straight draws aren't impossible since loose-aggressive players will play combinations like jack-nine or nine-seven, but they won't play them all the time, whereas most loose-aggressive players will at least see a flop with something like ace-jack suited or king-queen suited. So we have to rate the straight draws as less likely than the flush draws.

But if the flush draw is the most likely holding for Player C, we're in serious trouble, and if another diamond comes we just might have to lay our hand down if we check and Player C makes a big bet.

River: 6♣

Question: *What do we do?*

Answer: That's a perfect river card. We make trip sixes. The flush possibilities go away. Only two possible straights can beat us: nine-seven or seven-four. Player D's persistent betting throughout makes those holdings almost impossible for him. We can eliminate the seven-four holding for Player C since he was unlikely to call a raise with that hand on the flop, and even more unlikely on the turn since at that point he would have had just a gutshot straight draw with four outs. So if Player C has us beaten, he needed to start with nine-seven, call with a straight draw on the flop, make the straight on the turn and then slowplay. That's possible, but very unlikely.

What about Player D? He made a solid raise preflop after one limper, made a bet of about three-fourths of the pot on the flop against three opponents, and made another bet of about two-thirds of the pot on the turn against two opponents. His play has basically said "I started with a big pair, I've still got it, and I'm betting to chase away you pesky draws." The only other possible read is that he's on a courageous bluff and he's already been willing to fire two barrels.

So what's our play? We have three choices:

1. Bet. Our analysis indicates that we're against a player who missed his draw and a high pair.

2. Check. Hope that one of the other two players makes a value bet.

3. Check. Hope that someone else bluffs at the pot.

The logic for betting is clear. We have a good hand, probably best, and that's all we need. We think Player C will fold, but we hope Player D calls us with his pair. The pot is now $1,855. We have $2,200 left in our stack and Player D has $2,600. If we bet $600, we'll be offering Player D 4-to-1 odds to call; he might feel he was beaten, but he'll almost certainly call with those odds. We could bet $900 and be offering 3-to-1 odds. That's not so certain to be called.

What's the right amount? If we bet $600 and if he's 90 percent to call the bet with 4-to-1 odds, our expected profit on the bet is $540 (assuming that, indeed, we have the winning hand.) If we bet $900, he'd have to call at least 60 percent of the time for the bet to be as profitable. Of the two bet sizes, the $600 bet looks a little better to me. I've seen players lay down a high pair with just 3-to-1 odds on the end — in fact, I've done it myself, but 4-to-1 is almost embarrassing to fold. If you decide to bet, bet $600.

What about checking in the hope that someone else will bet for value, which you can then raise? The problem here is that if you've read the hand correctly, no one else *can* bet. Player C has probably missed a flush draw. If he had instead some sort of legitimate hand, it's a hand he's refused to bet so far, so it's not likely he'll bet it now. You've read Player D as betting a high pair. If that's correct, he probably knows that he's telegraphed his strength and wouldn't expect to get called except by a better hand. And if you've misread the hand, a bet represents a holding that beats you.

Checking in the hope that someone will bluff also isn't likely to make any money. There's a small chance that Player D has been bluffing the whole way and is now prepared to fire a third barrel on the river. But that's a really long shot. Player C has to worry that any bluff on his part will just get called by Player D.

Conclusion: You have a good hand and a reasonable-sized bet is likely to be called by Player D. So bet.

Action: You actually check. So do Players C and D. Player C shows A♦3♦, and Player D shows the Q♣Q♠. Your three sixes take the pot.

Failing to make good value bets on the river is one of the most common (and costliest) mistakes in deep stack poker. Remember, the pot is growing geometrically throughout the hand. Errors made on the turn are much more costly than errors made on the flop, and errors on the river are more costly yet. Player C could have made a bet of $600 and, in all likelihood, gotten a call from Player D. That mistake cost Player C *60 big blinds*, an error which dwarfs the effect of any number of bad preflop calls or foolish flop bluffs.

In passing, note that Player D did well not to bet on the end even after seeing two checks in front of him. He correctly realized that it was not likely that any hand he could beat was going to call a final bet.

Hand 7-4

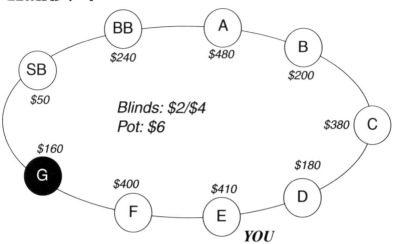

Situation: Medium stakes online game. The table has been tight. Player A appears to be an "opposite" player. He likes to bet his weaker hands and slowplay his stronger ones.

Your hand: A♥K♦

Action to you: Player A calls $4. Player B calls $4. Player C folds. The pot is $14.

Question: *Do you call or raise?*

    Answer: Raising is obviously the standard play, but calling should be done occasionally for diversification. I like a mixture of 70 to 80 percent raises and 20 to 30 percent calls.

       With two limpers already in the pot, your raise should be larger than the "standard" three big blinds. I would raise to five or six big blinds.

Action: You raise to $24. Everyone folds around to Player A who calls $20. Player B folds. The pot is $58.

Flop: Q♣T♦7♥

Action: Player A checks.

Question: *What do you do?*
    Answer: Except for a gutshot, we missed the flop. Let's see how we think the flop impacted Player A.
    Player A's call preflop marks him as having a pretty good hand —a pair or two high cards, but not a great hand — aces, kings, or queens. If he has a pair of tens or sevens, he just made a set. If he has any other pair below tens, he probably doesn't like that flop, and he should fold to a bet.
    A lot of the high card combinations hit the flop and won't fold. Some, like ace-king and ace-jack, missed the flop like we did. But king-jack now has an open-ended straight draw. However, they won't be eager to call a bet out of position.
    It looks like a continuation bet will chase away a lot of hands that are currently beating us while creating an image of strength which, coupled with position, might make some money later in the hand. Let's bet a little over half the pot and see what happens.

Action: You bet $32. Player A calls $32. The pot is now $122.

Turn: 7♠

Action: Player A checks.

Question: *What do you do?*
    Answer: There are not a lot of hands that Player A can hold that we can't beat. The pot is getting large and we don't have anything, so let's be glad we get to see the river card for free.

Action: You check. The pot remains at $122.

River: A♠

Action: Player A checks.

Question: *What do you do?*
   Answer: The arrival of the ace changes the picture considerably. There are now a lot of hands we can beat, and a few that are beating us. Let's make a list.

- We can beat any ace except ace-queen, ace-ten, or ace-seven.

- We can beat a hand with a single queen or a single ten.

- We lose to aces, queens, tens, or any hand containing a seven.

   The hands that we can beat containing an ace will probably call us, which is good. It's very hard to hit your ace on the river and then fold to a bet. Unfortunately, there shouldn't be too many of these left. Most should have folded on the flop.
   Hands containing a single queen or a single ten are our real profit center. Those hands fit the betting reasonably well. They should have called our flop bet, and probably checked the river when the ace arrived. Hands containing a queen might have wanted to bet the turn. Hands containing a ten would most likely have checked, fearing a queen.
   The hands we really fear are aces, queens, and tens. But would any of those hands have checked the river? In order for a check to make a profit over simply betting, a series of events have to occur:

- We have to have an ace in our hand (otherwise we're afraid of the ace and won't bet).

- We have to have a big ace (otherwise we're afraid he might have a better ace, and won't bet).

- We have to bet.

- We have to call his raise. (If we won't call his raise but would have called a bet, he would have done just as well by betting first.)

That's a long sequence of events, and the probability they all occur is pretty small. Another possibility is that a check may induce a bluff, but that's also a small chance. Clearly, the smart play for those hands was to bet the river. So we're probably not facing a set, and we're probably better. Let's bet.

Action: You bet $40. Player A raises to $130. The pot is now $292 and it costs us $90 to call.

Question: *What do you do?*

Answer: It's hard for a hand we can beat to make that raise, but we're getting 3.25-to-1 on our call. That's a good price, and we've already decided that the holdings that beat us probably wouldn't have played this way. When you see a discrepancy, you have to take a good price and call, because a discrepancy frequently means a bluff.

Action: You call, and he turns over T♣T♠ and wins the pot.

Sometimes bad plays get rewarded. Checking his full house on the river was objectively a bad play, but you had the hand that made it work. Unlucky.

Hand 7-5

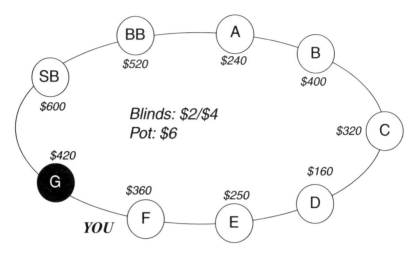

Situation: Medium stakes online game. The table has been tight. The small blind and big blind both appear to be tight, straightforward players.

Your hand: A♥9♥

Action to you: Players A through E all fold.

Question: *Do you call or raise?*
   Answer: In the cutoff seat, with everyone folding in front of you, ace-nine suited is good enough to raise.

Action: You raise to $12. The button folds. The small blind calls $10 and the big blind calls $8. The pot is now $36. You have position after the flop.

Flop: A♣K♥6♠

Action: The small blind checks. The big blind bets $32. The pot is now $68.

Question: *What do you do?*

    Answer: You hit top pair with a good, but not great kicker. You're losing to some of the aces, but beating most of them. Of course, your opponent may not have an ace at all, and just be betting to see if he can win the pot by showing strength.

    If he has a good ace, his play is a little unusual. Since you were the preflop aggressor, he could just check and expect you to bet. Still, you have position and it's definitely too soon to go away (with top pair). You should call.

Action: You call $32. The small blind folds. The pot is now $100.

Turn: 9♣

Action: The big blind checks.

Question: *What do you do?*

    Answer: That's a great card for you giving you a strong two pair. Now you're only losing to ace-king or the various sets that are possible.

    You should bet here, and you should bet a reasonable amount. The best guesses you can make about his hand are that he has an ace with a good kicker (better than your nine — ace-king, ace-queen, ace-jack, or ace-ten) or an ace with a weak kicker (everything from ace-eight on down). Why do you know that? Because those are the hands that are most likely to take the betting lead after an ace flops.

    However, an ace that bet the flop doesn't want to fold just because a nine arrived on the turn. These hands are overwhelmingly likely to call, so you need to make a good-sized bet, about 70 percent of the pot.

Action: You only bet $50. The big blind calls. The pot is now $200.

River: T♠

Action: The big blind checks.

Question: *What do you do?*

    Answer: You need to bet again. It's a pure value bet. You're both marked with an ace, and probably a medium-to-high kicker. You can beat ace-queen, ace-jack, and anything below your ace-nine. You lose to ace-king and ace-ten. (You also lose to queen-jack and various sets, but those hands don't fit the betting very well.) Since you can beat the majority of hands you may be facing, you should bet. If you then get raised, you'll have a difficult decision on your hands, but you have to respond to the evidence you've seen. If the big blind had a big hand, he should have bet the river, but he didn't. That last piece of evidence has to guide your play.

Action: You bet $70. The big blind calls and shows A♠Q♥. You win the pot.

Hand 7-6

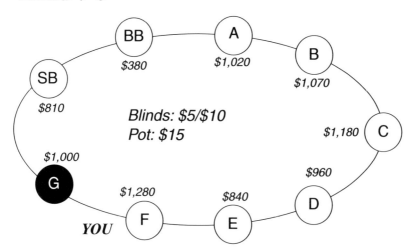

Blinds: $5/$10
Pot: $15

BB $380
A $1,020
B $1,070
C $1,180
D $960
E $840
F $1,280
G $1,000 — YOU
SB $810

Situation: Medium stakes online game. The table has been tight. The small blind seems tight and moderately aggressive. He hasn't done anything unusual so far.

Your hand: K♣K♥

Action to you: Players A through E all fold.

Question: *Do you call or raise?*
    Answer: Certainly you can raise with your pair of kings. Calling is a deceptive play which I might make here about 20 percent of the time.

Action: You make a mini-raise to $20. The button folds. The small blind calls $15 and the big blind calls $10. The pot is $60.

Flop: T♠6♦4♣

Action: The blinds both check.

Question: *What do you do?*
    Answer: A mini-raise from late position is an unusual play because it gives the blinds good pot odds to enter with marginal hands. On the positive side, the move appears weak and makes your hand a little more deceptive.
        Right now you can certainly bet. The flop is fairly harmless, although there could be some straight possibilities at the low end.

Action: You bet to $55. The small blind calls $55. The big blind folds. The pot is now $170.

Turn: 7♠

Action: The small blind bets $110.

Question: *What do you do?*

    Answer: The small blind starts to put on a little pressure. You have a strong overpair, but it's far from the nuts. If your opponent called with a couple of medium or small cards, he could have a set, two pair, a straight, or various draws. (Any five in his hand gives him an open-ended straight draw, while an eight gives him a double belly-buster. There's also the possibility of a spade flush draw which is a less likely threat since there was only one spade on the flop.)

    Since you have position, you'll get to see your opponent act first on the river. Coupled with the 2.7-to-1 pot odds, that's certainly a reason to call. If you call, the pot will be $390 and your stack will be almost $1,100, so pot commitment isn't a problem yet.

    Notice, by the way, why you really want to reduce the field when you have a premium pair. Unless you make your set, almost any random board can produce a lot of scary threats.

Action: You call $110. The pot is now $390.

River: A♦

Action: The small blind checks.

Question: *What do you do?*

    Answer: You should bet. Most players fall down in this situation and refuse to bet. They were worried on the turn, and now another scary card came, higher than their kings, so they think their situation has gotten worse. But it hasn't. In fact, it's gotten better! Let's see why.

    The key to untangling this problem is to match your opponent's actions to the cards on the board. Although we had bet the flop, he took the lead and made a good-sized bet on the turn. At that time, the board was T♠6♦4♣7♠. Did he take the lead because he had ace-six, ace-four, or ace-seven and was now proud of his middling-to-low pair? Almost certainly not. He might have bet with ace-ten, but why bother? On the flop, in an arguably better situation, he had just checked and then called our bet.

It's even less likely that he has a hand like ace-queen or ace-jack. Now taking the lead on the turn makes no sense after the strength we've shown. If on the turn he likes his pair of aces and thinks he's now best, a better plan was to check, and raise after we bet. So our conclusion is that the ace probably didn't help him because it doesn't explain his turn bet very well.

What about our other worries on the turn? If he had a draw, the ace didn't make his hand. If he had a straight or a set, why did he check the river? We slowed down on the turn, only calling his bet. He doesn't have any reason to assume that we'll take the lead and bet on the river, so if he wanted to make some money on the river, he needed to at least lead out with a small bet. But he didn't.

So what's a reasonable conclusion? He probably didn't have an ace in his hand because the turn bet doesn't make sense, and he probably doesn't have a big hand because the river check doesn't make sense. The best guess is that he has a pair, maybe with an inside straight draw of some sort, and he bet the turn in the hope that our bet on the flop was just a continuation bet with two high cards. When we called and an ace came on the river, he gave up on the hand.

If that's our analysis (and it fits the observed facts pretty well), then our best play is to make a small bet on the river, one that he can call with his pair because of the good pot odds. Since the pot is $390, a good bet is $80 to $100, which offers pot odds of 5-to-1 or 6-to-1. Those are hard odds to turn down.

"Suppose we bet and get raised?" you ask. We'll worry about that when it happens. We've analyzed the hand, probably correctly, and now we have to act on our analysis, not on our vague and inchoate fears.

Action: You in fact check. The small blind shows 8♠6♠, and your K♣K♥ wins the hand.

On the turn, our opponent had a pair of sixes, a flush draw, and an inside straight draw. In fact, he had 18 outs. So his turn bet was very reasonable, although checking with the idea of raising would also have been an interesting play.

Our failure to bet the river probably cost us 8 to 10 big blinds.

Hand 7-7

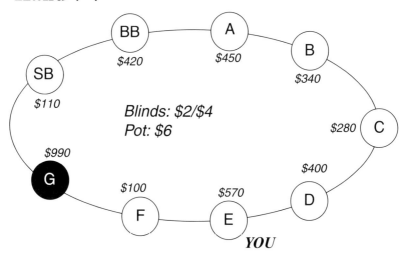

Situation: Medium stakes online game. The table has been extremely tight except for the small blind, a weak player, who has played over half the hands and has lost most of his stack.

Your hand: T♥8♣

Action to you: Players A through D all fold.

Question: *Do you fold, call, or raise?*

    Answer: A hand like ten-eight offsuit is a hand you want to play once in a while from any position when you're first in the pot. You're going to play it for deception value, for metagame value, and (as here) to take advantage of a very tight table.

    When you play the hand, you can either call or raise. Both have advantages. Calling lets you see a cheap flop. Raising lets you represent a genuinely strong hand when high cards fall, while giving you a chance to play a powerful hand that's extremely well concealed when middle cards fall.

    At a generally tight table, you can raise slightly more often with the hand since you'll steal a few more blinds.

Action: You raise to $12. Player F calls $12. The button folds. The small blind calls $10 and the big blind calls $8. The pot is now $48.

Flop: J♣7♣7♦

Action: The small blind and the big blind check.

Question: *What do you do?*

    Answer: The flop didn't entirely miss you as you now have an inside straight draw. It's a good bluffing flop, and if no one has a jack or a seven or two clubs, you may be able to take it down right here. The two blinds checked, which is a good sign. Make a continuation bet and see what happens.

Action: You bet $16. Player F folds. The two blinds both call. The pot is now $96.

Turn: T♣

Action: The small blind and the big blind both check.

Question: *What do you do?*

    Answer: Your bet on the flop was a little small, only one-third of the pot. Both blinds called your bet after initially checking. The small blind was getting 4-to-1 odds, while the big blind was getting 5-to-1. Those are big odds, but still they must have had something to call. Most likely one of the players had a flush draw, while the other hand a small pair or possibly a jack.

    If one had a flush draw, they just made their flush, so betting is out of the question. You do have the 8♣ in your hand, so if neither has a club, or if one has a low club as part of a pair, then your flush draw just might win the pot. Your best hope here is to see if you can check the hand down.

Action: You check. The pot remains at $96.

River: 5♣

Action: Both blinds check.

Question: *What do you do?*

    Answer: With four clubs on board, you just made a flush. However, that doesn't help you very much. If neither of your opponents has a club, they won't call a bet. If one does have a club, it's likely to be higher than yours.

    There's some chance you could make a big bet and chase away someone holding the 9♣, but you won't be able to chase away one of the big clubs, so betting doesn't look very cost effective. Just check and see if your flush is good.

Action: You check. The big blind shows 9♣9♠ for a higher flush. The small blind shows A♣9♥ for the nut flush.

    The small blind made a very bad play by checking the nut flush. He was hoping someone would bet behind him and he could raise. But a little thought would reveal a few problems with this idea. First, no one without a club will bet. Second, with the A♣, J♣, T♣, 7♣, and 5♣ all accounted for, the outstanding clubs (from the small blind's point of view) are the K♣, Q♣, 9♣, 8♣, 6♣, 4♣, 3♣, and 2♣. Which of those clubs would take the lead in the betting? Most likely only the K♣ and the Q♣. The other clubs might call a reasonable bet, but would prefer to just check the hand down (as we did with our 8♣). So to maximize his expectation, the small blind should bet (and hope he gets called).

Of course, the small blind didn't actually have the nuts. With a pair on board, someone could have quads or a full house. But there's absolutely nothing in the betting to suggest that there's some well-concealed monster lurking in the bushes.

What probably happened is that the small blind held two contradictory ideas simultaneously:

1. "I don't want to bet because someone might have the nuts."

2. "If I don't bet, I can trap someone and raise after they bet."

Not betting is better in all cases!

Absurd, of course, but players get caught up in this kind of thinking in the heat of battle. Make sure you decide what you really think is happening, then act consistently upon it.

Hand 7-8

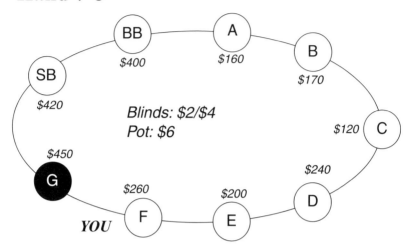

Situation: Medium stakes online game. The table has been fairly tight. The blinds have only played a few hands each.

Your hand: A♦A♣

Action to you: Player A folds. Player B calls $4. Players C, D, and E all fold.

Question: *Do you call or raise?*

    Answer: Limping with aces should be a rare option. The best time to limp is in early position at a loose-aggressive table when there's a good chance that someone will attack the limpers with a raise, and you can come over the top. (Some players make the same play with ace-king, representing aces.)

    Limping here is much less effective. With one limper already in the pot, it's more likely to encourage the button and the small blind to come in cheaply as well, the worst possible result for aces. I wouldn't always raise in this position, but I would hold my limping percentage down under 10 percent.

Action: You raise to $20. The button and small blind fold. The big blind calls $16. Player B calls $16. The pot is now $62.

Flop: A♥9♦3♠

Action: The big blind and Player B both check.

Question: *What do you do?*
> **Answer:** Good news: You hit top set! Bad news: You hit top set! How do you make any money on this hand? The preflop action showed that two players were interested in the pot, but no one had a big pair. The flop is totally devoid of draws, and now only one ace remains in the deck, and probably neither of your opponents has it. You took the lead before the flop, so if you bet now, both opponents will think you hit an ace, and will probably go away.
>
> You must check here. This isn't a metagame play; you're just trying to figure out how you can get a little more money in the pot. If you check, you're saying that the ace scared you too. That's a start.

Action: You check. The pot remains at $62.

Turn: K♦

Action: The big blind and Player B both check.

Question: *What do you do?*
> Answer: The K♦ is a good card for generating a little action. There's now a diamond draw on board, and the king could have given someone second pair.
>
> You need to bet at this point. If no one has anything and the bet wins the hand, so be it. There was no money to be made. But if someone has a king or even a nine, they may decide you're trying to steal the pot with your good position.

They could also think you have two diamonds and are making a semi-bluff. Either way, they have good reasons to call. The best scenario for you is that you're up against a hand that can not only call this bet, but one on the river as well. You should play as though that's the case because if no one has anything, it doesn't matter much what you do.

You don't want to make a big bet, however. Half the pot or a little less is the right amount. You're trying to make it easy for someone to stick around for the next street.

Action: You bet $28. The big blind folds. Player B calls $28. The pot is now $118.

River: 3♦

Action: Player B checks.

Question: *What do you do?*

Answer: First check Player B's stack. He started with $170 and he's put $48 in the pot so far, so he has $122 left.

With the arrival of the third diamond, you no longer have the nuts, but that shouldn't concern you too much. There wasn't any reason to suspect that Player B had the flush draw, and his check on the river pretty much confirms that. With a hand as big as a flush, most players will bet the river when first to act, rather than risk the hand being checked down. So as far as you know, you still have the winning hand, and you're going to make a value bet.

How much should you bet? The pot is $118 and your opponent has $122 left, so you could push all-in without severely overbetting the pot. However, this isn't the time for an all-in bet. The only strength your opponent has shown was his call on the turn. If the call wasn't based on a diamond draw, then your best guess is he has some sort of underpair: hopefully a king, but perhaps nothing more than a nine. Not only does he have to fear the ace which has been on board since the flop, but now he has to worry that you may have hit a flush.

In short, you can't bet very much here. Your ideal bet is something small enough so that he feels he can't let you steal the pot cheaply, if that's what you're trying to do. Bet $30 to $40, and you might get paid.

Action: You push all-in and Player B folds.

Hand 7-9

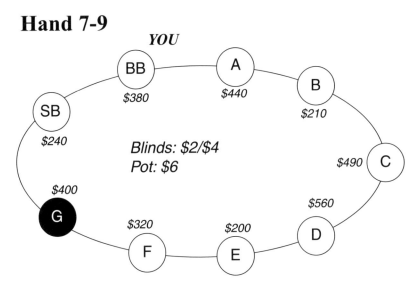

YOU

BB $380

A $440

B $210

SB $240

C $490

G $400

D $560

F $320

E $200

Blinds: $2/$4
Pot: $6

Situation: Medium stakes online game. The table has been fairly tight.

Your hand: T♣2♠

Action to you: Players A through E fold. Player F calls $4. Player G calls $4. The small blind folds. The pot is $14.

Question: *Do you check or raise?*

    Answer: Once in a while you can raise with a hand this weak in the big blind as a bluff, knowing that you can easily abandon the hand against resistance. For the most part, of course, just check and see a free flop.

Action: You check. The pot is $14.

Flop: J♣7♠3♥

Question: *What do you do?*

    Answer: It's a non-descript flop with few draws, but you've missed it and you're out of position. Trying to steal this from two opponents with no additional information is a distinctly negative equity play. Just check and see what your two opponents do.

Action: You check. Players F and G check as well.

Turn: K♦

Question: *What do you do?*

    Answer: You now have some evidence that no one has a strong hand, but there are two high cards out there and you have absolutely nothing. Check again.

Action: You check. Players F and G check also.

River: 7♣

Question: *What do you do?*

    Answer: You've reached the river and you have absolutely nothing, but a very good bluffing situation has arisen. Your two opponents have shown no interest in the pot, so if the first seven didn't help them, the second seven didn't help them either. Meanwhile, the second seven allows you to bet, and now your bet tells a consistent and believable story. "I had some junk hand like seven-four, I had second pair on the flop but I was out of position, and then I only had third pair on the turn so I didn't bet there either, but now I've lucked into trip sevens and I have to bet. Lucky me!"

It's a high-percentage bluff because you've combined your opponents' obvious weakness with the arrival of a river card that could plausibly have given you a great hand.

Contrast this hand with the following scenario: you're again in the big blind against two limpers and the board comes A♣J♥4♠. Everyone checks. Now an 8♦ arrives and everyone checks again. On the river, another ace comes and you bet out. This bet won't fool anyone with a pair because your story doesn't hold up. You're representing an ace in your hand, but with a good ace you might have raised preflop. After the flop, you declined to bet your pair of aces against two players, and then you didn't bet again on the turn. Now on the river, you make trip aces and decide to finally bet. Sorry, this story won't win any Pulitzers. Anyone with a jack or an eight will just look you up.

Action: You bet $10. Players F and G both fold. You win the pot.

Hand 7-10

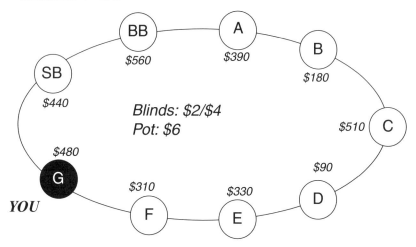

Blinds: $2/$4
Pot: $6

BB $560
A $390
B $180
SB $440
C $510
G $480 YOU
F $310
E $330
D $90

Situation: Medium stakes online game. The table has been fairly tight. You've been playing a tight-aggressive style.

Your hand: 7♦6♦

Action to you: Players A through C fold. Player D raises to $12. Players E and F fold. The pot is $18.

Question: *Do you fold, call, or raise?*

Answer: Suited connectors are playable hands in big stack poker. I won't play them all the time, but I'll play them in many favorable situations. You can lead with them for an opening raise in middle or late position (and even occasionally in early position), or limp with them in good position after a series of limpers. On rare occasions, I'll call a raise in good position.

Suited connectors have one very nice feature: they're self-limiting. Ignoring ace-king and king-queen, which are fine high-card hands, and ace-deuce and trey-deuce, which don't have enough straight potential, there are a total of 36 suited connectors from queen-jack down to four-trey. That's less than 3 percent of the total number of possible hands, which means a tight player can play suited connectors in any favorable situation without skewing his hand distribution too far towards junk hands.

Action: You call $12. The blinds fold. The pot is now $30.

Flop: A♥T♣5♣

Action: Player D checks.

Question: *What do you do?*

Answer: You missed the flop, except for a distant chance for a runner-runner straight draw. Player D checked despite being the preflop aggressor, so it's possible the ace scared him, but it's also possible he's trapping. You have nothing except position, and it's too soon to make a move. You want to know more than you do, and fortunately you have a chance to see another card for free, so take it.

Action: You check. The pot remains at $30.

Turn: 3♥

Action: Player D checks.

Question: *What do you do?*

Answer: The trey gave you an inside straight draw for a little extra equity. More important is the fact that Player D has checked a second straight time. He's saying pretty clearly that he doesn't have much, so you have a green light to try to take the pot down now. Bet somewhere between 50 and 70 percent of the pot and see if he goes away.

Action: You bet $16. Player D calls. The pot is now $62.

River: 2♣

Action: Player D checks.

Question: *What do you do?*

> **Answer:** You have only a seven-high hand, so it's almost impossible that you can win without betting. Since you bet last time, you've had three good pieces of information. He only called your bet on the turn, showing a hand good enough to call but not good enough to raise. Then the 2♣ came, putting the third club on board. That very likely did not give him a flush, but it did give you an extra threat. Finally, he checked again on the river, his third straight check.
>
> Player D hasn't shown any strength since his preflop raise, so you have to put him on a hand without much value, perhaps something like king-queen, king-jack, or jack-ten, where he's hoping the high card or the second pair will be enough to win the pot. It's reasonable to think that a bluff could win, so make another bet, 70 to 80 percent of the pot, imitating a solid value bet, sounds about right, and see what happens.

Action: You actually only check. He shows K♦Q♠, and his king plays and takes the pot.

Hand 7-11

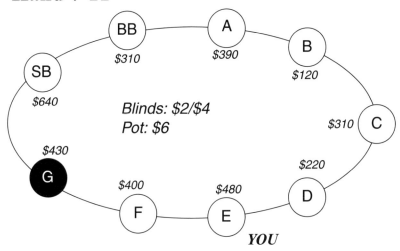

Situation: Medium stakes online game. The table has been fairly tight. You've been playing a tight-aggressive style.

Your hand: 4♠3♠

Action to you: Players A through D fold.

Question: *Do you fold, call, or raise?*
> **Answer:** If you've been playing tight, you should raise once in a while with suited connectors, especially if you're first one in . This looks like a perfect time to raise as the table has been playing tight and you've already had four folds.

Action: You raise to $12. Player F folds. Player G calls on the button. The blinds fold. The pot is now $30.

Flop: J♠7♠6♣

Question: *What do you do?*

Answer: That's a pretty good flop for you. You've got a flush draw plus a gutshot straight draw (needing a five). You took the lead before the flop, so there's no reason to slow down now. Make a good-sized semi-bluff bet of about three-fourths of the pot, and see if that takes the pot down.

Action: You bet $20. Player G calls. The pot is now $70.

Turn: K♦

Question: *What do you do now?*

Answer: Your bet didn't take the pot down, but you weren't raised either, so your opponent probably doesn't have a powerhouse. It's possible he has a flush draw or a straight draw just like you do. Or he doesn't have much, but wants to take the pot away on the turn. You have the same 12 outs to either a flush or straight you had before, so make another bet.

Action: You bet $40. Player G calls. The pot is now $150.

River: 2♦

Question: *What do you do?*

Answer: You've missed all your draws, and if you check and show the hand down it's hard to believe your 4-high will hold up. However, if your opponent was drawing, as you originally thought might be the case, then the king and the deuce didn't help him and he missed his draws as well.

Your bets have been completely consistent with an overpair or a top pair top kicker type hand. Your opponent's bets have at least been consistent with the idea that he had a draw, and if that's the case, he now has nothing. If you bet half the pot, he only has to fold one time in three for you to break even. My guess would be that this bet would do much better than that. Forget about the money you've already put in the pot and make a good bluff.

Note that although the pot is getting large, pot commitment isn't an issue because you will certainly fold if your bet gets raised.

Action: You bet $75. Player G folds.

Hand 7-12

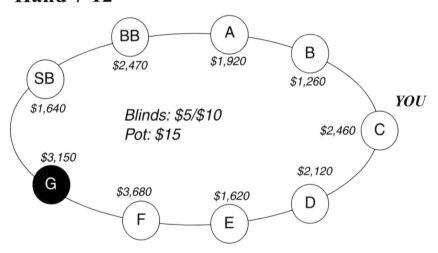

Situation: Medium stakes live game. The table has been mostly loose and aggressive. You've been playing a tight-aggressive style.

Your hand: T♣T♥

Action to you: Players A and B fold.

Question: *Do you call or raise?*

Answer: I would mostly raise with a pair of tens in third position, but mix in a few calls for deception purposes. When limping, I want to flop a set or at least an overpair to the board before I start pushing the hand.

Action: You call $10. Players D, E, and F fold. Player G calls $10. The small blind calls $5. The big blind checks. The pot is now $40.

Flop: J♠T♠9♣

Action: The small blind checks and the big blind checks.

Question: *What do you do?*
   Answer: You've flopped middle set, which is nice, but the board is uber-dangerous with potential made straights as well as straight draws and flush draws. You can't really consider giving the other players a free card here. So make a good solid bet.

Action: You bet $30. Player G calls $30. The small blind folds. The big blind raises to $150. The pot is now $250.

Question: *What do you do?*
   Answer: Combined with the board you're facing, that's a scary bet. Of course the big blind knew it would look like a scary bet, that's probably why he made it. Before we panic, let's take a look at the big picture.
   There are only two flush cards on board, not three, so he doesn't have a flush. His bet really represents a straight, in which case his hand needs to be king-queen, queen-eight, or eight-seven. Since he only checked preflop, any of those hands are possible.
   Now we have to ask, what other hands are possible? The answer here is pretty obvious. Many different semi-bluffs are possible on that board. It's a natural way for a semi-bluff to

play the hand — check to let players come in with bets, then come over the top with a big raise.

When I see a dangerous board and a big bet, my thinking is semi-bluff first because there are a lot more possible semi-bluffs than made hands. That's the assumption we should make here. We're probably looking at a flush or straight draw, or maybe both. If that's the case, here's a little summary of just how we stand against some possible hands:

- If he has Q♠5♠, for a flush draw and an open-ended straight draw, our winning chances are 61 percent.

- If he has Q♠5♥, for just a straight draw, our chances go up to 73 percent.

- If he has 8♣5♥, for a straight draw on the low end, our chances go up a little more to 76 percent.

- Finally, even if he has 8♦7♦ for a made straight, our chances are 36 percent.

Right now the pot is $250 and we have to put in $120 to call, so we're getting a little over 2-to-1. That's not a bad deal considering we're mostly a favorite, so we call.

We haven't mentioned Player G, who is still active behind us. Mostly, he's going to fold. If he pushes all-in, we'll get to see the big blind act before we do, but sometimes that will be a semi-bluff as well, and we'll have to call it.

Action: You call $120. Player G folds. The pot is now $370.

Turn: 7♦

Action: The big blind checks.

Question: *What do you do?*

    Answer: Not a great card for us. If he had an eight and was drawing to the low end of the straight, he just made it. But he didn't bet. It's just possible he was trapping, but trapping after a big bet on the previous street is unusual.

    We could bet, but we aren't really sure where we stand, and if we bet and get hit with a big raise, we won't like it at all. The pot is already pretty big and there will probably be more action on the river, so let's act weak and see if a little deception helps us on the end.

Action: You check. The pot remains at $370.

River: 3♦

Action: The big blind bets $200.

Question: *What do you do?*

    Answer: The flush never arrived, so your three tens now beat everything except a straight or a higher set of jacks. The jacks are a real long shot, so let's focus on the chance that the big blind has a straight.

    If he has a straight, he either had the straight on the flop (by holding king-queen, eight-seven, or queen-eight), or he made the straight on the turn when the seven hit because he had an eight in his hand. In either case, we have to ask, "Why check the turn?" At that point you had indicated unambiguous strength with a bet and a call of a big raise on the flop. You might have been drawing to any of these hands:

- A flush (with two spades)

- A better straight (with a king or a queen if he held the low end of the straight)

- A full house (with a set of jacks, tens, nines, or eights)

- A full house (with any two pair)

That's an awful lot of potential draws. With a straight, would you allow an opponent a free draw in those circumstances? Few players would, yet what else could you have, given your flop play against a very threatening board? With a straight on the turn, the big blind would have to see you with a strong draw, or a strong hand plus a strong draw, and figure he had to charge you then because he couldn't be sure of getting any money out of you on the river.

So we have all the components in place for calling a potential river bluff: a weak card on the river that couldn't help a draw, a story that didn't ring true, and a hand good enough to beat anything but a real powerhouse. You must call.

Action: You call. He shows Q♠4♠, for a busted flush, and your set of tens take the pot.

Hand 7-13

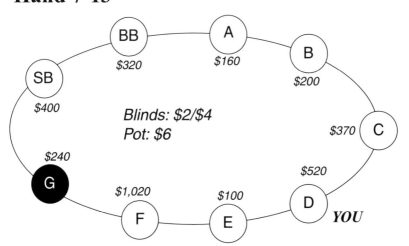

Situation: Medium stakes online game. The table has been mostly loose and aggressive. The button and the big blind are both calling stations and will call hands down a long way with just a low pair.

Your hand: K♠Q♥

Action to you: Players A, B, and C fold.

Question: *Do you fold, call, or raise?*

> **Answer:** King-queen in fourth position is a good enough hand to raise, especially at a loose table, where it rates to be better than many of the hands that might call you.

Action: You make a mini-raise to $8. Players E and F fold. Player G, on the button, calls $8. The small blind folds and the big blind calls $4. The pot is now $26. Three players are left and you're in the middle.

Flop: J♣T♠4♣

Action: The big blind checks.

Question: *What do you do?*

> **Answer:** You were the aggressor preflop and there's no reason yet to think you're beaten. You have an open-ended straight draw and two overcards to the board, so your king-high hand may be best right now. Make a continuation bet and see what happens.

Action: You bet $12. Player G calls $12. The big blind folds. The pot is now $50.

Turn: 6♥

Question: *What do you do?*

    Answer: You got rid of one player, but now you're up against a known calling station. If he has a small pair, which is likely, he'll stay around to the end, calling but not betting. If he doesn't even have a pair, he won't call your bet. Save your money and see if you make a hand on the river.

Action: You check. Player G checks. The pot remains at $50.

River: 3♠

Question: *What do you do?*

    Answer: You only have king-high and you know your opponent is the sort who will call with a pair. Don't try to bluff a calling station. Just check and see if you can check the hand down.

Action: You check. Player G bets $4.

Question: *What do you do?*

    Answer: You're being offered 54-to-4 odds, or 13.5-to-1. Those are huge odds, but what hands can you actually beat? You can't beat any pair and you can't beat an ace, so the only hands he might have played that you can beat are queen-nine or nine-eight, where he missed a straight draw. Would a calling station bet those hands on the end with a tiny bet that's just begging to be called? No. Even though the amount is only one big blind, save your money.

    If a sophisticated player made a minimum bet on the end, you might consider calling. It's a known play, designed to take a pot with a very weak hand by risking the minimum. You hope that your opponent doesn't have much and is prepared to fold to any bet without considering the odds, or else he's a little better than that but figures that since the bet is begging for a call, it must be a trick.

Action: You fold.

Hand 7-14

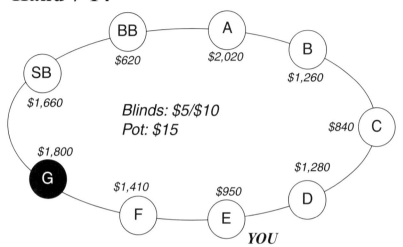

Situation: Medium stakes online game. The table has been pretty loose. Player G, on the button, is particularly loose and aggressive.

Your hand: A♣8♣

Action to you: Players A through D fold.

Question: *Do you fold, call, or raise?*
> **Answer:** In fifth position, ace-eight suited is just good enough to raise. Calling is also reasonable. I would not throw the hand away.

Action: You raise to $40. Player F folds. Player G calls $40. The blinds fold. The pot is now $95.

Flop: J♥J♣8♥

Question: *What do you do?*

> **Answer:** That's not a bad flop since you hit your eight. You were the aggressor preflop and you hit your hand, so you should mostly bet here with just a few checks.

Action: You bet $60. Player G calls $60. The pot is now $215.

Your first job is to consider what hands might have legitimately called on the flop, and how you stand against those hands. There are actually quite a few, but we can put them into a few broad groups:

- **A jack.** If he's trapping with a jack, you're almost dead. Against a hand like Q♦J♦, for instance, you're about a 24-to-1 underdog.

- **An eight**. Here you're doing well because you have the ace as your kicker. Against 9♦8♦, for instance, you're a 4-to-1 favorite.

- **A straight draw**. The only reasonable straight draw comes when he holds exactly the ten-nine. Against the T♦9♦ you're a slight favorite before the turn at about 5-to-4. (You're only a small favorite because he holds two overcards to your eights.)

- **A flush draw**. If he has two hearts, he's got a flush draw. If the cards are overcards, perhaps the K♥Q♥, he's about even money. If he has undercards, like the 6♥5♥, you're about a 2-to-1 favorite. If he's lucky enough to hold the T♥9♥, he has a straight flush draw and he's about a 3-to-2 favorite. That's such a long shot, however, that it won't factor seriously into your calculations.

- **An overpair**. If he holds a pair from aces down through nines, you're in bad shape. If he holds the kings, queens, tens, or nines, you're about a 3-to-1 underdog. If the holds the aces, he takes away most of your outs and you become a 7-to-1 underdog. However, the aces, kings, and queens are unlikely since he didn't raise you preflop.

- **An underpair**. If he holds anything from a pair of sevens down to of deuces, you're between a 6-to-1 and a 7-to-1 favorite.

That's a lot of possible hands. Our next job is to order them by likelihood. Some hands, like the straight draws with ten-nine are unlikely because there aren't many of them in the deck. Others, like the high pairs, are unlikely because of the way the hands has been played. If we group the hands by likelihood, here's what we get:
The most likely hands:

- A flush draw,
- An underpair, and
- An eight.

These hands are likely because there are a lot of them and they fit the betting well.
The least likely hands:

- A jack,
- An overpair, and
- A straight draw.

A jack is unlikely because there are only two left in the deck and because he didn't raise on the flop. (He didn't have to, of course, because the hand was perfectly strong enough to slowplay. But he could have, and since he didn't, the likelihood drops.) An overpair is unlikely because he didn't raise either preflop or on the flop. A straight draw is unlikely because there are so few of them.

Arranging the hands this way is encouraging. We're beating the most likely hands, and losing to the least likely ones! That's good news.

Turn: 9♦

Question: *What do you do now?*

> **Answer:** The arrival of a nine that isn't a heart doesn't change our evaluation too much. While it might look like a dangerous straight card, it was a card that he was already supposed to have in his hand if he was playing a straight draw. The only hand on our list it affected was the straight draw with ten-nine, which has now made an overpair and is ahead of us. Since we thought that was his least likely holding, we're not worried much about the card.
>
> Although our hand isn't a monster at this point, the nine shouldn't have helped him, so we're entitled to bet again and charge the draws.

Action: You bet $100. Player G calls. The pot is now $415.

River: J♦

Question: *What do you do?*

> **Answer:** We've now made jacks full of eights, but we have to figure out just how good that hand might be. The call on the turn and the jack on the river adds some more important information to the picture. Some of the most likely hands suddenly got a little less likely.
>
> • **A jack.** The appearance of the third jack has caused the likelihood of the case jack in our opponent's hand to drop. Of course, four jacks are now the nuts.

- **An underpair**. The likelihood of the small pairs (sevens through deuces) just dropped because he called a second consecutive bet on the turn. If you had a pair of treys, for instance, how many bets would you call against that board? One perhaps because your opponent might be bluffing, but two? While some adventurous souls might persevere, most would be gone at this point, so we have to downgrade the underpairs considerably. Any underpair that remains now has a full house, but has to worry that it's not the best full house.

- **An eight**. Most of the eights that would have called on the flop might still be hanging around. Hands like queen-eight, ten-eight, and eight-seven might still have been playing with the straight possibilities. Of course, nine-eight has become a winning full house (jacks full of nines), while the other eights have now made jacks full of eights, and tie us.

- **An overpair**. We thought this was unlikely before, and its failure to raise on the turn makes it a bit less likely still. Any overpair, however, now has a better full house than ours.

- **A flush draw**. The probability of a flush draw went down a little bit with the call on the turn since they weren't getting the right expressed odds, and couldn't be sure of getting implied odds on the river if the flush card landed. Now, of course, the flush draw didn't get there.

- **A straight draw**. We thought the only plausible straight draw on the flop was the ten-nine holding. That hand has now become a better full house.

Now let's try to put all this information together and see where we stand.

The hands that we thought were likely before, and that we were beating, became less likely with his call on the turn. The underpairs would mostly have folded after our turn bet, the flush draws might have folded, and the eights would probably still have called. After the river card made three jacks, the eights are now splitting the pot with us and the other hands are losing.

The unlikely hands, except for possibly the jack, have become more likely because they were strong enough to call a turn bet. All those hands, the last jack, the overpairs, and the straight draw, are now beating us.

So what should we do? We only have two options: check, hoping to check the hand down, or make a blocking bet, hoping to get to the showdown at minimal cost. (Note that a big bluff won't work here. The hands that we're beating won't call, and the hands that are beating us won't fold.)

First. let's assume we check:

- All the hands better should bet. The worst of these hands is now the straight draw (ten-nine) which became a better full house, jacks full of nines. Even that hand, though, should think it's probably best. The pot is now $415, so let's estimate that these hands will make a $300 bet.

- The hands worse than us should be happy to check the hand down. The missed draws might consider bluffing as their only way to win, but would then probably realize that they're facing a full house at this point, which won't go away. So we'll assume that the hands worse than us will check.

- The hands that tie with jacks full of eights should check as well, based on the same reasoning we're going through.

  If we check and our opponent bets, we should fold. We're getting odds of $715-to-$300, or about 2.4-to-1. We only need to win about 30 percent of the time to call that bet. But it looks like the bet will be coming almost exclusively from hands that beat us, so winning 30 percent of the time could be a tall order.

  Next, let's assume we make a blocking bet, say about $150.

- Of the hands that beat us, some will call this bet and some will raise. None will fold. The raisers will be the fourth jack, obviously, and jacks full of aces. Jacks full of kings might also choose to raise. The other hands will probably just call. We'll fold to the raisers and lose to the callers.

- What about the hands that lose to us? The busted flushes will fold, and the underpairs will probably all fold as well. They'll be facing a third consecutive bet on a board with all overcards, so if they didn't fold the turn they will probably fold now.

- How about the eights which tie us? With a full house, they'll probably call because of the big pot odds even though they'll think there's a good chance they're beaten. We'll split the pot.

Looking at the two choices, the blocking bet doesn't work *because the board is too strong*. We can't slow down the hands that beat us since they're too big and they know at this point that they're too likely to be best. At the same time, we can't get calls from enough weaker hands because facing a monster board, there's too little chance their hand is good. The best play is to simply check.

The general lesson to take home from this hand is that a blocking bet is a reasonable play on a board of moderate strength. The stronger the board, the less effect the bet has because the great hands will ignore it and raise anyway, while the weaker hands can't call.

Action: You actually bet $150. Player G raises to $750, and you fold.

Part Eight

Tells and Observations

Tells and Observations

Introduction

When you're playing poker online, you don't have access to much information about your opponents except for their betting patterns. You can see how often they enter pots, how they bet their hands, and how they respond to the action at the table. Once in a while, a hand will go all the way to the showdown and you'll be presented with a wealth of information as to exactly what your opponent saw during the hand and how he responded. From these clues, you should be able over time to construct a pretty good picture of his habits and inclinations.

In live games, however, a whole new world of information becomes available. By actually seeing your opponents, you can watch their reactions as cards fall and bets are made. Watching them carefully might let you find a "tell," a non-verbal clue about the cards they actually hold. In poker movies and literature, spotting tells is usually the key to success at the table.

In this section, however, we're going to take a contrarian approach to the business of tells. Rather than try to provide you with a catalog of tells, we're going to explain why the whole science of spotting tells is more difficult and less useful than most people suppose. As compensation, however, we'll provide some bullet-proof advice for defending yourself at the table, to make sure that no one can gain any advantage by observing you.

A different, but closely related topic is the art of conversation at the poker table. We'll close this section by showing how players use conversation to their advantage, and how you can avoid falling prey to seemingly innocuous remarks.

Evaluating Tells

The simple truth about tells is that, in general, they're not as important an element of the game as most people think. A player who can't read his opponents at all, but who has mastered the mathematics, tactics, and logic of no-limit hold 'em, as we've described, and who can make a reasonable effort not to give anything away with his mannerisms, will do just fine. Reading tells should be seen as just a little bit of icing on the cake, something to get you that last fraction of a percent of vigorish, and not as the game's main course.

To some of our readers, this last paragraph will seem like heresy, but I assure you it's true. Let's look at some of the problems with evaluating tells.

Problem No. 1: Finding a tell. Spotting tells isn't nearly as easy as the books on tells would have you believe. Most players are making at least a modest effort not to give any information away. Even when you see someone do something that might be a tell, you may have no idea what it means.

Suppose, for instance, you see a player bet with a slightly exaggerated motion, shoving his chips toward the center. You think "Aha! A tell." But his opponent folds the bet, so you never get to see his cards. His mannerism might have meant something, but was he bluffing, or did he have a big hand? You won't know until you see him do it again, and see his cards, and then see him bet in a different manner later, and then see those cards.

And remember, you're supposed to be looking for tells for everyone at the table. It's a daunting task.

Problem No. 2: Real or random? A player shifts in his seat as he plays a hand. Is that a tell? Or did he just shift in his seat? People do move around from time to time. The player on your right just scratched his chin as he contemplated a raise. A tell? Or was he just scratching an itch? Watch someone sitting in an airport, waiting for a plane, and under no pressure at all. Chances are you'll see him shift, scratch, fidget, and blink within a minute or so — all perfectly natural, all meaningless.

Problem No. 3: Real or deception? Some of your opponents will actively send out false signals. (We'll describe a good method of doing just that later in the chapter.) Can you tell the real from the fake? You may have to observe someone for quite a while before you can sort things out.

Problem No. 4: What does it mean? Let's assume you've found a tell on Transparent Ted, sitting across the table from you. It's passed all the tests — you spotted it, it's not random, and you're sure Ted's oblivious to his tell, so it's not deceptive. Whenever he has a strong hand, he drums his fingers on the table, and if he has a weak hand, he doesn't.

Great. Now let's put our tell into practice. Follow the next hand as it develops and let's see how Ted's egregious tell can help us.

Sample Hand

We're in our favorite $2-$5 game at the local casino, seated across from Ted. Our stack is $700, Ted's is about the same. Ted, in early position, bets $15, and we call with

The hand is heads-up. The flop comes

giving us a set of treys. Ted checks, we bet $30, and Ted calls. The pot is now $97.

The turn card is the 9♥, giving us a full house, treys full of nines. Ted checks again. We bet $80, and Ted calls. The pot is now $257. We have about $575 left in our stack.

The river card is the T♠, putting straight and flush draws on board. Ted flashes the tell that lets us know he has a big hand, and bets $250. What are we supposed to do? Should we call, raise, or fold?

We have diligently studied Ted's play and developed a very reliable tell as to the strength of his hand on the end. We believe that the tell is 100 percent reliable. Now we're in a huge hand and he's flashed the tell. But there's a slight problem. We know Ted thinks he has a big hand. But is his big hand

- Trips?
- A straight?
- A flush?
- A better full house than ours?
- Quad nines? Or,
- A straight flush?

Simply knowing that Ted thinks he has a "big" hand isn't terribly useful because we have a big hand too, but not the nuts. So some of Ted's potential big hands beat us, while others lose.

While our tell isn't all that helpful, some knowledge of Ted's betting patterns would help a lot. For instance, what does he do when he flops a set? Will he check, or does he tend to bet out? If he tends to bet rather than check, then we can downgrade the likelihood that he now has quads or a full house. Does he routinely semi-bluff with a straight or flush draw? If he doesn't, then it's likely that he has one of those two hands. If he does semi-bluff, then the fact that he didn't this hand means that we may well be beaten.

Knowledge of an opponent's betting patterns is in many cases more reliable than information based on tells since it can give us some very specific clues that enable us to eliminate certain classes of hands. Knowing that an opponent has a hand that he considers "strong" or "weak," however, can be pretty murky. It's useful if we have a hand like a single pair, and we want to know if he's bluffing with nothing or betting with something. But if we have a real hand and so does he, we haven't really gained much.

Consider the last example again. He bets on the river and his tell says he has a big hand. But the combination of the bet and his board says exactly the same thing. The board is so threatening that hardly any bettor would consider bluffing into it. So our physical tell hasn't added any information between what the simple bet tells us.

Mason Malmuth has pointed out that tells are only useful when they cause you to make the right decision when otherwise you would have made the wrong one. That's a stiff test to pass. In this example, even the existence of a 100 percent surefire bulletproof tell on the river was not helpful to us. Instead, we needed to revert back to consideration of the betting pattern to see what to do.

Playing in Live Games

My general advice for someone sitting down in a cash game for the first time in a new casino is simple but heretical — forget about picking up physical tells on your opponents. Just play poker, observe betting patterns, and make good common sense decisions. If you think someone is actively trying to send you a message with their body language — if their behavior seems unusual, unnatural, or stilted — then revert to Mike Caro's basic criteria: strong means weak and weak means strong, and act accordingly.

Remember that trying to observe eight other players constantly for hours is, in fact, extremely draining. Poker requires a fresh alert mind, and if you're planning on playing in a live game for several hours, you may be much better off focusing on hand reading and betting patterns and letting the tells take care of themselves.

Keep in mind as well that many tells, even if you can spot them accurately, may only duplicate the information you've gained from observing the play of the hand. Suppose, for instance, that your opponent has played a hand inconsistently, and as a result you've decided that you'll have to call a river bet to pick off a possible bluff. If you then pick up a tell that says your opponent is in fact bluffing, the tell won't do you any good; you'll make the same play you would have made anyway.

Many major tournaments have now been won by players from the online world, who couldn't be expected to have well-developed tell-reading skills. The most famous example is Chris Moneymaker, who won the 2003 World Series of Poker main event in his first try at a live tournament. It's highly unlikely that skill in picking up tells was a big part of his game.

Disguising Your Own Play

Players like the idea of reading their opponents' many tells. Much more important, however, is the art of disguising your own play and minimizing your own tells.

Why is it more important? For a very simple reason. Even if you've picked up some very reliable tendencies on a player in your game, you and he won't be involved in a lot of hands together over the course of an evening. Let's say you're in a live game and the pace is fairly quick, say 40 hands per hour. Suppose you're a fairly tight player and you get involved in one hand out of four. And suppose this other player has about the same tendency. That means you'll be in a pot with him about one hand in 16, or about 2.5 hands per hour. In a six-hour session, you and he will play about 15 hands together. And in most of those hands, nothing significant will happen. Say you both stay for the flop, and when the flop comes, you bet and he folds. You may have had a tell that told you he was going to fold before he folded. Very nice, but it didn't make you any money.

But if you have tells, those tells are going to be on display *every hand you play*. That's disastrous. Perhaps you'll be lucky and most of the players at the table will be unobservant. But if even two or three players know what you're doing, your profit margin might be wiped out.

The lesson is clear: controlling your own tells is "Job Number One." Only after you're sure you're not giving any information away should you start to invest energy studying your opponents.

I'll outline a couple of separate approaches to defend against giving away tells. Let's start with Patrik Antonius.

Defending Against Tells:
The Patrik Antonius Way

Patrik Antonius from Finland only appeared on the world poker scene about four years ago. (I first heard of him in 2004.) But in that short time, he's established himself as a major force, and many already consider him the best heads-up player in the world. Those of you who've seen the excellent show *Poker After Dark* might remember a long heads-up session he won against Brad Booth, a fine Canadian player.

Antonius' defense against tells is classically simple. After he makes an important bet, he just sits at the table, stiff as a board, and stares silently at a fixed point in space. He doesn't respond to questions, taunts, or feeble attempts at humor. In fact, he gives a good impression of a catatonic trance, until his opponent finally calls or folds. After that, Patrik reenters his body and rejoins the living.

Most players actually try for some version of quiet passivity, (I do myself), but Patrik has mastered the art form like few others. It's a simple and effective solution to the problem of revealing the bare minimum of information.

Another Approach:
The Scripted Defense

Another way of dealing with the information problem is what I call the scripted defense. It's more active than the classic passive approach, but requires more planning as well.

Here's the basic idea. Imagine a series of unrelated, somewhat random, but noticeable physical movements. Here's a sample list:

- Moisten your lips with your tongue.

- Stare to your left for a few seconds.
- Drum the table surface with the fingers of your right hand.
- Shift position in your chair. And,
- Repeat.

Each motion should require a few seconds to execute before moving on to the next motion. When you reach the end of the list, go back to the first motion and repeat until your opponent finally makes a decision.

Call this first set of motions Script No. 1, and practice at home until you're able to perform it casually and routinely.

Now invent a second set of motions, which we'll call Script No. 2. The second script might look like this:

- Scratch the left side of your face.
- Play with your hair with your right hand.
- Jiggle your leg under the table.
- Blow your nose.
- Fumble with your chips. And,
- Repeat.

Again, practice this at home until it's second nature.

Continue inventing new scripts until you have five or six in your repertoire. Now put them to work. When you're sitting at the table and you are ready to make a big, important bet, say a pot-sized bet on the river or an all-in on the flop, first generate a random number with your watch and use the number to choose one of your scripts. Then, after you make the bet, begin executing the script.

While this approach may seem silly and elaborate at first, it actually has a number of important advantages compared to the strong silent method.

- **Concealment:** Suppose you try to be still and silent while your opponent is observing you, but in fact you actually have a tell that you're not aware of. (For instance, you might sit up straight when you have a good hand, but slump when you're bluffing.) When you're otherwise trying to hold yourself still, any real tell will tend to stand out, like a brush stroke on a blank canvas. But if you're consciously performing a series of scripted motions, any unconscious tell will be obscured. Your opponent sees you sit up straight, but he also sees you scratch your ear, and then start to moisten your lips. What's the real tell? He won't know.

- **Stress Reduction:** Trying to sit perfectly still and give nothing away is quite stressful, whether or not your opponent is needling you with comments like "Do you want me to call, Joe? Do you want a call?" With the passive defense, you have to just sit there and take it, all the while hoping you're not revealing anything. Executing scripts puts you back in control. You're being active, not passive, which has the dual benefit of reducing your stress and taking the initiative from your opponent.

- **Confusion:** The motions you're executing are random and meaningless since you chose them in advance. But your opponent doesn't know that. As far as he knows, you could be revealing important information. So he has to try to observe you carefully and make sense out of what you know is nonsense. You're forcing him to waste time which must by definition be good for you.

- **Control:** Because you've numbered and memorized your scripts, you can reproduce them when needed. Depending on how your opponents react, this could give you a big edge. For instance, consider this scenario. You have a big hand, and you make a big bet on the river. Your watch tells you to select Script No. 3. You execute Script No. 3. Your opponent studies you and eventually calls. You show the winning hand

and scoop the pot. Your opponent now may believe that Script No. 3 indicates a big hand on your part. You can test this by betting again with a good hand and this time deliberately executing Script No. 3. If the same opponent quickly folds, you can be pretty sure that he's decided "Script No. 3 = Big Hand." Now you have an enormously powerful weapon the next time you want to bluff this opponent.

Although this should be an obvious point, make sure that the motions in your scripts are subtle, in fact just barely noticeable rather than blatant. Blatant motions will look phony and won't fool anybody. Small subtle motions will get the job done. If you're serious about this approach, take the time to tape yourself with a video camera and make sure that the scripts look natural rather than forced.

Observing Betting Patterns

The best and most fruitful way to spend your time at the poker table is to observe the betting patterns of your opponents. Your opponents can't disguise their bets; they are out there for everyone to see. You don't have to worry trying to figure out if a bet is significant or not; it is by definition. Your opponents are forced to display their methods for all to see. You just have to organize the information into some coherent pattern.

When watching betting patterns of new players at the table, I like to focus on a few patterns in particular. Only when I know how they handle these key situations will it be prudent to look for more subtle trends. Here are the five major patterns to watch for:

- Loose or tight?
- Aggressive or passive?
- Straightforward or opposite?
- Fold or call?
- Top pair, top kicker?

Let's look at each in turn.

Loose or Tight?

A loose player plays a lot of pots. A tight player plays a few pots. After a few rounds at the table, I'll have noticed some players playing many hands. They're my loose players. If I haven't noticed a player after a few rounds, he's probably one of the tight ones.

A tight player is looking to play premium hands for the most part. If I can get an idea of just how often a tight player gets into a pot, that will give me a pretty good idea of just how tight he is. For instance, if a player seems to play only about 1 hand in 10, or less, I know he's playing only pairs and the very best non-paired hands, perhaps just ace-king, ace-queen, and ace-jack.

How do I know that? There are 1,324 possible hands in the deck. Of these, there are 6 of each pair and 13 possible pairs, which accounts for 78 hands. There are 16 ways to be dealt an ace-king, and the same number for any other non-pair. So ace-king, ace-queen, and ace-jack add another 48 hands. Someone playing a super-tight strategy of just pairs and the top three non-paired hands only has 126 possible hands.

$$126 = 78 + 48$$

That's just under 10 percent of the total possible hands. So if a person appears to be playing what seems to be about one hand in ten over a long period of time, I can be almost certain of their starting hand set.

By the way, I also know someone playing that tight has to be pretty weak. By playing too few hands, they're giving away too much information and won't get action on their good hands. Remember, other players besides me will spot what they're doing.

The loose players are playing four or five hands every round of the table. They're playing half the hands they're dealt, and there just aren't that many good cards. It's important to pay careful attention to them because if they're involved in that many hands, *when I decide to play a hand, it will probably be against these guys.* A tight player might be more dangerous, but if two tight players are at the table, the odds are they'll contest very few pots against each other. Mostly, they'll be playing pots against the loose players, and the loose players, of course, will mostly be playing each other.

The players to be most concerned about are the ones playing a couple of pots each round of the table. I know they're playing a lot of premium hands, but they're mixing in enough suited connectors and other hands to ensure that any flop could be a potential threat. Until I know better, it's best to assume that anyone playing at that rate is dangerous.

Aggressive or Passive?

An aggressive player likes to bet. He understands the concept of fold equity, and knows that betting gives him two ways to win: his opponent might fold now, or he might actually have the best hand.

A passive player tends more toward checking and calling. He may understand the idea of fold equity, but he's just uncomfortable putting money in the pot unless he really believes he has the best hand.

In tournament play, an aggressive style is very important because your time horizon is limited. Aggressive players pick up a lot of blinds, and in tournaments that approach helps to tread water until a big hand comes along.

In cash games, the aggressive style doesn't have quite the same advantages. The blinds are tiny compared to the stacks, and there are no antes, so scooping the starting pot isn't a particularly high priority. The aggressive style has a distinct downside: by pushing at the pot, you can jeopardize too much of your stack before you realize you're being trapped by a really strong hand. A good aggressive player has a keen sense of when to back off, while a weak aggressive player can easily find himself in a pit.

The passive style is just what it implies. The passive player is more inclined to check rather than bet with a moderate or weak hand, and call rather than raise. Passive play with a big hand can trap an over-eager aggressive player very easily. The optimal style is really a blend of aggressive and passive play that's very hard to read.

The quick way to spot the aggressive players is to look at how people behave when they're first to act in a pot before the flop. How often do players raise in that situation? Do they ever limp rather than raise? You'll find players who will raise 60 to 70 percent of the time if it's folded to them and they're first to act. Obviously, a lot of these raises are with total trash, so whenever you pick up a hand, you want to play with these folks.

Passive players won't do anything so blatant, so you'll need to observe them over time.

Straightforward or Opposite?

A straightforward player likes to bet or raise his strong hands, and check his weak ones. An opposite player likes to do just the reverse: he checks his strong hands, and bets his good to average hands. Straightforward players like to plow ahead and get money in the pot. Opposite players like the thrill of surprising their opponents.

An optimal strategy mixes both tendencies. Optimal play is predominantly straightforward because you need to keep getting money in the pot with your good hands, but mixes in some opposite plays because all betting sequences need to contain some strong hands to keep your opponents off balance.

You can't tell if a player is playing straightforward poker or opposite poker until the showdown, so *you must pay careful attention to all showdowns.*

As you watch a hand play out, keep a general idea in your mind of what each player did. "Preflop — he raised in early position, he called on the button." "Flop — both players checked." The hand usually goes slowly enough so that you can remember this much. Don't get confused trying to calculate the actual pot size or bet sizes. That's more detail than you need or can easily handle. Just focus on the actions of each player.

When the showdown comes, look at the cards (it's possible only the winner will show his cards), then go back through the hand and see how those cards conform to the player's action. What did he do preflop? How did the flop fit his hand? If he made a big hand, did he bet it or check it? You want to put some of these clues together so after the showdown you can say "OK, it looks like Joe may be an opposite player who bets big on the river with a good hand."

Remember that showdowns are invaluable sources of hard information, but the information is only useful if you have a general idea of how the hand was played — that is, who was betting, and on what streets were they betting?

Fold or Call?

If you bet at a player, can he fold if he has nothing, or will he call instead and hope for lightening to strike? This is key information, and you need it very quickly. If you know a player can fold, then you can make continuation bets at that person after the flop. That's valuable information.

But if he can't fold, that's even more valuable information! Why? A player who can't fold will lose his stack pretty quickly, and you want to get some of it before it's gone.

Not long ago I was in Las Vegas playing for a few hours at one of the casinos. A newcomer, who seemed to be a foreigner, sat down at the table and bought in for 50 big blinds. In his first hand he invested his whole stack, calling down to the river against one of the veterans. The board showed

The veteran turned over the

showing a king-high flush and hoping the newcomer didn't have the A♣ or a full house. The newcomer turned over

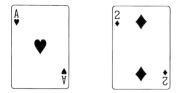

"I was hoping to catch an ace," he said. The newcomer continued to buy in for some time, while the other players jockeyed to get into his pots.

Watch what happens when a player limps preflop and gets raised. Does he always seem to fold? Does he have a mixed strategy? Will he always call? What happens when you bet into him on the flop? Will he go away or stick around until the turn? There are players who will always call preflop and on the flop, but give up on the turn unless they've hit something. Having a clear picture of just how someone reacts to a bet will make you a lot of money.

Top Pair, Top Kicker?

What I'm looking for here is how a player handles the top pair, top kicker holding on the flop and the turn. In particular, I want to know if he overvalues it to the extent that he'll go deep into the hand and lose a lot of money against someone with a set or two pair. If the answer is "yes," I need to know that as soon as possible since he can lose a lot of money quickly.

Overvaluing top pair top kicker is a tendency that doesn't always require a showdown to reveal. Consider the following hand:

Sample Hand

A player I don't know much about makes a standard raise from early position. He gets called by a tight player in late position. Those two are the only players in the hand on the flop. The flop is

The early player bets 75 percent of the pot, and the player in late position calls after some hesitation.

The turn is the J♥. The early player again fires, this time about 60 percent of the pot. The player in late position folds.

In a low or moderate stakes game, this pattern is pretty transparent. The early position player probably bet with ace-x, where 'x' is a good kicker, and the late position player called with a pair of some sort. The first player hit his ace and bet, the second player didn't hit a set, called one bet to see if the leader would fire again, and then folded after the turn bet. I'll tentatively classify the early position player as someone who could overplay top pair top kicker.

Why am I in a hurry to classify him after just a hand? Because the first hard evidence I'll have will come when he loses his whole stack to someone sitting back with a set, and that's just a bit too late. We're not looking for certainty in poker, just some good solid tendencies backed by some empirical data.

Conversational Gambits

Imagine you've just had a great stroke of luck. You go to Las Vegas, enter a couple of satellites for a major tournament, and win a free entry to a World Poker Tour tournament starting the next day. You enter the tournament and luck is on your side. You're playing well and picking up some good cards to boot. The field shrinks to 300, then 200, then 100. You're in the money, picking up steam. Your stack is growing, and the field keeps shrinking. Life is good. The announcer calls out "50 players left," then "30," then "10." The bubble bursts, the final table is set. You're in with a good solid stack. Tomorrow, you'll show the world you belong at a final table.

Tomorrow comes, and play starts. You're pysched, you're pumped, you're ready to show who's boss. There's a couple of world-class players at the table; you've seen them on TV plenty of times. The amateurs don't look too threatening. You've got the third biggest stack. You're in good shape. The cameras are running.

You don't pick up any cards the first time around the table. No problem, you've got plenty of time. Then, under the gun, you pick up a pair of aces. Whoo mama! Time to do some serious damage. In your mind's ear, you can hear Vince and Mike excitedly squealing "He's got a pair of bullets, the weapons of mass destruction…" Mustn't give anything away though, the whole world is watching. With infinite cool, you murmur, "Raise to 60" and push a few chips to the center of the table. You imagine how suave that motion is going to look on the broadcast.

One of the world-class players on the button calls you. Everyone else folds. The flop is

Not bad for you. Perhaps the world-class player has a straight draw with the jack and ten out there. You decide not to let him draw cheaply. You call out, "Bet 100," and slide another stack into the middle.

The world-class player, a young guy in his 20s with a big reputation, thinks awhile, then looks at you carefully, then thinks a little more.

"No problem," you think to yourself. "He can't read me. Let him try. I'm just going to sit here, calm and collected."

The world-class player says "Do you have a good hand?" He looks at you earnestly. "Should I call?"

You're a little puzzled. You hadn't quite expected that. It wasn't in your script.

He looks at you again, even more earnestly this time. "Have you got something good over there? Do you want me to call?"

You're starting to sweat a little. You look around the table. No one else is paying any attention. The dealer is just staring at the flop. What's the right response? You want to say something witty, a brilliant quip that will put him in his place, something James Bond would be proud of, but your mind's a blank. You're acutely aware that the cameras are rolling, recording every tick and stammer. I'm going to say something stupid, you think.

The world-class player asks again, very nicely. "Have you got a good hand? Do you want me to call?" You can almost hear him whispering "Just tell me if you have a good hand. We can be friends … such good friends …"

The temperature in the room seems to be rising. You realize you have to say something, put an end to this. You blurt out "Just call me and find out." It doesn't come out the way you intended.

Your voice cracks in the middle. You knock over a few chips. The world-class player smiles and says "That good, huh?" and folds.

Poker is a peculiar game. On the surface, it appears to be a sociable game. You have nine or ten people gathered in close quarters for hours at a time. The urge to break the ice, make a friendly comment or two, is irresistible to most normal people.

But the sociability ends when the cards are dealt. From that point until the pot is done, your goal is to win the other guy's money, and his goal is to do the same to you. That doesn't mean you have to be obnoxious or unfriendly, or behave improperly in any way. You shouldn't, and I wouldn't count anyone who behaved that way among my friends. But neither are you under any obligation to make your opponent's job any easier.

For a number of players, table talk during the hand is just another way to separate their opponent from his money. They've studied it, they're good at it, and they know pretty quickly when they sit down at the table just who is vulnerable and who isn't. If they size you up and think you're vulnerable, they come after you.

Just how they come after you depends on the player and the situation. Good players are adaptable and have the weapons available.

Some, for instance, just keep asking some variation on the question "What have you got?" "Should I call?" They can ask in such a sweet manner that you're supposed to feel that it's somehow unsporting or unfriendly to be silent. But it's very hard to make any response at all that somehow doesn't reveal how you feel about your hand.

Others will browbeat you mercilessly. "I can't believe you called with <fill in your hand>. What an idiot! Why do I play with idiots?" Remarks like this sound pointlessly vicious, but they have a clearly defined effect. Amateurs don't want to look foolish, so they buckle down and say to themselves "I'm gonna wait until I have a really big hand, then bust this guy!" Of course, that's the point. As players at the table raise their starting requirements, the nasty player both scoops more blinds, and gets a clearer idea of his opponent's hand range when he finally gets in a pot.

The Dangers of Table Talk: A Concrete Example

Some players pride themselves on being able to talk during the hand without giving any information away. One of the best players in this respect is Daniel Negreanu who can turn into a real chatterbox during hands, usually without revealing anything useful. However, talking is a dangerous, double-edged business, without a lot of useful upside, and I don't recommend it for the aspiring amateur.

Here's an example of just how easily a line of chit-chat can rebound in your face. During a hand in the first season of *High-Stakes Poker,* Antonio Esfandiari tried to pump Negreanu for information during a hand. It was a fascinating conversation because Esfandiari is one of the masters at begging for information and interpreting what he sees and hears while Negreanu is very confident in his ability to talk without revealing his hand in any way.

Sample Hand

The hand developed this way. The blinds were $300 and $600, with $100 antes. (Antes are very unusual in cash games, but they're useful for a televised game since they give players good pot odds to get involved, hence generating more interesting hands in a given amount of time.) With a full table of eight players, the starting pot was $1,700.

Jennifer Harman and Barry Greenstein both folded. Phil Hellmuth, in third position with a short stack of about $25,000, raised to $3,200 with

(Hellmuth continually got in difficulties through the session by raising with very marginal hands. It's been a successful approach for him in open tournaments where he can push weaker players out of hands with aggression, or duck bad situations with good reads. At a table of world-class players, it proved to be a recipe for trouble.)

Johnny Chan folded. In fifth position, Daniel Negreanu, with about $700,000 in his huge stack, called $3,200 with

Negreanu comments "He hasn't won a pot in awhile. I'm going to play with him." His implication is that he doesn't have a real big hand, but he doesn't need one since Hellmuth may be impatiently trying to steal the blinds with a weak hand. (All true, as it happens.) The pot was now $8,100.

On the button, Antonio Esfandiari picked up

His stack was $77,000, a little down from its original total of $100,000. After some thought, he asked Hellmuth "Is there a $5,000 chip, Phil, under there? Under the thousands, is that a five thousand? They're all thousands, right?"

Asking an opponent how many chips they have is a ploy to send a message of strength. Esfandiari doesn't really care whether Hellmuth has exactly $15,000 or $20,000 or $25,000 in his stack. With his jacks, he'd be happy if Phil got all-in against him with any of those amounts. His comment is directed more at Negreanu, who's already shown some interest in the hand, as well as Jerry Buss and Todd Brunson, sitting in the blinds and yet to act. Since Hellmuth, on a small stack, started the betting, Esfandiari assumes that his jacks are good and he's ahead of what Hellmuth has, but he doesn't want other players coming in the pot with good odds and drawing to beat him. Hence he's sending a message to the table that he's got a really good hand. Right now, he'd like to take his jacks heads-up against Hellmuth's small stack.

Hellmuth never responds (he was listening to music on headphones), so after another pause, Esfandiari raises to $12,000. Buss and Brunson quickly fold their blinds.

After another long pause, Hellmuth folded but Negreanu called. This must have come as a surprise to Esfandiari, who now has to wonder what sort of hand Negreanu actually has, to only call Hellmuth's small raise and then cheerfully call a much bigger one from a player with position. The pot is now $28,900.

Negreanu now announces he's checking in the dark. Players out of position do this occasionally when it's the player in position that has shown the early strength. As we saw in our chapter on heads-up flop play, checking is almost always the right play in any event.

The flop comes

It's not a bad flop for Esfandiari. There's only one overcard to his jacks, plus a possible flush draw. Since Esfandiari has two of the jacks, the possibility that Negreanu has a straight draw is reduced.

Negreanu hit middle pair, which is something. He might be ahead, he might be behind. It's certainly not a hand he's happy to play out of position, but he's not going to be in a hurry to fold middle pair.

Play is somewhat complicated by the stack sizes. Negreanu has a huge stack, but Esfandiari started with about $77,000, and now has about $65,000 left. The pot is now almost $29,000. If we get a bet and a call, the pot will be close to Esfandiari's remaining stack, meaning that the next bet will essentially be an all-in.

Since Negreanu checked in the dark, the first move is Esfandiari's. Now the conversation starts in earnest.

Esfandiari takes $15,000 of his chips, fiddles with them, and thinks for awhile. He looks at his cards again. (With two spades on board, this usually means "I know one of my cards was black, but was it a spade?" That's not the case here as Esfandiari actually has the jack of clubs.)

Negreanu chuckles. Esfandiari looks at him. Negreanu chuckles some more and says "He gave me a dirty look!" Then he says "You're going to bet 15, right?"

Esfandiari responds "What are you going to do if I bet 15?" It's a good response, revealing nothing and fishing for information.

Now Negreanu launches into a long monologue: "I'm not sure yet. After you bet 15, I'm going to say 'How much have you got left?' I'm not saying I'm going to put it in, but I don't really know. But I definitely have something there that I can play with. It won't be an easy decision, I promise. Either way."

Esfandiari says "All right", and bets $15,000. In essence, Negreanu has just said he'll move all-in after that bet, and Esfandiari figures that's probably not indicative of a super-strong hand, so he makes the bet he wants to make, about half the pot.

Negreanu, true to his word, asks "How much have you got left?" and Esfandiari replies "50."

After some thought, Negreanu indeed pushes all-in. Esfandiari grunts. Negreanu remarks "That was nice to hear. Ahhh. He had me scared for a second." (*Translation: Esfandiari can't have a set or an overpair because he would instantly call, not grunt.*)

Negreanu: "For me it was like a coin flip. I wasn't sure if I had you or not."

Esfandiari: "Do you have ace-queen?" "King-queen?"

Negreanu: "What have you got?"

Esfandiari: "Maybe ace-ten, huh?"

Negreanu: "By what you have to say, my guess is you have a pair of jacks. Correct?" (*Translation: You're afraid of a queen but not of a ten. But you're seriously thinking about calling. So you must have jacks.*)

Negreanu: "Must be jacks by the way he's talking."

Esfandiari: "You've got to have a queen. Can't have anything else, right?"

Esfandiari: "The old king-queen, huh."

Esfandiari: "Jacks any good?"

Negreanu: "You want to see a card?"

Esfandiari: "Yeah, just one time."

Negreanu: "I can't show you a card. I don't have a good one to show you, to tell the truth."

Esfandiari: "That's so gross if you show me a king-queen."

Negreanu: "I'll show you a card after you fold, how's that? Make you sleep better." (*Translation: Please fold.*)

On hearing the last remark, Esfandiari instantly called. Negreanu had figured out exactly what Esfandiari had, so Negreanu knows he's winning or he knows he's losing. Negreanu's last remark couldn't be made by someone secretly rooting for a call, unless he's one of the best actors and quickest thinkers in the world. So Negreanu wants him to fold, so Esfandiari should call.

Throughout this whole extended conversation, Negreanu was basically telling the truth. That's fairly typical of players who talk during hands. It's actually surprisingly difficult to actively lie while a hand is being played because your brain knows, almost on a subconscious level, that's it's hard to lie while telling a story that's completely consistent with what has happened at the table. The truth, on the other hand, is always consistent. So your brain realizes it's probably too dangerous to construct a lie on the fly, and keeps you saying somewhat truthful things. (Talking after the hand is another matter. With the tension gone, players mostly lie about the hands they held.)

Esfandiari doggedly stuck to the point: He kept trying to elicit information about what Negreanu had and whether his jacks were good. He also did well to just keep the conversation going. Negreanu was plainly willing to talk, so Esfandiari just kept him talking.

Curiously, Negreanu's excellent reading ability was his undoing. Once he knew Esfandiari's hand, and Esfandiari knew that he knew, Negreanu had an extra piece of knowledge: He knew whether he had a winning hand or not. By rooting for Esfandiari to fold when Negreanu should, if he had a queen, have been rooting for Esfandiari to call, he gave away one too many pieces of information.

Moral: Keep it simple and don't talk during the hand. If players on this level can give their hands away, so can you.

A Quick Glossary
of Conversational Remarks

Certain inquiries pop up again and again at the poker table. Here's a quick rundown of some of the most common, along with what they may mean and your best response.

Remark No. 1: "What do you have?" Meaning: I can't read you, so open up and say something or I'll pretend you're not my friend. Anything you say is sure to give me the information I need.
Response: Stare into space and recite the 23rd Psalm.

Remark No. 2: "Do you want me to call?" Meaning: Same as Remark No. 1.

Remark No. 3: "Do you have big chips back there?" Meaning: Actually has two meanings.

1. My hand is strong and I'm getting ready to move all-in, so you probably don't want to play this hand with me, and anybody else who's thinking about calling should stay away, and

2. Start counting your chips so I can see how nervous you are.

   Response: Point at your chips. Let the dealer count them for you.

Remark No. 4: "I can't call, so I must raise." Meaning: Intended to be ambiguous and confusing, but it usually means great strength.
Response: Fold.

Remark No. 5: "Will you show me your hand if I fold?"
Meaning: I'm sort of weak, but I will oh so reluctantly call and continue in the hand; of course you can bet confidently next round.

    Response: Don't put any more money in the pot.

Remark No. 6: Amateur gives a long, rambling speech.
Meaning: I finally have a hand so good that I can gloat after hours of excruciating tension.

    Response: Fold. The speech = the nuts.

Part Nine

Playing the
Loose-Aggressive Style

Playing the Loose-Aggressive Style

Introduction

Now it's time to look at the second major style in no-limit cash game play, the loose-aggressive style.

The loose-aggressive style is easy to describe. It's like the tight-aggressive style but you play more hands preflop, and you push them more aggressively both preflop and post-flop. When we defined the tight-aggressive style, we said the tight-aggressive player plays all the hands that have real value given his position. He also mixes in just enough non-standard hands like small pairs, suited connectors, and the occasional gapped cards to create the possibility that any particular flop could have hit his hand solidly.

The loose-aggressive player also plays all his strong hands, of course, but mixes in even more of the non-standard hands so that's he's raising a much larger percentage of his total hands than the tight player. In general, loose players play about twice as many hands as tight players. Whereas the tight-aggressive player might voluntarily put money in the pot 15 to 20 percent of the time, the loose-aggressive player might be entering 25 to 35 percent of the pots.

Strengths of
the Loose-Aggressive Style

A tight player wants one of two situations to occur when he enters the pot. Either

- He's a good favorite to have the best hand, or

- He's getting good enough pot odds to compensate for the inferiority of his hand.

The loose-aggressive player doesn't mind having the better hand or getting good pot odds, but he's looking to put other factors to work for him.

- He wants to be able to pick up the blinds when no one else has a hand.

- He wants to apply pressure, intimidate the table, and force other players to make mistakes.

- He wants to maximize the payoff on his really good hands.

- He wants to reap the rewards of volatility.

- He wants to see more flops, cheaply.

Let's look at these ideas one at a time.

Picking Up the Blinds

Over the course of a session, there will be a fair number of hands where no one at the table has a hand strong enough to stand up to a raise. That's free money lying around, and loose-aggressive players will take a lot of it.

Applying Pressure

A table of tight players is pretty sedate. Each player gets involved in a relatively small number of hands, usually with solid values. Most hands are over either preflop or on the flop. Pots are generally small. Pot-commitment decisions are rare. It's quiet poker.

Add a couple of loose-aggressive players to the mix and the game heats up. Hands are contested. Raises get reraised. Blinds are stolen. Pots gets big. Stacks are threatened.

All this activity puts pressure on the tight players. Some fight back immediately, but they're forced to enter pots with hands they consider too marginal for comfort. Other crawl into a shell, determined not to enter a pot until they have a hand so good they can stick in a big raise. Loose players have a good time, outmaneuvering the first group and stealing mercilessly from the second.

As naturally tight players react to the loose player, the relative value of the loose player's hands change. Against alert tight players, his strong hands go up in value because alert tight players know they must call his bets more often, and with weaker hands. Against passive tight players, his weak hands go up in value because they're more likely to steal the pot.

Some tight players perform well under extra pressure, but others do not. When tight players make mistakes, loose players make money.

Maximizing Payoffs

Since loose-aggressive players are playing a very wide range of hands, their genuine premium hands benefit and become much more certain money makers. A loose player will get dealt just as many aces and kings and have the same probability of flopping a set as anyone else, but their opponents can't assign a high weight to those hands because it's more likely that they made a play with suited connectors or nothing at all.

The next hand illustrates some of the problems that tight players face when trying to play against a loose-aggressive player.

Sample Hand

We're watching a $5-$10 table. Player B, who'll be second to act, is a tight-aggressive player who's been whittled down a bit. His stack is now $560. Player E, fifth to act, is another tight-aggressive player with almost his original buy-in, $960. Player F, in sixth position, is the table captain, a loose-aggressive player who's been pushing the table around for the last couple of hours. He plays about half the hands and has tripled his original stack to $2,900.

- **Player B:** The first player folded and Player B picks up the

He limps for $10. At this table, with Player F attacking relentlessly, he might have to call a raise later, but he's prepared to do so. If Player F comes after him and he can hit a set, he might make a big score. It's a reasonable play.

- **Player E:** The third and fourth players folded and Player E looks down at

It's good enough to call, so he puts in $10. He could raise, but he wants to see what F does first.

- **Player F:** Our loose-aggressive player picks up

Since no one has shown real strength, he's happy to raise and see if the limpers want to defend their position. If they continue and he hits his hand, it may be well disguised. He raises to $60.

The button and the blinds fold.

- **Player B:** He was prepared for this move. Player F has been attacking limpers, or any other sign of weakness, through the entire session. His pair is a good enough hand to play under the circumstances. He calls $50.

- **Player E:** Player E was also not surprised. Like B, he decides that his hand, ace-queen offsuit, is good enough to call a raise. He calls $50.

Given Player F's track record, both players could have considered raising with their hands. A raise from Player B would have been dubious: he only has a low pair, so he's unlikely to be much better than a coin flip against Player F. In addition, he has Player E to worry about.

Player E was in a better position to raise because he had already seen that Player B did not raise. In all likelihood, a raise from Player E would have forced Player B to release his hand whatever Player F chose to do. But sticking in a second raise with ace-queen offsuit is not a comfortable play for most tight players. (A fact, of course, which greatly benefits Player F, and in this case Player B.)

The pot is now $195.

The flop is

missing both Player B and Player E, while giving Player F three tens.

- **Player B:** Checks. He's aware that with his pair of sixes, he may well have the best hand on this flop. But he's out of position, and it's not a hand he wants to bet against two opponents who could have more or less anything. So he waits.

- **Player E:** He's missed the flop, but he has two overcards and an inside straight draw. His ace may give him the best hand right now. If not, any ace, king, or queen may well give him the best hand. Again, it's not a betting situation, but he's not likely to go away easily with a reasonably good holding.

- **Player F:** He's hit three tens and both players have checked in front of him. The checks shouldn't discourage him from betting. Since he's been pushing the table around with constant bets and raises, it would be natural for an opponent to check a good hand and wait for him to bet before raising. In addition, both opponents must know that it's a good stealing flop, and he would certainly be betting at this flop if he had nothing. Only a check here will look unnatural, so he must bet.

  He actually bets $80. It's a small bet, less than half the pot, and probably looks like an attempt at a cheap steal. If either Player B or E has something, that bet shouldn't be enough to chase them away.

- **Player B:** Loses heart and folds. He thinks his sixes might be best, but doesn't want to take them into a growing pot while out of position, and without knowing what Player E is going to do. It's a very reasonable decision. Small pairs play well in position when you can see what odds you're getting, and poorly out of position, especially with multiple players to act behind you.

- **Player E:** Decides he can't fold his ace-queen for the small price that's being charged. Against Player F, his ace-high may well be best right now. In addition, he has six outs to a probable winning hand, and four outs to a monster. Against someone playing almost half the pots, this is a pretty good situation. He calls $80.

The pot is now $355. Player E has $820 left, Player F has much more. Player E isn't pot-committed yet, but each future bet has to be considered in that light.

The turn is the J♥, putting two pair on board.

- **Player E:** Checks. He didn't improve his hand, but he may still be best. If Player F was playing a low pair, it just got counterfeited, so the value of his ace has risen dramatically. However, he's happy at this point to just check the hand down and see who wins.

- **Player F:** Player F made a full house, but his relative situation actually got worse. Player E called last turn with something. If he called with a jack, then he just made jacks full of tens and is now trapping. If he doesn't have a jack or a ten, then he may not even be able to call a bet. So Player F checks.

Note that as we get deeper into the hand, there becomes less and less difference between the "tight" play and the "loose" play. So much information is now available in terms of the board cards and the betting history that the distinction between tight and loose play disappears and gets replaced by "correct" and "incorrect" play. Player F makes exactly the same play any tight player would make, for the same reason.

The pot remains at $355. The river is the Q♣.

- **Player E:** The queen hits his hand and he now has two pair, queens and jacks. Should he bet? No, absolutely not. No one with a jack or a ten will fold their full house, although someone with a ten (like Player F) might call feeling he was probably beaten.

The only hand that might call which Player E can beat is king-queen. That hand does more or less fit the betting. Player F might have raised preflop, bet on the flop with an open-ended straight draw, then checked the turn with the same draw. But that's a long shot, and mostly Player E will either lose this bet, or the bet won't get called but Player E would have won anyway. Player E actually bets $230.

- **Player F:** Player F has a full house but can't be sure he's winning. Player E called on the flop, a sensible move if he had a jack. He might have had other holdings as well, of course. Player E's bet on the river indicates some strength, and a bet with just a pair of queens wouldn't make much sense, so what other strength can he reasonably have? There's some chance he hit a straight on the river, but even a straight should be reluctant to bet with the obvious full house danger.

In short, Player F can't be confident of winning, but he's getting pretty good odds to call. ($585 to $230, more than 2.5-to-1.) It's a crying call, but he'll make it nonetheless.

The players show their hands and Player F's full house beats Player E's two pair.

In this hand, Player F's loose-aggressive style resulted in his winning a much larger pot than he could have won otherwise. Against a tight-aggressive player, Player B folds preflop with his small pair out of position, and Player E might have folded after the bet on the flop. Pots like this help to balance the pots where F's loose-aggressive play runs up against strong hands that can't be chased away, resulting in the loss of an extra bet or two.

Reaping Rewards of Volatility

Some will read this headline and say "Rewards of volatility? What's that all about? There's just too much volatility in the game. I'm trying to learn how to avoid it!"

Which of course is exactly the point. Most people, in any endeavor that blends skill with some sort of randomizing agent (dice, cards, price fluctuations) that causes huge volatility, want to somehow extract the skill and its rewards, and leave the volatility behind. In effect, they're willing to pay to reduce the volatility, so they can sleep easier at night.

Let's say you're good at poker, you think you have a long-term edge, but you can't stand the swings. You'd pay someone if you could just reduce the volatility somehow. But who is there to pay? Answer — the loose-aggressive player! He's busy making plays that increase volatility — bidding up pots with nothing, raising your well-considered value bets, forcing you to defend your blinds with hands you don't really want to play. In order to reduce your volatility, you must pay him, by surrendering pots you could choose to defend, if it weren't so tough. Better to wait for really good hands; one is bound to come along in a little while. Then you'll defend your hand. Sure, that's the ticket.

Courting volatility is inherently profitable. The more volatility you can endure, the higher your expected return in a skill/chance arena. The clearest example is the financial markets where over time growth stocks outperform value stocks, and value stocks outperform corporate bonds, and corporate bonds outperform municipal bonds. In each case, the better-performing investment also has the higher risk.

In poker, the volatility is extreme, and many, if not most, players are willing to pay a little bit to reduce it. At any table, the long-term collectors of this "volatility tax" are the loose-aggressive players. Note however, that when a loose-aggressive player pushes the envelope too far, the tax becomes a tax worth paying and not worth collecting.

Seeing More Flops Cheaply

Although all of the points mentioned so far are advantages to the loose-aggressive style, there is an overarching advantage which is less obvious. Behind all the blind-stealing, bullying, and small ball maneuvering, the loose-aggressive player is actually seeing a lot of flops, usually at a cheap price and usually with the initiative. We know from our previous discussions that really big hands are usually necessary to win your opponent's whole stack, and flopping really big hands is more a matter of luck than careful card selection. If the goal is to flop a monster, ace-king doesn't have any advantage over eight-seven. The more flops you can see, the more monsters you expect to get in the course of a long session.

Although a good loose-aggressive player can make a small profit from all the little action going on, the real profit comes from the big hands where they can win an entire stack. By seeing more flops, they can see more big hands than a tight player.

By the way, this is precisely the reason a loose-aggressive style does not do as well in limit hold 'em. Now when you flop a monster, you can only win a few more bets. But in no-limit your reward can be much higher. Yet in both games, the price to the flop is similar. So while a loose-aggressive style can be very rewarding in no-limit, (if you can implement it properly), do not expect the same results in a limit game played at a full table.

Drawing Limits: How Far to Pursue Weak Hands

Loose-aggressive players will bet their good hands strongly, of course. But what about the weak hands? If you're playing a loose-aggressive style, you need to develop some sense for when you can keep betting and raising even though you don't have much, and when you need to back off and go away. Most loose-aggressive players follow a couple of simple rules:

- Keep betting as long as your opponent doesn't show strength.

- If your opponent is still with you on the turn, and the board doesn't show obvious draws, back off.

What constitutes "showing strength?" It's a play that indicates you really want to get more money in the pot as opposed to any play that simply indicates you want to see another card, or a play that says "I want you to go away cheaply, please." For instance:

- Checking doesn't show strength.

- Calling a bet doesn't show strength.

- Making an initial bet might or might not show strength. If you called a bet on the previous street and now start off the next street by betting, that indicates strength.

- A raise shows strength.

"Attack as long as the opponent hasn't shown unambiguous strength" is a quick and easy rule of thumb for a loose-aggressive player. It should win a lot of pots, while enabling you to get out before sinking too much money into a lost cause.

Slowing up on the turn is reasonable because of the size of the bets involved. If you raise preflop and get called, then bet again on the flop and get called, the pot is getting pretty big. Although your opponent hasn't shown any great strength, he has shown that he's got some interest in this pot. If you don't have a hand by now, the turn bet may cost a lot of chips for what might be a lost cause.

The Tactics of the Loose-Aggressive Style

Playing a loose-aggressive style requires stealing a lot of pots with nothing or not very much. A good loose-aggressive player has to have a repertoire of moves that are useful for this purpose. Here's a list of the nine main moves that loose-aggressive players employ for their weaker hands.

Keep in mind that if you're trying to play a loose-aggressive style, you need to play most of your hands the same way. Avoid the temptation to fool around with your weak hands, but bet strongly with your good ones; opponents will quickly catch on to that approach.

There's nothing about these moves that's unique to loose players. Tight players need to know them and employ them as well. But since tight players in general have stronger hand distributions after the flop, they don't need to make these moves quite as often.

Move No. 1: The First-In Bluff

Setting: Preflop, no one has acted before you.

Action: You raise to take down the blinds.

The simplest of all bluffs. You raise if you're first to act and see if anyone wants to stand up to you. I've seen loose players who will make this bet a solid majority of the time when they're first in the pot. Against weak passive players, it can be a profitable approach. But against good players raising this often should be a losing strategy.

How much should you bet? In practice, most players who employ this bluff use smaller than usual raises, either twice the big blind or 2.5 times the big blind, rather than the "standard" raise of three times the big blind. The smaller bet gives them a slightly better risk-reward ratio, and in truth most players who will fold to a standard raise will fold to a mini-raise as well.

Move No. 2: The Squeeze Play

Setting: Preflop, after a first-in raise from a loose player and a call from anyone.

Action: You make a big raise, hoping both fold.

Another simple bluff which can be very effective. The idea is that the caller probably doesn't have a really big hand, or he would have raised himself. The loose player probably doesn't have a big hand because he plays lots of hands. The loose player has the additional problem that the caller is still to act behind him, but the real point is that he is often making first-in raises with marginal hands, and now has gotten far more action than he wants.

The raise should be big, at least five times the raise from the loose player. If anyone sticks around, they've demonstrated they probably have a high pair and you can proceed accordingly after the flop.

Move No. 3: The Continuation Bet

Setting: Post-flop, where you were the aggressor preflop.

Action: You bet if first to act, or if your opponent checks and you have position.

You're bluffing that you either have a premium pair, so your hand is strong enough to bet whether you hit the flop or not, or that you hit the flop and now have a strong hand. It's a powerful bluff because it simply continues your preflop action.

Most players will make a continuation bet 50 to 60 percent of the time if they raised preflop. Loose players tend to bet somewhat more, but that carries the risk that their post-flop bets contain too few strong hands. In my view, 60 percent represents an upper limit regardless of style, unless you're at a table so tight that players are laying down without a big hand.

Move No. 4: The Bad Board Bet

Setting: Post-flop, if the board lacks an ace and is unconnected, like Q♦8♥2♣ or K♠5♦3♠.

Action: Bet if you are first to act or if your opponent checked.

This bet can overlap with the continuation bet. The board is more likely than usual to have missed your opponent, so your bet has a better than average chance of succeeding. The key is to have just one high card on board which is not an ace. Since players play a lot of aces and hands with a couple of high cards, these flops tend not to be helpful, and this bet tends to have a better chance of success than the standard continuation bet.

Move No. 5: The Check-Raise Bluff

Setting: You're first to act post-flop. Either you or your opponent might have been the preflop aggressor.

Action: You check. If he bets, you raise.

Obviously indicates a very big hand, either two pair or a set. More effective for loose players than tight players since loose players could hit two pair on any random board. Costly if it doesn't chase your opponent away, but works a high percentage of the time. Of course, you must do this with some real hands as well.

Move No. 6: The Check-Call Bluff

Setting: Post-flop, you are in position. Your opponent was the aggressor preflop where he raised and you called in position.

Action: He bets. You call. On the turn, he checks and you bet.

A strong move which says "I hit my set, and my call on the flop was just a slowplay to induce you to bet again. Since you haven't bet on the turn, I must now regrettably claim the pot rather than give you a free card."

A very effective bluff aimed at collecting continuation bets from players who will fire one barrel on the flop but won't fire two barrels. (But note that this play is better if the flop has no obvious draws.)

Move No. 7: The Double-Barreled Blast

Setting: You were the aggressor preflop and are first to act on the flop.

Action: You bet the pot on the flop. If he only calls, you bet the pot again on the turn.

Basically a higher-octane continuation bet. It will mostly work because his call on the flop indicates that he fears he may be beaten. The move also picks up the pot from anyone who is playing Move No. 6. This play is a very necessary weapon in the arsenal of a loose-aggressive player because as players see what you're doing they will be less and less willing to concede pots to you on the flop.

If this move gets called on the turn, you have to decide whether to throw in the towel or proceed to Move No. 8…

Move No. 8: Three Barrels

Setting: You were the aggressor preflop and are first to act on the flop.

Action: You bet the pot on the flop. If he calls, you bet the pot again on the turn. If he calls that, you either bet the pot or push all-in on the river.

This move simply says you have at least close to the mortal nuts. It's highly effective in the right situation because your opponent has had three chances to raise and hasn't exercised any of them. That kind of self-restraint is rarely seen.

There are several situations where you can't employ this move. Here are a few:

- Don't try this against weak players. They won't realize how good a hand you're supposed to have to call.

- Don't use this against one of the short stacks. They could be pot-committed (or have simply decided in their own mind to stake their stack on this hand) by the river.

- Don't use this if your bets don't tell a consistent story. Remember, you are representing the nuts on the end, but the board has to support that thesis. For example, suppose you bet and he calls preflop. The flop is

You bet, he calls. The turn is the Q♦. You bet, he calls. Now the river is the J♦. The turn and the river have put both straight and flush draws on board, but you can't represent those hands because you were betting strongly preflop and on the flop where there was no hint of a flush or a straight. A good player will see that your bets don't add up, and call you if he has something.

Move No. 9: Switch to Tight Play

Setting: You've been playing loose-aggressive for some time and the players at the table have figured you out and started to react.

Action: Switch to a tight-aggressive style. Play strong hands that represent good value for your situation.

Since your opponents will now be playing a wider range of hands, your switch should put you in a situation that's even more profitable than a good tight-aggressive player normally enjoys.

The sudden move to tight play is the most profitable move that a loose-aggressive player can make. After you've shown down a few high-value winning hands, you can switch back to loose play with better effect.

How to
Play Strong Hands

Since loose-aggressive players play more weak hands preflop than tight-aggressive players, their post-flop distributions tend to be weaker as well. As a result, most of the theory of playing the loose-aggressive style revolves around salvaging as many weak hands as possible with artful bluffing moves.

Playing strong hands isn't really a problem. In general, all the advice we gave in the chapters on tight-aggressive play applies equally well here. One caveat must be noted:

> Loose-aggressive players should slowplay less than tight-aggressive players.

This insight is counter-intuitive for most loose-aggressive players *who think of themselves as primarily trappy players*. Since they bluff aggressively with their weak hands, they like trapping and slowplaying with their strong hands. However, the reverse approach is actually better. The reason has to do with the idea of balance which is fundamental and applies equally well to loose players as to tight players.

Imagine that a tight player and a loose player are both sitting at a table of primarily loose-aggressive players. The tight player says to himself, "I need to figure out how I should play very strong hands after the flop, hands like sets, straights, and flushes. At this table, players are very active, so if I flop a strong hand and check, there's a good chance that someone behind me will take the lead in the betting and I can raise, or even just call and bet or raise on the next street. I'm going to slowplay these hands more often than usual (for me). I'll use a mix of 50 percent bets and 50 percent checks if I'm first to act post-flop."

The tight player is trying to exploit the table, but he realizes that he still needs to bet with some of his very strong hands to balance the times he bets when he only flops a pair or a draw, or even when he makes a continuation bet after missing the flop entirely. That way both his post-flop bets and his post-flop checks represent a balanced mixture of weak, average, and very strong hands.

What about the loose-aggressive player? He needs balance just as much as any other player. But notice that by playing more weak hands, and playing them aggressively, his post-flop betting hands tend to have a distribution that's skewed to the weak side. To compensate, he needs to bet, rather than slowplay, a *larger* percentage of his strong hands. So while the tight player at the table described above decided that a mixture of 50 percent bets and 50 percent checks was right for his strong hands, a loose-aggressive player at the same table might want to play his strong hands with something like 75 to 80 percent bets and 20 to 25 percent checks, thereby strengthening his betting distribution with more high-octane powerhouse hands.

Downsides to
the Loose-Aggressive Style

Every style has downsides as well as upsides. Let's look at some of the downsides inherent in loose-aggressive play.

Downside No. 1: Calling raises and reraises. Loose-aggressive players tend to play a lot of marginal and sub-par hands, particularly preflop. There's no great harm in this when you're first in the pot, or limping in the pot after some early limpers since one of the points of the strategy is to see a lot of cheap flops.

Problems arise, however, when the pot has been raised or reraised in front of you, especially if it's a normally tight player doing the raising. Now someone has announced that they have a good hand. Calling raises requires a better hand than opening the pot or limping, and many loose-aggressive players are slow to make the adjustment. This is especially true if they opened the pot and got reraised. Now they often feel compelled to call the reraise and see the flop.

At first glance this would seem to be an easy problem to solve. Just attack a lot of pots, limp into a lot of pots, but if you get raised or reraised, just keep your premium hands and throw the rest away. While that looks like an easy solution, it has some problems of its own.

The other players at the table, if they're paying attention, will see how many pots you're entering. If your percentage is far above what would be expected if you played only good hands, they'll know that a lot of your moves are being made with suspect hands, and react accordingly. That means they'll be raising you with hands that are decent, probably better than yours, but not necessarily premium. If you start folding your sub-par hands to their raises, they'll gradually force you to stop playing sub-par hands, which in turn, would force you to become a tight-aggressive player.

For many loose-aggressive players, the solution is simply to defend their sub-par hands with calls once they get raised. The post-flop play then becomes a battle between two players, each of whom may be playing a hand slightly out of their comfort zone. A good loose-aggressive player figures that in such a confrontation his skills will give him an advantage. (And he might be right.) The tight player who made the raise or reraise initially compensates by relying on his generally greater hand strength.

There is no "correct" answer to this problem; it's endemic to the loose-aggressive style. The best that can be said is that a loose player has to be ready with a response when players start raising him more and more often. Calling these raises is risky and comes with a cost, but folding carries its own cost.

Downside No. 2: The altered table dynamic. The arrival of a loose-aggressive player at a previously tight table alters what we call the *table dynamic*, the way in which the players are reacting to each other. Some of these alterations are favorable to the loose-aggressive player, while others are not.

We've already elaborated on the ways in which a loose player alters things in his favor — tight players are moved out of their comfort zone and forced to either let pots be stolen or fight back in ways that aren't totally natural for them. However, the loose player isn't the only beneficiary of the changing dynamic. The alert tight player can reap benefits as well.

The loose player, because of his level of activity, draws the attention of everyone at the table. He's raising from all positions, sweeping up blinds, and betting at many pots after the flop. The other players will notice quickly. They don't like being pushed around, and they have to figure out what to do about it. They'll start studying the loose player — how often does he call a raise, what hands does he show down, how does he react to a check-raise?

At the poker table, you don't really want to be the center of attention. People will pick up your habits faster and they'll start to tailor their play to counteract you. In effect, the extra attention creates a headwind that you have to fly against.

Meanwhile, everyone else at the table is getting a pass. If you're a tight player sitting at the table and playing just your usual quota of good hands, you can be pretty sure that no one's watching you closely. In effect, everyone who's not the loose player will be regarded by the table as a generically tight player. You can use that knowledge by being aware that pots will be easier to steal once the loose player has shown that he's not interested in a hand.

Downside No. 3: Going over the edge. Poker players often discuss "playing on the edge," and the need to avoid going over the edge through carelessness or hubris. Here's what we mean.

Imagine that you're a tight, conservative player who nonetheless plays a sound, alert game of no-limit hold 'em. You play only solid, premium hands. You don't get a lot of action, but all the hands you play are individually profitable, and over time you have a slight edge and your game makes you some money.

But you'd like to make more money, so you start to tweak your game. You add a few hands like suited connectors and ace-small suited hands to your mix, trying as much as possible to add them in position so you don't get caught with too many tough decisions. What happens?

Actually, two good things happen. Your new hands are profitable in themselves, partly because they benefit from the cover provided by your old hand selection. But in addition, your old, premium hands become more profitable because players slowly become aware that you may be holding weaker cards than before. You benefit two ways, and your net profit rises.

Excited by this new trend, you make some more adjustments. You begin playing weaker hands in earlier and earlier position, and you mix in even more substandard hands like unsuited connectors and one-gap hands.

More changes occur. Your premium hands become almost completely unreadable, and hence are even more profitable than before. But the new hands are weak enough so that, considered on their own, they are actually money-losers. However, the total effect is positive and your net profit rises again.

In the next iteration, you add still more hands to the mix. Your premium hands continue to rise in value as you get little credit now for having any premium hands. But your new hands become money-losers, and the net effect, for the first time, is negative for the bottom line rather than positive.

With this last iteration, you "went over the edge," playing too many hands to sustain a profitable style. Over time, you can watch a lot of promising players make exactly this mistake, pushing the edge of the envelope until they go from steady winners to broke. Poker is an especially treacherous game because it's very hard to get the perspective required to see when your style is going off the rails. No matter how you play, you'll always have some good winning sessions (confirming that your latest approach is valid), while your losing sessions will always look like bad luck. If you try a loose-aggressive approach, remain aware that there is indeed an edge and you need to be careful not to cross it.

Adjusting to
a Loose-Aggressive Player

If you're a tight player and you're facing an opponent who's playing a loose-aggressive style, you'll need to adjust your basic approach. At a tight table, you need good values to enter a pot after it's been opened in front of you. If you're sitting behind a loose player and you keep those same standards, he'll chase you out of too many hands. When you do get involved, he'll know you started with a premium hand, and let his hand go unless he hits a strong flop.

Playing your natural style will leave you playing too few hands and conceding too many pots to an opponent holding weaker cards. Here are some of the adjustments you'll need to adopt to accommodate the loose player at the table.

Adjustment No. 1: Calling or raising with medium-strength hands. When you're in a heads-up hand with a loose-aggressive player, many of your hands increase in value. The hands which show the greatest increase in strength are the hands which we call the "trouble hands," those with two high cards. Against tight players, hands like AJ, AT, KQ, KJ, and QJ are trouble to play because they can be easily dominated. But against players who will cheerfully raise with queen-ten or jack-nine, these hands are now more likely to be dominating than to be dominated.

Other hands are affected to a lesser degree. Middle pairs do slightly better because a loose player's distribution contains fewer premium pairs on a percentage basis than a tight player's distribution. (Loose players get exactly as many high pairs as tight players, but their effect is diluted by the number of marginal hands that a loose player is playing.) Plus the middle pair is a little more likely to be higher than one of the loose player's cards. Small pairs play about the same. They mostly still need to hit a set to be playable post-flop. Suited connectors also don't change in value much.

Premium pairs also play better, oddly enough. Loose players know that their style is forcing tight players to play more hands. Therefore premium pairs form a smaller percentage of a tight player's distribution than would be the case if a tight player is matched against another tight player. Injecting loose play into a tight game puts a sort of fog over the battlefield and every player, loose and tight, becomes harder to read.

If you're in a multi-way pot with a loose player and a tight player, the situation becomes even less clear. Is your tight opponent playing his normal tight game? Or has he started to react to the loose player and opened up his starting requirements? Is he still betting legitimate hands, or has he increased his bluffing frequency? Evaluating the loose player might be straightforward, but the tight player may have morphed into an unknown quantity.

Remember that the overriding long-term goal of a successful loose-aggressive player is to see a lot of flops cheaply, searching for the monster hands that will let him double up. To thwart that strategy, you have to make the flops expensive, rather than cheap. To do that, you have to be willing to raise, rather than call, preflop.

Adjustment No. 2: Position. When one player is entering a lot of pots, the idea of position changes meaning dramatically. "Position" now means "Position relative to the loose player." If the loose player is sitting in Seat 4, the best seat at the table is Seat 3, the seat to the *right* of the loose player.

At first this seems distinctly counter-intuitive. Why would you want to act before the active player? But when one player is extremely active, he becomes the pivot point at the table. Each hand in effect doesn't start until he's made his play.

Consider a table where a very loose player is sitting at Seat 4 and you're on his right in Seat 3. Let's assume that Seat 1 is under the gun. The first two players fold and the action is on you. You pick up a pair of kings. Instead of raising, you just limp. The loose player behind you now raises, as expected. His raise now drives the action around to you. Before you act again, you'll have seen how everyone at the table reacted to his move. If his raise leads to a couple of calls and then a large reraise from the big blind, you're in position to make a big third raise.

Had you been sitting to the left of the loose player, your advantage wouldn't be so great. True, you'd always get to see what he does before you act, which is worth something. But if he's very loose and aggressive, you often know what he's going to do ("I raise!") so actually seeing it isn't that informative. And from that position, you have to act before seeing what everyone else is going to do.

As an example, suppose you're on his left, the action is folded to him, and you have a medium pair. He raises. If you're last to act in the hand, a medium pair is good for a reraise against his range of hands. But if several players are left, you don't know what to do. If you raise and someone behind you has picked up a real hand, you're in trouble. If you limp, someone behind you might see his raise and your call and decide this is a perfect time to bluff. Because the loose player is the fulcrum of all the action, sitting to his left is, in effect, sitting in early position.

Adjustment No. 3: Check-raising with good hands. Loose-aggressive players usually take their cues from your actions. Since they play a lot of mediocre to weak hands, they have to win a lot of these hands to make their preflop activity profitable. The best time to attack is when you show weakness, so they're looking to attack players who limp preflop or check post-flop.

To combat a loose-aggressive player, you have to be willing to check-raise or limp-raise more often, and with weaker hands, than you would use in a tight game. To make good decisions, you need some idea of just how often a loose player is getting into pots. A player who's involved in 25 to 30 percent of the pots is loose, but I'd make only moderate adjustments in my strategy to combat him. A player who's getting into 40 to 50 percent of pots (or more) has a big target on his chest. Now I'm looking to get involved much more often.

The caveat here is to remember that there are other players at the table who may or may not be reacting to the loose player. Interpreting exactly what they're going to do can be a problem.

Adjustment No. 4: Calling for information. When a loose player arrives at the table and announces himself by attacking many pots and playing many hands, you need to assign extra value to calling on the river in order to see his hole cards. Recognize that you're going to be playing a lot of hands against this player over the course of a long session, and the more you know about his habits, and the sooner you know it, the better.

If you get to the river and your analysis of the hands indicates that a call is probably only slightly incorrect based on the pot odds, go ahead and make the call. The extra knowledge will probably compensate for any lost equity in the hand itself.

Sample Hand

You're playing at a $5-$10 table and you're under the gun. There's a very loose player in fifth position who's been involved in more than half the pots. You pick up the

You decide to limp, hoping that the aggressive player will raise so you can reraise him.

The player in third position limps as well. The loose player in fifth position raises. Everyone folds to the big blind, who makes a big reraise! *What do you do?*

There's no easy answer to this question because there are now too many variables. The third player could have nothing or he might be copying you and hoping to sandbag with a big hand. The loose player probably has to go away, but loose players get just as many big hands as anybody else, so maybe he really has something. The big blind might have a very strong hand or he might just be reacting to what he's seen, two limps followed by a raise from a loose player. My best recommendation would be to fold the tens because you're not likely to be much better than a coin flip here, although it's completely possible you have the best hand.

Here's a useful guide:

> The more players still involved in the hand, the more you want to play normal poker (whatever you think that is). The fewer players still involved, the more you focus on fighting the loose player.

What Style is Best?

So what style is better, loose-aggressive or tight-aggressive? As you might imagine, this is a trick question with no good answer. To worry about what style is best is really to miss the point of poker. The idea is to be a player who is both good and unreadable, and who can morph from style to style as the situation demands. Here are a few style guidelines that may be helpful.

- At a table of loose players, tight play will make money.

- At a table of tight players, loose play will make money.

- At any table, alternating your style with periods of tightness followed by periods of looseness will make money.

- Playing loose when you have a good table image (players have seen you show down a lot of winning hands) will make money.

- Playing tight when you have a bad table image will make money.

- At a table of both loose and tight players, all of whom play about equally well, the players in the middle will make money — the loosest tight players and the tightest loose players.

The Problems

Hand 9-1

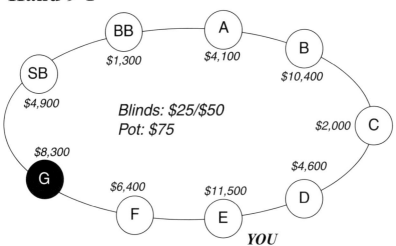

Situation: High stakes live game. You are loose-aggressive and like to take chances and push the table around. So far this session you've been doing well. Players B and C are tight-aggressive players who seem sharp and savvy.

Your hand: K♥J♠

Action to you: Player A folds. Player B limps for $50. Player C limps for $50. Player D folds.

Question: *Do you fold, call, or raise?*

Answer: Calling looks good here. As a loose-aggressive player, you want to see more flops than a tight player does, so limping here is natural. In fact, most tight-aggressive players would take a look at a cheap flop with this hand.

Action: You actually raise to $750. Players F, G, and the blinds fold. Player B reraises to $2,500. Player C folds. The pot contains $3,375 and it costs you $1,750 to call.

Question: *What do you do?*

Answer: You fold. A tight-aggressive player will notice your style and lay traps for you. In this case he limped, then hit you with a big raise when you attacked the limpers.

There are only a couple of hands that can legitimately make this play: aces and kings. (It's a more speculative play with kings, but I've still seen it done.) Some players will make the move with ace-king, representing aces but figuring they're doing all right as long as their opponent calls with something less than specifically aces or kings.

It doesn't much matter which of these hands he has. You're a 3-to-1 underdog against ace-king, a 6-to-1 underdog against aces, and a 10-to-1 underdog against kings. In fact, you're a 2.5-to-1 underdog against queens and a 2.2-to-1 underdog against jacks. So only if he's running some sort of elaborate bluff are you getting the calling odds you need.

The biggest mistakes made by loose-aggressive players are their willingness to call raises and reraises with mediocre hands. Sticking in a raise with a hand like king-jack can never be a really big mistake because of the fold equity inherent in the bet. But calling a reraise can be a monstrous mistake, especially against a tight-aggressive player who's carefully picking his spots.

Action: You call $1,750. The pot now contains $5,125. Player B has $7,900 left and you have him covered.

Flop: J♣T♥9♣

Action: Player B goes all-in for his last $7,900. The pot is now $13,025 and it costs you $7,900 to call.

Question: *What do you do?*

Answer: The flop is reasonably good for you, giving you top pair and an inside straight draw. But Player B pushed all-in anyway, and against his most likely hands, you're not doing to well. Here are your odds against his top five hands.

- Against aces, you're a 2-to-1 underdog.
- Against kings, you're a 5-to-1 underdog.
- Against queens, you're a 6-to-1 underdog.
- Against jacks, you're a 6-to-1 underdog.
- Against ace-king, you're a 2-to-1 favorite.

The pot is offering you 1.65-to-1, so you're only getting good odds against ace-king or some sort of semi-bluff.

Should you call? The most likely hand for him to have is actually aces. It's the hand that matches best with his preflop play, and it fits the flop bet as well, since that's a dangerous board and he wouldn't feel he could wait around to get the money in. You're much worse off against the other pairs, but it's less likely he made the play with one of those hands.

In the absence of any specific knowledge about Player B except that he's been tight-aggressive, calling is probably right. You're not quite getting the odds you need against his most likely hand, but his second most likely hand is probably ace-king, and you're doing fine there, a 2-to-1 favorite and getting odds besides.

Action: You call. The turn is the A♠. The river is the 4♦. He turns over A♣A♥, and scoops the pot.

Hand 9-2

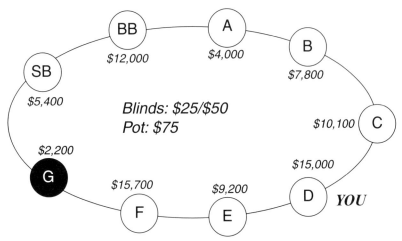

Situation: High stakes live game. You are loose-aggressive and have been doing well this session. The table is generally good with a mix of tight and loose players. The big blind is particularly tight and aggressive.

Your hand: Q♥J♥

Action to you: Player A folds. Player B raises to $350. Player C folds.

Question: *Do you fold, call, or raise?*

    Answer: The typical opening raise occupies a range between two big blinds (a mini-raise) and four to five big blinds. Here Player B has raised to seven big blinds, an unusual number. Larger than usual raises generally indicate one of three things:

1.   A hand of modest strength and the raiser would like to take the pot down right now, but the hand retains some chances in case of a call, or

2.   A very strong hand which is fishing for a call, or

3.   A complete bluff.

A good player will mix a few of these larger bets into his strategy to make himself even more dangerous and difficult to read.

I don't recommend calling such a bet with anything less than a very good hand. If your opponent is willing to lay big odds to steal the blinds, let him. You don't need to pick off very many of these raises to show a profit. Remember as well that unless you call or raise with a premium hand, you're vulnerable to anyone behind you who wakes up with a big hand.

How big a hand do you need? In general, you need a very big hand to call a raise and retain positive equity. Many loose-aggressive players run into trouble here precisely because they're used to trying to steal pots with weak hands. While that approach works fine if you're first in, and may work if a weak-tight opponent has made a tenuous initial raise, it doesn't work against a tight opponent who has made a solid initial raise. It's too dangerous to assume they're bluffing, and if they're not bluffing you'll have to spend too much money to find out.

In this case, queen-jack suited is barely strong enough for a correct initial raise from fourth position. It's nowhere near a good enough hand to call a big raise from early position. Remember, Player B knows he's at a table with a bunch of aggressive players. You have to assume he's ready for some loose action behind him, and he chose his bet accordingly. Fold.

Action: You actually call $350. Player E, another tight-aggressive player, calls $350. The cutoff, button, and small blind fold. The big blind raises to $3,000. Player B folds. It costs you $2,650 to call.

Question: *What do you do?*

Answer: Now you really have to fold. The big blind has made a significantly larger than pot-sized raise. (The pot was $1,125 when the action got to him. He needed to put in $300 to call, making the pot $1,425, and then another $1,425 to make an exact pot-sized raise, for a total of $1,725. He actually put in about $1,000 more than this.) This is a known tight-aggressive player betting into three opponents, each of whom has already either made a large raise or called a large raise. Unless you have some other reason for thinking there's a significant chance he's bluffing, you have to put him on a hand from a relatively small group: aces, kings, queens, jacks, or ace-king. Of that group, queens and jacks are the least likely since you have a queen and a jack.

The pot is currently offering you $4,125 to $2,650, or about 3-to-2 odds. Here are your chances against his most likely hands:

- Against aces: 4-to-1 underdog
- Against kings: 4-to-1 underdog
- Against queens: 5-to-1 underdog
- Against jacks: 2-to-1 underdog
- Against ace-king: 3-to-2 underdog

In short, if you were pretty sure he didn't have one of the four top pairs, and you didn't have a live player still to act behind you, you'd be getting about the right odds to play. Factoring in both the chance that he may have a big pair, and that the player behind you might want to make a move, turns the decision into a big pass.

Action: You call $2,650. Player E folds. The pot is now $6,775.

Flop: T♥7♠6♦

Action: The big blind bets $4,500.

Question: *What do you do?*

> **Answer:** The big blind just bet half of his remaining stack. If you call, the pot will be almost $16,000 and he'll have just $4,500 left, so his bet has left him pot-committed.
>
> Meanwhile, you have nothing. Since he's pot-committed, you can't bluff him out, so you have to fold.
>
> The loose-aggressive style is ideal for stealing a lot of pots and maneuvering with small bets while trying to determine if the opponent is really married to his hand. When bets get very large quickly, you have to let the marginal maneuvering hands go.

Hand 9-3

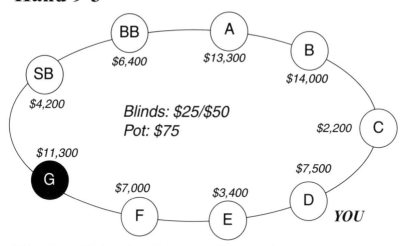

Blinds: $25/$50
Pot: $75

Situation: High stakes live game. You are loose-aggressive and willing to take chances. It's your first hand at this live table but some of the other players know your style from previous games. Player F is also a loose aggressive player who likes to take the lead when his opponents show weakness.

Your hand: Q♥8♥

Action to you: Players A, B, and C fold.

Question: *Do you fold, call, or raise?*

> **Answer:** A tight player would fold, but you're not a tight player. You have two suited cards somewhat connected, and three players have already folded. It's your first hand, so although five players remain to act behind you, some of them may not know your style, and your bet could be interpreted as a good hand. This is a pretty typical situation for a loose-aggressive raise.

Action: You raise to $175. Player E folds. Player F, who is familiar with your style, calls $175. The button and the blinds fold. The pot is now $425.

Flop: T♦8♦5♦

Question: *Do you check or bet?*

> **Answer:** As we discussed in the chapter on heads-up tight-aggressive play, flops with three of a suit are good bluffing flops. If you're a loose-aggressive player, they're less advantageous for you because players assume you'll be betting anyway.
>
> Here you don't have any diamonds, but you do have middle pair plus an overcard. You're going to make a continuation bet anyway, but in addition you have a bit of a hand, so you're in objectively good shape. If Player F doesn't have a diamond either, he may decide to give up the hand even though he knows you could be betting with nothing.

Action: You bet $350. Player F calls $350. The pot is now $1,125.

Turn: Q♠

Question: *Do you check or bet?*

Answer: You keep on betting. Now you have top pair and third pair, so you have an excellent hand, almost certainly best here. But for a loose-aggressive player, checking strong hands is rarely an option. Because you bet a lot with nothing, you need to bet most of your strong hands, more than a tight player would, to achieve balance. These bets are the real point of loose-aggressive play. You get to make strong value bets which look like bluffs and which will often be called for that reason.

Action: You bet $1,100. Player F calls. The pot is now $3,325.

River: A♣

Question: *Do you check or bet?*

Answer: Check. Your opponent has been calling with something. If it was a diamond draw, he missed it and he won't call your bet unless he held the A♦. If he had something like a pair and an ace, he just made a better two pair than you, in which case he'll at least call any bet you make. There are almost no hands that could call the flop and the turn that you can beat and that will call a bet here, so just check and see what happens.

Action: You check. Player F checks. He shows J♠T♥, and his pair of tens loses to your two pair.

On the flop, Player F hit top pair with a mediocre kicker. He called, figuring you didn't have a flush. On the turn, he just called again, although with more trepidation. An overcard to his tens had come and you were firing a second bullet in addition to your preflop raise. The ace on the river probably looked like a card that beat him if he hadn't been beaten already. You didn't cost yourself any money, as he would have folded your river bet.

Hand 9-4

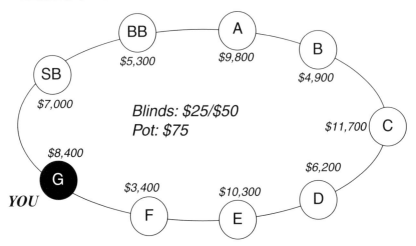

Situation: High stakes live game. The players are tough and observant. Player C is loose-aggressive and joined the table about an hour ago. He's been pushing the table around and picking up a lot of pots. If first to act in the hand, he mostly raises. Some of the players are visibly getting annoyed.

Your hand: J♦J♥

Action to you: Players A and B fold. Player C raises to $125. Player D calls $125. Player E folds. Player F raises to $400.

Question: *Do you fold, call, or raise?*

> **Answer:** At a table of tight players, a pair of jacks wouldn't look very good here after a raise in early/middle position, a call and then a reraise. If these actions all came from tight players, you would seriously have to consider folding.
>
> At a table with a loose-aggressive player, however, the dynamic changes considerably. Player C's raise only means he has a better-than average hand. Player D called, rather than reraised, so he probably doesn't have a powerhouse, just

a hand that would like to see a flop. Player F's raise says he has a better hand than those two, but he doesn't need a premium pair to say that.

In a tournament, with a limited time horizon, this would be a great spot to make a substantial raise. But in a cash game, even one being driven by a loose-aggressive player, the situation is much more difficult. Your hand might be best, but there's been a lot of activity so far and it's not at all clear where you stand. A raise might win the hand, and it might also cost you a lot of chips,

Since you have position, the prudent course is to treat the jacks as a small pair and just call, reevaluating after the flop. In cash games, you want to get your money involved when you have some good evidence that your hand is best. Here the evidence so far is unclear, so play the hand small for now.

Action: You raise to $1,200. The blinds fold. Players C, D, and F all fold.

Hand 9-5

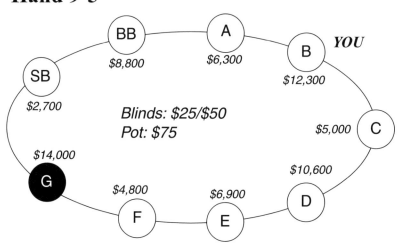

Situation: High stakes live game. The players are mostly tight. Player D is loose-aggressive and he's been playing many pots and attacking limpers relentlessly.

Your hand: A♣A♠

Action to you: Player A folds.

Question: *Do you call or raise?*
> **Answer:** Call. In a tight game you would raise here about 80 percent of the time for all the obvious reasons. Aces play very well heads-up, but not so well in a crowd, so raise to thin the field. The calls you would make would just be for deception and to provide balance for the times when you limped with a genuine limping hand like a small pair or suited connectors.
>
> With a known loose-aggressive player in the game, however, your strategy changes considerably. Now limping becomes the prevailing option in the hope that you get a raise from him. If for some reason you don't, the pot may still get raised by someone else. In this environment, raising becomes the balancing play.

Action: You call $50. Player C calls. Player D raises to $200. Players E and F fold. Player G calls. The small blind raises to $600. The big blind folds. The pot is now $1,150, and it costs you $550 to call.

Question: *What do you do?*
> **Answer:** You'll raise, of course. It's only the exact amount of the raise that you need to calculate. Making a pot-sized raised would require you to put in $2,250, $550 to call the existing raise, creating a pot of $1,700, and then another $1,700 for the raise itself. That's not a bad move, but you want to look at the stacks of the other players before you decide. There are still four other players alive in the hand,

and it's possible that one of them holds a hand like kings, queens, or ace-king that might make one further raise, which you would certainly welcome. The ideal result would be to make a raise that would chase away three people and allow the fourth to put you all-in.

The remaining stacks are as follows:

- Player C (limped behind you): $4,950
- Player D (the loose-aggressive guy): $10,400
- Player G (called the loose-aggressive guy): $13,800
- Small blind (raised to $600): $2,700

Usually, one stack will be more important to you than any of the others. In this case, the important stack is Player C's $4,950. Do you see why?

- Player D isn't important because he's the loose-aggressive guy. He probably raised with not much, and now he'll just go away. Even if he doesn't, his stack is big enough so you can raise any reasonable amount and he can still come over the top with a big reraise.

- Player G isn't important because he already had a chance to reraise Player D and he didn't do it. Now the pot has been raised and reraised behind him, so he'll be folding.

- The small blind might have a big hand since he's already reraised. But his stack is so small that your raise is going to put him essentially all-in, so he doesn't matter.

- Player C is the important one. He limped after you with the loose guy still to act, so he might have been sandbagging just like you were. Now he may feel he has a hand worth taking all-in. So let's figure out how your raise looks to him.

If you make a pot-sized raise, you'll put $2,250 into the pot. The pot will then be $3,400 (= $1,150 + 2,250), and he needs to put in $2,250 just to call, leaving him with $2,700 in his stack and a pot of $5,650. So he could raise a little less than half the pot, not a very impressive raise.

If you raise less, you make his possible raise look a little stronger, which is what you want. But you can't raise too much less because you don't want to make the pot so inviting that more than one player tries to get in.

I'd put about $1,950 into the pot. That's $550 to call, and a raise of $1,400. If Player C then goes all-in, he might feel he's got some fold equity, while the small blind would still be committed to the pot if he decides to play.

Action: You put in $1,950, raising the pot $1,400. Player C moves all-in. Players D and G fold. The small blind folds. You call.

The board comes K♥9♠4♠J♥2♣, and your opponent turns over A♦K♣. You take the pot.

When loose players get in the game, it's not unusual to see tight players moving all-in with weaker hands than they might play at a tight table, even when they're against other tight players.

Hand 9-6

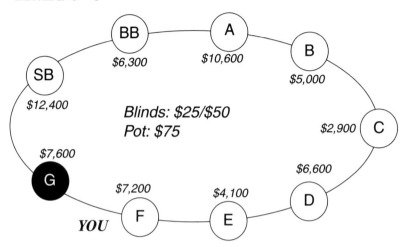

SB $12,400
BB $6,300
A $10,600
B $5,000
C $2,900
D $6,600
E $4,100
F $7,200
G $7,600 — YOU

Blinds: $25/$50
Pot: $75

Situation: High stakes live game. Player D is a tight player. The small blind is loose and aggressive. You've been playing tight.

Your hand: K♠Q♠

Action to you: Players A, B, and C fold. Player D raises to $150. Player E folds.

Question: *Do you fold, call, or raise?*
  Answer: Your hand isn't really strong enough for a reraise of a tight player. A call is perfectly in order, however.

Action: You call $150. Player G folds. The small blind calls $150. The big blind folds. The pot is $500.

Flop: Q♥7♦4♥

Action: The small blind checks. Player D checks.

Question: *What do you do?*
    Answer: You have top pair, good kicker, on a board with relatively few draws. That's a pretty good flop for you. The heart flush draw could be a problem, and the loose small blind might have called with something that could connect with the 7♦4♥ combination.
    If you were against one opponent, you could check if you wanted, keep the pot small, let your position work for you, and plan to bet on the turn. There are only two overcards to the queen, and you hold one of them. So a king on the turn won't hurt, but an ace might. Of course, betting would be perfectly reasonable as well.
    But with two opponents, the dangers of a board with even a few draws starts to multiply. Each player had something preflop. Possibly you're up against one player with an ace, while the other might have middle pair. You may be ahead of both players now, but each may have some draws to beat you, and the cumulative effect of two draws could be large.
    I would make a bet here of about $300, around 60 percent of the pot. If the bet doesn't win the pot, your opponent will probably check to you on the turn, so you can decide then if you want to bet again or take a free card and see the river.

Action: You actually check. The pot remains at $500.

Turn: J♣

Action: The small blind bets $400. Player D folds. The pot is now $900.

Question: *What do you do?*
    Answer: You're certainly not going to fold your top pair. The small blind is loose and aggressive, so it's possible the

jack gave him two pair and a better hand than yours. It's also possible he has only a pair, or even nothing at all, but figures the two checks on the flop gave him a green light to take the pot.

You shouldn't be happy raising and reopening the betting with your top pair, but you can't fold it either. Just call.

Action: You call $400. The pot is $1,300.

River: 5♣

Action: The small blind bets $1,200.

Question: *What do you do?*
Answer: There are too many ways you can win this hand to fold. The small blind could have made a pair of jacks and be putting you on a middle pair since you didn't bet the flop. Or the small blind could have nothing and think betting a solid amount is the only way to win. Or the small blind could have a middle pair and think you'll lay down your pair of jacks. Or you could be beaten. But your hand is good enough to call against a loose-aggressive player.

Action: You call. He shows A♣Q♦ and wins the pot.

The small blind initially checked as a trap, hoping that Player D would make a continuation bet. When that didn't work, he just bet out with his top pair, top kicker, realizing that it was unlikely that either of two tight players would have a better hand on an innocuous board. Note that a hand that wouldn't have been especially dangerous in the hands of a tight player becomes a good money-maker for a loose-aggressive player.

Hand 9-7

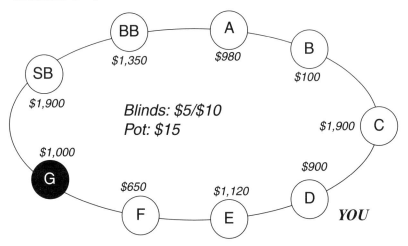

Situation: Medium stakes online game. Player C is very loose-aggressive. He raises most pots if he's first to act. If challenged, he'll let a weak hand go, but play with his better hands. After the flop, he'll fold to a bet or raise unless he has something. You're a tight player, but you've modified your style to challenge the constant aggression from Player C.

Your hand: A♦K♥

Action to you: Players A and B fold. Player C raises to $20.

Question: *Do you call or raise?*

   Answer: Raise. You have a very good hand and you want to get more money in the pot. Player C mini-raises with good and bad hands alike, so you don't have any idea what he has, but your ace-king is a huge favorite to be better than what he has.

   A normal reraise would be to about $60. You want to make a somewhat bigger than normal raise, both to clarify the situation and to take the pot down right now. You don't have a pair, and if you get called and miss the flop, you'll be in a more difficult situation than you would against a tight player.

Action: You raise to $90. Everyone folds to Player C who calls for $70. The pot is now $195. You have position after the flop.

Flop: 8♣7♥3♥

Action: Player C checks.

Question: *What do you do?*

    Answer: Player C called a big bet, so he has something, as you've seen him lay down preflop on several occasions after a bet and a big raise. If he has a pair, you're losing, but if he called with two high cards, you're winning.

    Against a tight player, you could check here because he might check on the turn. Against a loose-aggressive player, you have to bet. If you check, he's almost guaranteed to bet the turn, and if you still haven't hit your hand (and you have only six cards to hit) you'll either have to fold or call a big bet with no idea of what your opponent has. Betting at least offers you reasonable chances since your opponent has to be concerned that you made your initial reraise and flop bet with a premium pair.

Action: You bet $110. Player C raises to $350.

Question: *What do you do?*

    Answer: You raised preflop and made a good-sized bet on the flop, and Player C is raising you anyway. You've done all you can. If he's bluffing, so be it. You still have to give him the pot.

Action: You fold.

Hand 9-8

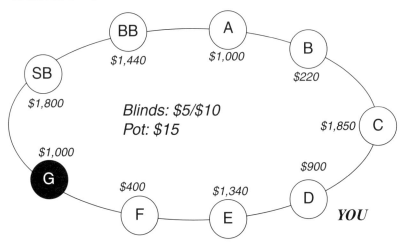

Situation: Medium stakes online game, same table as the last problem. Player F is an extremely tight player who has played only a few hands, but has always shown big cards.

Your hand: 6♣6♥

Action to you: Players A and B fold. Player C raises to $20.

Question: *Do you call or raise?*

> **Answer:** Call. Many players get over-anxious with a loose player in the game and try to raise him with any playable hand on the theory that he's always playing junk. In fact, of course, loose players aren't always playing junk. They get just as many good hands as anyone else, but the good hands are better disguised.
>
> But another reason for caution is that the other players at the table get to pick up hands as well. Five more players yet to act are sitting behind you. Your pair of sixes certainly wants to see a flop, but they're not strong enough to be raising anybody.

Action: You call $20. Player E folds. Player F raises to $60. The button and the blinds fold. Player C folds. The pot is now $115 and it costs you $40 to call.

Question: *What do you do?*

Answer: Player C has gone away and now we're left to face Player F. We know that Player F plays good cards. If he has a pair, it's almost certainly better than ours. It's hard to imagine a tight player coming over the top of two opponents with a pair lower than sixes. If he has two high cards we're theoretically better than even money. However, if we don't hit our set, and we're 7½-to-1 underdogs to do so, we'll have a problem continuing in the hand.

Suppose, for instance, the flop comes K♦J♣4♠. We'll be first to act. If we check and Player F bets, can we call? His pairs now beat us and so does any high card hand including a jack or a king. True, he might have raised with something like A♠Q♥ or A♣T♣, in which case we'd be folding the better hand. But we're not going to stick around to find out.

The key, as is so often the case, lies in the pot odds we're offered. Right now the pot is laying us just a little less than 3-to-1. We have some implied odds if we hit our set, but we don't know how much. I would certainly call getting 5-to-1 odds heads-up, and I might call with 4-to-1 odds, but 3-to-1 doesn't seem like enough to me against a generically tight opponent. I would fold.

Action: You fold. Player F takes the pot.

Always remember this key rule: *The more players left to act in the hand, the more you make the "normal" play, and the less you tailor your play to counteract the loose player.*

Hand 9-9

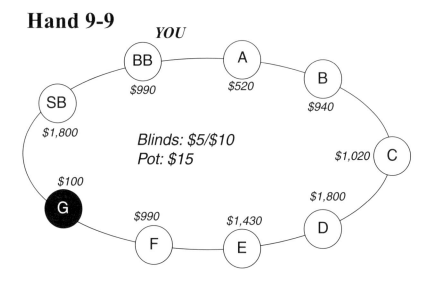

YOU

BB $990

A $520

B $940

SB $1,800

C $1,020

$100

G

Blinds: $5/$10
Pot: $15

$990

F

$1,430

E

$1,800

D

Situation: Medium stakes online game. You arrived at the table a short while ago. The small blind has been a dominating loose-aggressive player, raising almost every pot that is folded to him. While you've been at the table, he hasn't had to show down many hands.

Your hand: 9♣5♣

Action to you: Players A through G all fold. The small blind limps for $5.

Question: *Do you check or raise?*
> **Answer:** You check. You're certainly not strong enough to raise anybody in this position, even a complete maniac. However, you are curious about the hand. The small blind has been raising more than half the pots you've seen, and now he just calls. Your first guess should be — he probably has a big hand. Now see if events back up that guess.

Action: You check. The pot is $20.

Flop: 9♥4♥3♠

Action: The small blind bets $10.

Question: *What do you do?*
    Answer: You have top pair, weak kicker. It's certainly a good enough hand to hang around and call, but I would not raise. You might have the best hand, but you're in information-gathering mode against this loose-aggressive player, and you'd like to see what his bets mean.
    It's true there are some possible draws on board, and if you have the better hand right now, you might be giving him a free card for his draws. But it's actually likely he has no draw at all, in which case he has very few outs if you stand better, and you have few outs if he stands better. So raising here doesn't rate to lose or gain much at all. Be glad that you can see more of this hand at a very cheap price.

Action: You call $10. The pot is $40.

Turn: 7♦

Action: He bets $20.

Question: *What do you do?*
    Answer: The seven actually gave you an inside straight draw, and of course you may still have the best hand. He's made another cheap bet, so just call and hang around.

Action: You call $20. The pot is $80.

River: Q♥

Action: He bets $70.

Question: *What do you do?*

Answer: Finally, a non-cheap decision. We have second pair, which might or might not be best. The small blind might have had a better pair than us all along, he might have hit his queen, or he might have hit a flush on the end, or even a straight with a couple of low cards in his hand.

On the other hand, our calls haven't indicated much strength either. The small blind might be bluffing on the river with a hand like ace-jack, or might have hit a pair lower than ours on the flop and be betting to take us off a higher pair.

We're getting a little better than 2-to-1 odds on our call which would make me indifferent to the decision against a normal opponent. Against this opponent, however, I definitely want to call. Even if I'm not quite getting the odds I need, I want to see what his hole cards are and integrate that knowledge with how he played the hand. I know that's going to be a big help in the rest of the session.

Action: You call $70. He shows A♦A♥ and wins the hand.

So what did we learn? Basically, we learned that this particular loose-aggressive player is an "opposite bettor." We've previously seen him bet at a lot of pots, probably with nothing or not much. With a huge hand, he limped preflop, then made small suck bets on the flop and turn to keep us involved. His big bet on the end was his last chance to make some real money, and he took it.

The last bet was a bit of a gamble; we were calling with something, and if the something was a heart draw, we made our hand. But the most likely case was that we had what in fact we did have, namely a pair that we couldn't lay down.

In the future, we'll assume (unless more observations put things in a different light) that his bets mean the opposite of what they appear to mean, and proceed accordingly. It's good knowledge, worth the small theoretical price we paid.

Hand 9-10

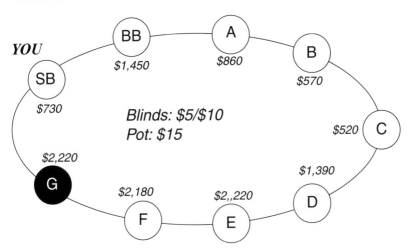

Situation: Same game as the previous problem, a few hands later. Player G, now on the button, is the loose-aggressive player whom we now suspect is an "opposite" player, tending to play his hands in a way opposite to their real strength.

Your hand: J♠T♠

Action to you: Players A through F all fold. Player G raises to $20.

Question: *Do you fold, call, or raise?*

Answer: We predicted that Player G would raise before he did since he almost always raises when first to act. When you can predict your opponent's actions before they happen, you're usually in good shape at the table.

Jack-ten suited, even out of position, is a good enough hand to play against an opponent who might have any two cards. It's not a reraising hand, however, since we are out of position and it's only slightly better than average in some respects. So we just call.

Action: You call $20. The big blind folds. The pot is $50.

Flop: Q♦9♦9♠

Question: *What do you do?*
> **Answer:** We now have an open-ended straight draw, which is a pretty good semi-bluffing hand. We have the luxury of knowing that if we check, our opponent will bet, whether he missed the hand or not. (He probably missed it since most flops miss most hands.) So our best course is to check, and hope he bets so we can check-raise.
>
> Betting is distinctly a second-best play. It will probably chase him away, but this is a good spot, against this player, to collect at least one extra bet.

Action: You check. Player G bets $20.

Question: *What do you do?*
> **Answer:** We'll raise, of course. It's an excellent chance to semi-bluff. How much should we raise? His bet made the pot $70, and calling his bet will make the pot $90. We should raise about two-thirds of the pot at least, so we'll put a total of $80, making the raise $60 to him which is enough to deny odds to a possible diamond draw.

Action: You raise to $80. Player G folds.

As expected, he had nothing and missed the flop. A little aggression on our part collected $40.

Hand 9-11

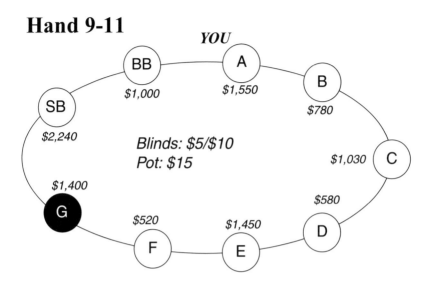

YOU

BB
$1,000

A
$1,550

SB
$2,240

B
$780

$1,400

G

C
$1,030

$520

F

$580

E
$1,450

D

Blinds: $5/$10
Pot: $15

Situation: Medium stakes live game. You're a loose-aggressive player. You've been playing for about an hour and doing well. You've stolen a lot of pots with your moves and the other players at the table don't seem to be reacting to you. You've only taken a couple of hands to the river, and each time you've shown a strong hand. The big blind has just arrived at the table. This hand you're under the gun.

Your hand: 6♠5♣

Question: *Do you fold, call, or raise?*
> **Answer:** A tight player would almost always fold this hand, but if you're playing a loose-aggressive game, you will raise a little more often.

Action: You raise to $30. Players B through G and the small blind fold. The big blind calls $20. The pot is now $65.

Flop: K♥K♠K♦

Action: The big blind checks.

Question: *What do you do?*
    Answer: Your raise in first position indicated that you're supposed to have a good hand. The big blind only called, and checked on the flop, so he hasn't shown any strength. He just sat down at the table, so you don't know anything about him. He might just be a player who doesn't like to give up his blind without at least the semblance of a fight. You're supposed to have a good hand here, and the flop didn't change your status relative to the big blind except in the very unlikely event he has a king. So you should bet. I would make a small bet which looks like you have a big hand and you're trying to suck your opponent into the pot.

Action: You bet $25. The big blind calls. The pot is now $115.

Turn: 2♥

Action: The big blind checks.

Question: *What do you do?*
    Answer: Time to slow down. If the flop bet didn't win the pot, your opponent may have something he's willing to take to the end. Your six-high certainly isn't best and you may not even have any outs. Check the turn and then reassess on the river.

Action: You check. The pot remains at $115.

River: 9♦

Action: The big blind checks.

Question: *What do you do?*

    Answer: Now it's time for an unusual play. You don't have the best hand, but you don't want to show the hand down either. Divulging to the table that you raised under the gun with six-five offsuit, bluffed on the flop, and then lost the hand will reveal how you've been playing.

    Instead, you should make a small bet, in the neighborhood of $20 to $25. This could work out for you in two ways:

1.   Your opponent could fold, giving you a huge payoff on a pot you had lost.

2.   Your opponent could raise, allowing you to think for awhile, then lay down your worthless hand, preserving your image.

    "How could he lay down his hand if I give him 6-to-1 pot odds?!" you may ask. It happens. Not everyone calculates pot odds. Some players just decide to lay down their hand if there's a bet, and don't pay any attention to the amount. Others assume there's a deep trap involved and decide they just won't fall for it. Whatever the reasons, players will sometimes fold to tiny bets, so your little bet could really win you the pot.

Action: You bet $25. The big blind raises to $100.

Question: *What do you do?*

    Answer: You fold and keep your hand concealed.

Action: You fold.

Hand 9-12

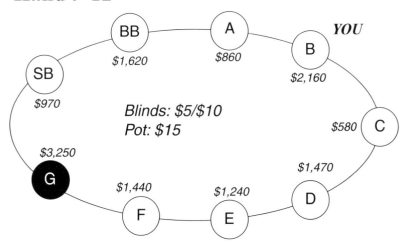

Situation: Medium stakes live game. You're a loose-aggressive player. So is Player D. Player G bought in for a big stack and has been trying to buy some pots lately.

Your hand: 8♣8♦

Action: Player A folds.

Question: *Do you fold, call, or raise?*

> **Answer:** As a loose-aggressive player, you're not folding this hand, so your choices are calling or raising. Either is reasonable. You've been raising a lot lately, so you decide to switch gears and call.

Action: You call $10. Player C folds. Player D calls $10. Players E and F fold. Player G raises to $50. The blinds fold. The pot is now $85.

Question: *What do you do?*

Answer: Player G has been pushing the table around. You have a real hand, so you're certainly not inclined to fold even though you're out of position. On the other hand, a reraise is pretty speculative. Just call.

Action: You call $40. Player D calls $40. The pot is now $165.

Flop: 8♠7♦6♣

Question: *What do you do?*

Answer: You have top set, but it's a fairly dangerous board with a lot of potential straight draws. The standard play is to bet here to make sure that the draws have to pay for their chance to hit a hand.

An unusual play would be not to bet. Now you're sending a message that you either

- Have nothing, so you don't really care if the draws get a free card or not because you're not sticking around in any event,

- You have a weak hand like bottom pair or an underpair, which might stick around for a bet, but which doesn't want to invest any more money in the hand than necessary, or

- You have a draw, but you don't want to semi-bluff.

Of course, once you call a bet the first possibility will go away and your opponents will be left guessing whether the second or third choice is the case.

Not betting is an aggressive play designed to win a big pot at some risk. Its merit is that it's highly deceptive. Suppose, for instance, that the button doesn't have a draw but does have something like a pair of queens. He may bet thinking you have a draw. If a blank comes on the turn, he'll decide you missed and put in another bet to make sure you don't get a free card. In effect, you're letting anyone with a hand that's not a draw build the pot, perhaps leading to a big win.

Checking here is an unusual but highly interesting play with a potentially big upside. It's a good deception play that needs to be in your repertoire for occasional use at the right sort of table — an aggressive one.

Action: You check. Player D checks. The button checks. The pot stays at $165.

Turn: J♠

Question: *What do you do?*

Answer: The flop action was a little surprising. No one bet which probably implies that there are no high pairs or sets out there, the hands that would most want to deny a free card to a straight draw. It's entirely possible that no one has anything.

At this point, you need to bet. If no one has anything, you may take the pot right here, which isn't a disaster. But if the jack hit either of your opponents, you should collect at least another bet. It's also possible your bet will be seen as a possible steal, in which case you might collect a bet from a low pair.

Action: You bet $160. Player D raises to $400. The button folds. The pot is now $725. It costs you $240 to call.

Question: *What do you do?*

Answer: You don't have the nuts. You're losing to someone who just made a set of jacks, or who played originally with ten-nine or five-four. (Also possible but unlikely, even at a loose table, is nine-five.) However, your play was designed to look like a steal, so you can't be worried because you got the action you craved. Your opponent might have paired jacks, have a smaller set, two pair, or be semi-bluffing with a flush draw.

You need to raise, in part to charge him if he's semi-bluffing, and in part because if he's on a draw and misses, he won't call any bet on the end. So you need to get the money in now. The key question is — can you raise anything less than all-in, or is all-in the only reasonable move?

To answer this question, we just have to look at the numbers. If you call his bet, you put in $240 and the pot becomes $965. A minimal raise for that pot is about $500, so the pot would be $1,465. If he calls, the pot becomes $1,965, and his stack shrinks to $520. If he puts you all-in on the turn, you need $520 to call a pot of $2,485, almost 5-to-1 odds, so you're definitely calling with your set. If he has anything at all, even a draw, he's calling the same 5-to-1 odds as well. So all the money is going in on the turn or the river no matter who bets, so you lose nothing by putting him all-in now.

Action: You move all-in on Player D. He folds. You take the pot.

While you don't know what Player D had, it's likely he didn't have enough to call a standard flop bet from you. The button didn't have anything at all. Your cagey check on the flop likely made you an extra $400.

Part Ten

Beating Weak Games

Beating Weak Games

Introduction

A typical letter to a poker advice columnist:

Dear Action Dan:
I play very small stakes games online like 5¢-10¢ but I just can't beat them because when I bet or raise my opponents call even when the book says they're supposed to lay down their hand and its really frustrating especially when they call a big bet with complete garbage and I don't have anything either but they have to be crazy to make calls like that and then sometimes they even draw out on me and I don't know what to do so should I move up to higher stakes where people will play good and respect my raises?

Good Player Who Is Losing to Feebs

So far in these books we've laid out a strategy for playing online and live games against reasonably competent opponents. We've discussed concepts like selecting good hands, randomizing your betting patterns, controlling the pot size, using deception and leverage, analyzing your opponent's bets, and a variety of other topics designed to maximize your winning chances against opponents who are knowledgeable about the game and are actively looking to gain some knowledge about you and your approach.

But what if you're not playing in a game like that? What if you're playing weak players who don't really do any of these things? Should you still just play as we've described, or should you play differently; and if you play differently, how differently?

For most games with a large skill component, this question doesn't really arise. A chess grandmaster who sits down to play a relative beginner doesn't need to do anything different from what he would do in a top level tournament. In fact, he doesn't really need to do anything at all. He can just play the first decent moves that comes to mind, and his opponent will quickly blunder the game away.

Backgammon plays much the same way, although here the outcome isn't certain anymore, and even a complete beginner will win a certain percentage against a top player. But a good player has no need to deviate from what he thinks is correct strategy.

No-limit hold 'em, however, is something of a different story. Now there is no such thing as a correct strategy that exists in a vacuum. Good strategy, by definition, is a strategy that constantly adjusts to the strategies of your opponents.

On a very simple level, you begin to adjust by observing your opponents and trying to do the opposite of what they do. If they are very loose, you adapt by playing strong hands in early position, but opening up in late position where the table may give you many chances to play suited connectors and one-gap hands at a cheap price. If they are tight, on the other hand, you play a little looser. Now you pick up lots of blinds and win pots on the flop when your opponents miss their hand; over time, these gains should more than compensate for the fact that on average you will have a worse hand than your opponents when you see the flop.

In weak games, however, the situation is a bit different. You will encounter both tight players and loose players, aggressive players and calling stations. But most of all, you will meet *unobservant* players. They aren't really paying attention to what you're doing. Instead, they're picking up hands and betting their cards in accordance with some strategy that makes sense to them.

Some players will flop a set and always bet it because they have a strong hand. Other will flop a set and never bet it because they love the idea of trapping their opponent. The same holds true for other types of hands. They have an idea of how hands should be played, and they will play their hands that way.

Could you beat a weak game by playing as we've suggested so far in this book? Yes, you could. But you can do better, with less effort, by adapting to this new environment. If your opponents are playing linear strategies, your counter-strategies should themselves be linear. Balance and deception become less important. The main skill is figuring out just what this particular opponent is trying to do, and exploiting his tendencies as directly as possible. So in the rest of "Part Ten: Beating Weak Games," we'll describe these games in some detail and show you how to beat them as easily as possible.

What's a Weak Game?

So what are the characteristics of a generally "weak" table? After playing in games at all stakes, both live and online, we settled on the following key traits as characteristic of a genuinely weak game:

- **The game is easily beatable by straightforward, tight play**. If you can sit there for hour after hour, patiently wait for good hands or draw to promising hands with great odds, make no particular effort at deception, peddle the nuts when you get them, and show a large win rate over time (15 big blinds per hour or better), then you're in a weak game.

- **Opponents are unobservant**. If you play the same locksmith style for hour after hour, your opponents should notice and give your bets more respect. If they can't adapt to your obvious methods, you're in a weak game.

- **Opponents are extreme and one-dimensional**. Whatever style an opponent has, he sticks to an extreme version of that style. The tight players always play very tight, waiting for premium hands. Loose players might enter half the pots or more, playing any suited or connected cards.

- **Opponents don't respect raises**. If a player limps into the pot and gets raised, he simply calls. He's decided that his cards are good enough to play the hand. Price doesn't matter.

- **Opponents will chase draws to the river, then fold**. An opponent might call a pot-sized bet on the flop, and another on the turn, then fold to any bet at all on the river. He had a draw, and wanted to see if his draw hit. It didn't, so he folded the river bet. Pot odds don't matter.

If you're at a nine-player table and three or four players fit this description, you've found a weak game. While there may be one or two good players besides yourself, there is still plenty of money to be made.

At What Stakes
are Weak Games Found?

The answer to this question was a bit surprising, and depends very much on whether you are playing live games or online games. In live play, the weak games are found at the $1-$2 and $1-$3 level. This seemed to be true for all casinos and all locations, whether in Las Vegas, Atlantic City, or the smaller casinos scattered across the country. Moving up a level to $2-$5, produced more of a mixed bag. It's not unusual to find games at this level where most of the players were competent, although in the right situation the table could be pretty profitable. In general, however, the play in the $2-$5 games was far better than at the $1-$2 tables.

By the time you reach the $5-$10 tables, you'll now find a lot of good players and only the occasional fish. You need to be a pretty good no-limit hold 'em player to beat these games consistently.

Online play was quite a different story. Here we found generally competent play at the 25¢-50¢, 50¢-$1, $1-$2, and $2-$4 tables. Some players at this level were quite good, and were clearly accumulating money as they worked their way to higher levels. The $3-$6 and $5-$10 tables were a bit tougher, and stakes above those were mainly for the professionals.

The 10¢-25¢ online game seemed to be a transition level, with some competent players mixed with some complete beginners. (Play in these games was roughly equivalent to the $1-$2 live games.) Games below this level (5¢-10¢ and under) were uniformly very weak. These evaluations seemed to hold across the different web sites. We didn't notice any significant difference in play moving from site to site at equivalent levels.

On the whole, online play had much improved from the 2003 to 2005 period when there were many weak players at levels as high as $5-$10. Today those games are very tough and require very sharp play to grind out steady profits.

For the rest of this chapter, our advice is aimed at those players playing in either the 10¢-25¢ online game or the $1-$2 live game. (If you're playing in even smaller online games, the advice should apply equally well.)

General Advice
for Beating Weak Games

Imagine that you're a mounted knight in the Middle Ages. You're alone and about to cross 100 miles of hostile territory. You're wearing a full suit of armor, and your steed is armored as well. Your armor slows you down, but it's necessary. Behind every rock and tree could be another soldier or thief, ready to waylay you. Without your armor, you wouldn't stand a chance.

After some travels, you come to a new country. Here, you are informed, the rule of law prevails. There are no thieves, no brigands. The local constabulary enforces the law firmly but without prejudice. You can lay down your armor and proceed without risk. After the initial leap of faith, you discover you and your horse can make much faster progress without the heavy weight of armor.

Playing in weak games is like that. It's basically pure offense (properly understood) without the need for heavy layers of defense. What is offense in poker? It's basically only one thing — betting and raising pots with what is likely to be the best hand. Everything else is defense.

What we've taught you so far in these books are strategies that are heavily defensive, designed to conceal the identity of your hand and protect your stack. Consider:

- *Why vary your betting patterns?* Defense. You don't want your opponents to be able to interpret any particular sequence of bets as indicating the true strength of your hand.

- *Why play the occasional weak hand in early position?* Defense. You're creating the threat that any particular flop

269

might have hit you, thus slowing your opponents from betting you off hands.

- *Why bluff at pots?* Defense. Your opponents need to know that you can bluff, so they will sometimes pay off your good hands.

The list goes on. Most of the moves we've explained in the book are actually defensive in nature, designed to prevent your opponents from reading you correctly, and ensuring that your actual value bets with good hands make you money.

If your opponents aren't reading you, aren't paying attention, and aren't modifying their play, then the road is clear. You can make your value bets and get paid without the need for elaborate (and sometimes costly) defensive maneuvers. If you like, think of defense as a tax you pay to survive, and weak games as a tax-free zone.

Don't take these comments to mean that in weak games the money just rolls in. It doesn't. Although in weak games you will notice a higher win rate (in big blinds per hour) and usually a lower variance, you'll still experience prolonged stretches where you don't get any cards and nothing happens.

One last, very important note. What almost never works in weak games are attempts to bully the table. Suppose you pick up

in early position. You make a raise of four big blinds and get called by a player in middle position with

If the flop comes

and you bet, he won't go away. As far as he's concerned, he's done pretty well. He made a pair on the flop, and that's a good hand. Your continuation bet won't make any impression. He's got a hand, and he's not going to let you bluff him out.

If the turn comes the 6♣ and you bet again, he'll call you again. Why not? He's still got a pair.

What's happened here is that you've played right into his strength. Like most weak players, he hates the idea of being bluffed out of a pot. So he'll keep calling with medium or low pairs, even if the board is scary. That's a weakness, in fact a huge weakness, but it won't cost him a thing if you keep betting when you have nothing and he has something. All you've done is force him to make "really great calls," which he will automatically do.

The way you exploit that weakness is to check when you miss the flop and bet when you hit it. Suppose the flop had come

Now you have top pair and a four-flush, and when you bet this flop, you'll still get called. That's where you're going to make your money.

In general, you want to start a weak game by playing tight. This will change later as you learn more about the players, but until you have very specific information on a given player's habits, you must play tight. You will not, in general, be able to bluff players out of pots once they have shown an interest. (In this respect, our letter writer at the beginning of this section was completely correct.) As a result, your approach will be to play strong cards, push your good hands mercilessly, and give up on a hand when you miss the flop.

As you play, you'll continue to observe your opponents carefully and make notes on their play. This process will be easier than in tough games because the other players won't be making any great effort to disguise their play.

Preflop Play
in Weak Games

Let's start by looking at proper preflop play and how it differs from the games we've discussed so far.

- **Playing premium pairs:** Premium pairs (tens through aces) are much stronger in weak games than in tough ones. Your opponents are calling and raising with weaker hands on average, so your premium pairs are more likely to get action.

  Limping with a premium pair up front is a stronger play than in a normal game. In weak games, certain players in late position will attack a chain of limpers with any reasonable hand. If you limp, get raised, and reraise, you'll get calls from hands like ace-ten, king-jack, or even medium pairs.

  Except for the case of limping in early position, you want to play premium pairs very fast because larger-than-usual raises and reraises do not inspire fear. Raising an initial limper to six or eight times the big blind, for instance, won't necessarily chase the limper away and may even get a call from a player in late position or one of the blinds. Remember, unlike what we've taught so far in this book, players are mostly playing their cards and not the situation. If a weak player believes that K♦T♣ is a playable hand, then he'll play it after a raise just as easily as if he's first in. So try to get as much money in the pot as possible with premium pairs, and don't worry about looking too strong and chasing away opponents. If they want to play, they'll play.

- **Playing middle pairs:** A simple rule of thumb for these hands is to limp from early or middle position when first to act, and raise from late position. If your limp gets raised, you want to call. If the pot has already been raised, you call.

You're partly playing these hands for set value, and partly because they may currently be the best hand at the table. After the flop, these hands can be somewhat tricky. If you flop a set you can just bet and keep on betting on later streets. If someone else at the table has anything they'll stay with you. If you miss the flop and overcards come, you'll need to be careful. The flop betting will be your guide. If no one bets, your pair is probably good. If someone does bet, they most likely have something and you can go away.

- **Playing small pairs:** You'll handle these much like middle pairs. In general you're willing to call a raise to see the flop because your implied odds when you flop a set are so big. If you don't flop a set you'll try to check the hand down, and if you can't, you should let it go.

- **Playing ace-king and ace-queen:** These hands are much more profitable than in tough games. If you raise with ace-king in early position, it's much more likely that someone with an ace-four will call in late position, and then call a good sized bet when an ace flops. It's also the case that a flop like ace-ten-seven will not discourage someone with a pair of tens from calling off a lot of chips.

  The mistake many players make with these hands is continuing to push them after missing the flop. If you miss the flop and are first to act, continuation bets don't work much in these games. Unless you specifically know that a particular opponent will fold after missing a flop, check. If other players start betting, fold. You don't need to press in these games.

- **Playing two high cards:** In our previous chapters we cautioned against playing high card combinations that were potentially dominated by even better combinations. King-jack, for example, is dominated by ace-king, ace-jack, and king-queen, all hands that tough players are more likely to be playing.

In these games, however, the value of a hand like king-jack rises because you will encounter players who think that king-ten or king-nine are strong hands. Does king-jack therefore become profitable? In general, no. But if you're in a pot against a player that you have seen play hands like king-nine aggressively, you can upgrade the value of your high card combinations.

- **Playing suited connectors:** Suited connectors are stronger than usual because they have a better chance of being paid when you hit a big hand. They're worth calling a raise preflop in most of these games unless a weak-tight player opens in early position.

- **Playing ace-x suited:** This is a great hand to play cheaply in a pot with a lot of limpers. You'll mostly have to play this from late position, however, since limping in early position invites players to attack the limpers.

- **Playing ace-x unsuited:** In tough games, the standard (and good) advice is to avoid weak aces unless most players in the hand have already folded, so the odds that one of the remaining players holds an ace is greatly reduced.

  In weak games, these hands are more playable. Suppose a player in middle position raises preflop and you call with

The flop comes

He bets. Should you call? In a tough game, it's difficult to play this hand very far because by betting on that board he's saying he has at least an ace, and if he has an ace, it's probably not worse than yours.

But in a weak game, he may well have an ace worse than yours, and be betting or raising thinking that if he has a pair of aces, he has a strong hand. He might also be betting with middle or bottom pair despite the ace on board, gambling that you don't have an ace.

So what do you do? On balance, it's a tough call. More often than not, your pair of aces is probably the best hand. But you might have to invest a lot of your stack to find out, and there will almost certainly be safer opportunities down the road to make money. You don't need to avoid these hands in weak games, but you do need to play them carefully.

- **Playing other connected cards and gappers:** In tough games, you play these hands occasionally both for deception and to help your metagame image. In weak games, let these hands go. Your idea is not to get involved with a lot of marginal hands, but to play good cards and to bet strong holdings.

Initial Raise
Sizing in Live Games

The $1-$2 live games differ from other live and online games in one key respect. The initial preflop raise is larger than in other games, and despite being bigger, they do not get much respect.

As we've discussed before, the initial preflop raise is normally anywhere from two to four times the big blind. Some players like to make a mini-raise of twice the big blind in early position and then gradually increase their raise size to three or four big blinds if they're the initial raiser in late position. The logic here is that your initial raise should be proportional to the amount of information you have. In early position, you have the least information, so you make a small raise. In late position, more players have folded, so you have more information, so you can make a larger raise. Other players like to raise to three big blinds whenever they're first in the pot, denying information by keeping their raise sizes the same.

In the $1-$2 live game, however, the typical initial raise can be to $10, $15, or even on occasion $20! Those are huge raises, equivalent to five or ten big blinds, and very unlike initial raise sizing in any other cash games. (In the $2-$5 games, the next highest level, typical initial raises are $15 or $20, equivalent to a more normal three or four big blinds.)

Initial raises that are high affect the selection of starting hands. Premium pairs, middle pairs, and high card combinations, the hands most likely to make the best hand on the flop, all rise in value. Hands that are likely to make good drawing hands, or that otherwise require good implied odds to be successful, like small pairs, ace-x suited, and suited connectors, all fall in value.

Games with large initial raises should play very tight. Optimal strategy is to wait for good starting hands and then push them hard. In fact, many of these $1-$2 games are very loose, and that disconnect helps makes them highly profitable.

The Power of Observation

In our earlier chapters we discussed the importance of observing your opponents and making notes on their styles, tendencies, and betting patterns. Curiously, in weak games, careful notes are even more valuable than in tough games! This notion seems counter-intuitive. What does it matter if you watch weak players closely? Won't they just give their money away anyhow?

Well, they will of course, but they'll give it away much faster if you watch them. The reason is simple: Weak players make much less effort to diversify their play. When you see a tough player do something, you don't really know what weight to assign to what you just saw. Was that part of his style? Did he just play opposite to his "real" style for deception? Was it part of some complex idea related to the metagame? You just don't know. You'll have to observe him for a long, long time before you feel confident that you understand his approach. But if you see a player in a weak game check a set on the flop and bet it on the turn, you have very likely seen how he handles sets in general.

Remember that players in weak games tend to repeat the same actions over and over. If they limp and get raised, they'll either call most of the time or fold most of the time. Once you see what they do in one or two instances, you can predict their future play pretty accurately. So in general, you're looking to classify the players in these games into three broad groups:

1. **Weak-tight:** The weak-tight player plays pretty good starting cards but won't continue with a hand without something good on the flop. They will bet or raise with an obviously strong hand, call with a weaker hand like middle or bottom pair, and give up to a big bet on the turn or river if their weak

pair hasn't improved. In most games, a majority of players will fit this description.

2. **Calling stations:** The calling station thinks the object of the game is to see who wins when the hand is shown down on the river. They'll make small bets along the way to head off bigger bets by you. They'll call all the way down as long as your bets aren't "too big."

3. **Loose-aggressive:** The loose-aggressive player plays lots of hands, bets and raises aggressively, and check-raises a lot. They'll call bets with weak hands under the assumption they can bluff you out of the hand later or under the assumption that you play just like they do and that their weak hand can beat your bluff. The loose-aggressive players constitute a minority of players at the table, but your overall results will be skewed by your results against them since they're involved in so many pots.

Once a player's profile is clear, you can decide whether you want to try and bluff them or not. You can chase the weak-tight players out of the pot when they miss their hand. You can't bluff the calling stations unless you're willing to make a big bet, out of proportion to the size of the pot. This is tricky, however, because they'll check and call their straights the same as their ace-high hands. Trying to bluff the loose-aggressive players is completely futile. But until you can accurately put a player on a profile, you're better off just value betting good hands.

You don't need to make much of an effort to conceal your own play. The weak-tight players and the calling stations aren't paying much attention. They're playing their own cards according to their own strategy. The loose-aggressive players aren't watching closely either. They're trying to take the pot away in any manner possible and will frequently assume you play just like they do.

Since you're not being observed, don't draw any conclusions from the number of hands you've played or haven't played. Suppose you sat out the last 20 hands with bad cards and now you pick up a pair of aces in early position. Just go ahead and bet if you want. Chances are no one at the table knows you've been folding for a long time. If anyone has noticed, they may think you're no threat because you don't seem to win a lot of pots. Tight play gets no respect.

One last point. Take the game seriously. If in a weak game you think you're a lot better than your opponents, and use that as an excuse for playing fast and casually, watch out! Poker is tough, and sloppy play will cost you money at any level. If you're going to spend some time at the table, take it seriously, observe your opponents carefully, and apply the common sense rules we've explained in this chapter.

The All-In
Move in Weak Games

In a tough game, pushing all your chips into the middle is serious business. When a player pushes all-in, he either has a very big hand for the situation, or he's making a carefully considered bluff. Either way, all-in moves are not commonplace. You might watch a session for several hours without seeing any of the deep-stacked players get all their chips involved.

Weak games are different. For many players, poker is a test of manliness, and the ultimate insult is to be bluffed out of a pot. Push all-in against such a player, and he will assume you're just trying to buy the pot. A player like that won't need much to call; middle pair or bottom pair might be enough.

As a result, all-in moves which might be silly in a tough game become positive equity plays in a weak game. Whether they become the *best* play is another question. Let's take a peek at a sample hand and see how this works in practice.

Sample Hand

Small-stakes online game with blinds of 10¢-25¢. The first two players fold. Player C, with a stack of $12, limps for 25¢. Player C limps in a lot of hands. He'll play any two suited cards or hands like jack-eight unsuited. He tends to raise with his very strong hands.

Player D, with a $16 stack, and Player E, with a $40 stack, also limp. They're not quite as loose as Player C, but they also like to limp into a lot of pots. The cutoff and the button fold.

The small blind, with a stack of $14, picks up a pair of

and raises to 75c. He's right to think he probably has the best hand, but his raise is much too small. My general rule of thumb is to make a raise of three big blinds when I'm first in the pot unless I'm in early position when I'll sometimes raise to two big blinds. For every extra player who's limped in, I'll increase my raise by one big blind. So with three limpers, my standard raise would be to six big blinds. The reason for the larger raise is to cut down on the pot odds given to the first limper and make his call a difficult decision. (If the first limper calls, then the remaining limpers are getting both good expressed odds and good implied odds, so they will tend to call as well.)

In a small-stakes game, I would raise even more because players there are more likely to limp and then call a raise than players in tough games. In this situation, I think the small blind should raise to 8 or even 10 big blinds. Note also that a pair of jacks, while an excellent hand preflop, is vulnerable when overcards fall. Hands like jacks and tens thus have more interest in making a big raise, while hands like aces and kings can afford to make a smaller raise.

In any event, the small blind raises to three big blinds, the big blind folds, and the three limpers all put in an extra 50¢ to call. The pot is $3.25 and the small blind is first to act after the flop.

The flop is

That's not a bad flop for the jacks. No overcards fell, and there's no flush draw on board. A normal bet here would be $2 or $2.50.

Instead, the jacks push all-in! Player C promptly calls for his last $11.25! Players D and E fold. The turn and river are the J♦ and the 7♦. The small blind turns over his jacks, and Player C reveals that he called with

He called the all-in bet with middle pair and no draw.

What can we make of all this? In a tougher game, we could just dismiss these as hopeless plays on all sides. But in a small stakes games, these sorts of hands happen with some frequency, so to play well at these stakes, we have to take these possibilities into account.

Player C showed the tendency we commented upon earlier. He's not really playing to win money; his goal is not to be pushed around. He called with five-deuce suited in early position hoping to flop a flush, and finally was willing to call an all-in with middle pair. Players with similar profiles aren't common, but you'll probably run into one every second or third session. Identify them quickly, as they represent the easiest money at the table.

Now what about the small blind's all-in bet? At a tough table, the move only gets called by someone who has flopped a reasonably good hand, like two pair or a set. As a rough estimate, that will happen about one time in 20 for a random hand, so with three limpers at the table, there's probably about a 15 to 20 percent chance that your jacks were beaten on the flop. The ratio of your stack to the pot is about 4-to-1, so the play is probably a marginally break-even play at a good table.

At this table, it's almost certainly profitable since some hands with just a pair factor into the calling mix. Is it the best play? Almost certainly not. A pot-sized bet should get you as much or more profit in the long run with much less risk. However, if you had run into Player C before and knew for certain that he could call with middle pair, you'd probably be right to move all-in.

It's easy to construct scenarios in small stakes play where a quick all-in is the right move. For example, you sit down at a table, you're on the button in the third hand, and you pick up a pair of aces. Five of the seven players in front of you limp into the pot. In this case, you should push all-in with your aces. There's a reasonable chance that an opponent will read your raise as just a bluff by someone who sat down at the table to steal a few blinds, and call you with a pair or a couple of high cards.

Adjusting to the Tactics of Low-Stakes Games: 16 Hand Examples

Example No. 1

You're playing in a live $1-$2 game at a major Las Vegas casino. You bought in for $200 and your stack is now $300. A new player recently sat down and bough in for $100 (50 big blinds). He's a middle-aged guy wearing a lot of jewelry, and seems like he might have had a drink or two recently. He's currently on the button. There are ten players at the table.

Action: The table folds to you in fifth position. You have the T♣T♦, and raise to $15. The player right behind you, who hasn't been very active and has a somewhat smaller stack than you, calls $15. The next player folds and the new guy on the button goes all-in for $100.

Question: *What should you do?*

Answer: You'll see this sort of move more often than you might think in both live and online low-stakes games. The story running in his head sounds like this: "Poker's not about math, it's about balls! I'll show these mopes who's got the big ones at this table." He might have a genuinely big hand, but usually not. Most likely he has a small pair or an ace with a medium or small kicker. That way, even if someone calls, he thinks he has some outs.

Your tens are almost certainly good against this guy, but what about the player right behind you? He has some sort of reasonable hand, and you'd really like to play this pot heads up against Mr. Viagra. Push all-in. It's very unlikely the player behind you can call two all-ins, and you should be able to get the showdown you want.

Result: You move all-in and the player behind you folds. The board comes K♦Q♣7♥7♦4♠. Your opponent turns over a pair of deuces and you win the pot.

Example No. 2

You're playing at a 10¢-25¢ online table. Your stack is $25 and Player B, second to act in the hand, has about $15.

Action: The first player folds and Player B limps for 25¢. The third, fourth, and fifth players fold and you're in the cutoff seat with 9♠8♣. You've observed Player B for some time. He limps about 70 percent of the time if the pot is folded to him. He will call with almost the same regularity if the pot is raised in front of him. He won't, however, call a raise and a reraise without a premium hand. After the flop, he will open the pot for the minimum bet and call all moderately-sized bets. He won't call an all-in without a big hand. He also won't call on the river without at least a pair.

In small-stakes play you'll meet players with this or very similar profiles with some regularity. For them, poker is entertainment, and the idea is to deal out seven cards and see who wins. Calling a bet is a little like buying a ticket to a play; as long as the theater doesn't overcharge, they'll purchase the ticket. Now back to our hand.

Question: *Should you call with your 9♠8♣?*
Answer. Yes. You definitely want to play pots against someone with Player B's profile whenever you have a reasonable hand. You probably have the worse hand now, but

if you hit your hand and Player B doesn't, you can collect bets on at least two streets. If you miss your hand, Player B won't get any more money out of you. The danger in calling is that you may get a raise behind you, but that's a danger worth taking.

Action: You call 25c, and the players behind you fold and the big blind checks. The pot is 85¢.

The flop is T♠7♣6♦, giving you a straight. The big blind checks and Player B bets 25¢.

Question: *What should you do?*

Answer. Raise to $1. There's no need to be coy here. Player B will call "reasonable" raises to see what happens. Keep shoveling money in the pot, but don't overdo it.

Action: You raise to $1, and the big blind folds. Player B calls. The pot is now $2.85. The turn is a 3♣. Player B bets 25¢ again.

Question: *What do you do?*

Answer. Your opponent has some number in his head which represents the most he'll call on the flop or the turn to see the hand through. If you observe Player B long enough, you'll learn what those numbers are. We know the flop number was at least a dollar. Let's try $2 and see what that does.

Action: You raise to $2, and Player B calls. The pot is now $6.85. The river is the Q♥. Player B checks.

Question: *What do you do?*

Answer. The check is a bad sign indicating that the queen didn't help him, and now he's lost interest in the hand. The right idea is to make a small bet, but there's not much chance that it will be called.

Action: You bet $1 and Player B folds.

It's nearly impossible to put Player B on a hand here. He might have had king-jack, or ace-eight suited, or anything else that didn't make a pair. If he had bet another 25¢ on the end, you'd know that he had some sort of pair and would call at least a bet the size of your turn bet. However, pushing all-in would be a big mistake. That bet wouldn't get called unless Player B had what to him was a really big hand, and if he had a hand like that he would have made a bet somewhat larger than the minimum.

Example No. 3

You're playing at a 10¢-25¢ online table. Your stack is $22, and Player A, first to act in the hand, has about $12.

Action: Player A limps for 25¢. The next four players fold and it's your turn to act. You have K♦Q♥. You know that Player A plays a lot of hands and generally raises with his good hands. He tends to limp with hands like jack-ten, ace-six suited, or seven-five offsuit. He doesn't pay much attention to position.

Question: *What should you do?*
    Answer: Raise. Your K-Q offsuit is better than most of the hands Player A might be playing. Raising gets more money in the pot when you probably have the best hand. It might also discourage hands from coming in the pot behind you, but not to the extent it would in a higher-stakes game. If someone wants to play, they'll probably play whether you raised or not.

Action: You raise to 50¢. The remaining players and the blinds fold. Player A calls for another 25¢.
    You shouldn't read anything special into the call. Most players at this level will call a raise once they've entered a pot.

The pot is now $1.35. The flop comes A♠J♥T♦. You have the nut straight. Player A checks.

Question: *What do you do?*

> **Answer.** Good players at weak tables tend to make the mistake of checking very good hands too often. They're keenly aware of just how strong their hand is, and they don't want to chase their opponents away by telegraphing their strength.

> To succeed at weak tables, you need a slightly different mindset. Ask yourself "What cards could my opponent have that would let him call a bet here?" On this flop, there are lots of cards that would let a weak, unobservant player call. Any ace, jack, or ten gives him a pair, and he'll certainly call with a pair. Any king or queen gives him a draw to the nuts, and that's worth a call. Keep in mind that pot odds aren't playing much of a role here. The key questions are "Do I have a hand?" or "Can I get a hand?" A "yes" to either question is a good reason to stick around. As a result, this is a great flop for getting more money in the pot, and you should bet.

Action: You bet 70¢. Player A calls. The pot is now $2.75. The turn is the 6♦. Player A checks.

Question: *What do you do?*

> **Answer.** Nothing has changed from before, so keep betting.

Action: You bet $1. Player A calls $1. The pot is $4.75. The river is the 9♦. Player A pushes all-in for $9.80.

Question: *What do you do?*

> **Answer.** Call. An all-in bet on the river means that the river card helped his hand in some way. While it's true that he might have hit a flush and that would be very bad news, it's much more likely he had ace-nine, jack-nine, or ten-nine, has

called you down with a pair, and now has two pair. Of these, ace-nine is less likely because he probably would have bet on the flop with top pair. He doesn't have a set unless he just hit a set of nines because he would have raised with a set as well.

Action: You call, and he shows J♦9♠ for two pair. Your straight wins the pot.

This is an important hand because it shows how hands are valued for a wide swath of low-stakes players. Middle pair was good enough to call two bets despite your pre-flop raise and the ace on board. Two pair was good enough to get all-in despite the flush and straight draws on board, not to mention possible better two pairs or sets. A hand that wouldn't be good enough to bet in a tough game warranted an all-in move in a weak game.

Example No. 4

You're playing at a 10¢-25¢ online table. Your stack is $20, and you're in second position.

Action: Player A, in first position, limps for 25¢. You have A♠8♠.

Question: What should you do?
  Answer. Table observation plays a big role here. Are players willing to limp in to see a flop, or do you have some players who like to attack limpers with big raises? If the latter, you have to fold. If you think it's likely that your limp will let the hand get limped around, then calling with ace-x suited is a good play.

Action: You limp for 25¢. Player C raises to $2. Players D and E fold but Player F calls for $2. The rest of the players and the blinds fold. Player A folds.

Question: What do you do?
   Answer. Fold. You might have the best hand, but you're out of position and not looking to play A-x suited in raised pots.

Action: You fold.

Example No. 5

You're playing at a 10¢-25¢ online table. You just sat down a few hands ago, and your stack is $24.50. You're in fourth position. The first three players fold. You pick up K♣J♥ and raise to 75¢. The two players right behind you call, and the blinds fold. The pot is $2.60. You don't know anything about the other two players.
   The flop comes Q♣T♠6♠. You're first to act.

Question: *What do you do?*
   Answer. You have a nice drawing hand, an open-ended straight draw with an overcard. If someone has a pair, you have 11 outs. Make a small bet, in the range of 75¢ to $1. Some players at the table will fold if they miss the flop. You need to know quickly who those players are because they will almost always fold when they miss. Others will almost always call on the flop and at least stay for the turn, while a few more will just call all the way to the river once they put some money in the pot. The sooner you can characterize players, the better. Since you have outs to a big hand, this is a good place for a semi-bluff type bet.
   There's no need to bet more because pot odds don't play much of a role in these games. If someone has decided to fold, they'll fold whether the pot is offering odds of 2-to-1 or 5-to-1 odds.

Action: You bet $1. The fifth player folds but the player in the cutoff seat calls. The pot is now $4.60.

The turn card is the K♥.

Question: *What do you do?*

Answer: You're now in good shape with top pair plus your open-ended straight draw. Keep betting.

Action: You bet $2.50. Your opponent calls. The pot is now $9.60.

The river card is the 2♦. (You have $20.25 left in your stack and your opponent has $18.00.)

Question: *What do you do?*

Answer: You're certainly going to bet. The deuce probably didn't help your opponent, and the action so far indicates that his most likely hand is second or third pair. Most players won't call an all-in with that hand, but they will call a bet they consider reasonable. Bet somewhere between $2.50 (your last bet) and $4, and you'll probably get called.

Action: You bet $3 and your opponent calls. He turns over T♦9♦ for third pair. You win the pot.

Example No. 6

You're playing at a 10¢-25¢ online table. You've been playing for a little while. The table seems more tight than loose with relatively few players seeing flops. In third position, you pick up 6♠6♣. The first two players fold.

Question: *What do you do?*

Answer. Raise and try to take advantage of what you've seen. If the table is tight, perhaps you'll pick up the blinds.

Action: You raise to 75¢; Player B in fifth position calls. So do the players in sixth and seventh position (the button). The blinds fold. The pot is $3.35.

The flop comes J♥4♣3♠.

Question: *What do you do?*
> **Answer.** With three opponents, you can't bet at this flop with your sixes. Just check and see what happens.

Action: You check, and the other three players check also. The turn is a T♦.

Question: *What do you do?*
> **Answer.** Checking down the hand would be a great result. Keep checking.

Action: You check, as does everyone else. The river is a 2♥.

Question: *What do you do?*
> **Answer.** Check. You could make some money here by betting, as someone with a four or a trey would call, and they might not bet. But no one with a better hand than yours is going away, so I would just check.

Action: You check. The player in fifth position bets $5. The other two players fold.

Question: *What do you do?*
> **Answer.** In these small games, bets tend to mean just what they appear to mean. This looks like someone with no hand betting to steal the pot. Let's review the betting and see if it supports this theory.

- **Preflop:** We raised and got three calls. There were no reraises, so we don't think Player B had a premium pair.

- **Flop:** A jack and two small cards flop. If Player B had a jack, would he have bet? Probably.

- **Turn:** A ten appears. Player B again didn't bet even though no one had showed strength on the flop. Some evidence he doesn't have a ten.

- **River:** A deuce appeared. Did the deuce give him a big hand? It's possible he called with a pair of deuces, checked the flop and turn with an underpair, and is now betting his set. But why such a big bet? Since no one has showed strength through three rounds of betting, will anyone call that bet? Does he really think someone has been trapping up to now, and is ready to call a bet of twice the pot? Or does he just want everyone to go away? That's my guess. I'd call.

You call, and he shows K♠7♠. You win.

When you make a good call, be prepared for a mountain of abuse. "How could you make that call with a pair of sixes, you moron! I hope to play against you all day! Blah blah blah." Take it in stride. You might even want to type "I always feel lucky on Tuesday" or something like that. Sends them over the edge every time.

Example No. 7

You're playing at a 10¢-25¢ online table. The table is about average for this level, with a collection of loose and tight players. Your stack has grown to about $30. Under the gun, you pick up J♥T♥.

Question: *What do you do?*

   Answer: I would just lay this down. The key to success in these games is not playing difficult hands, but just sticking to very solid cards and betting strongly when you get good flops. Limping with this hand in first position isn't appetizing since at small stakes tables there are many players, especially when they are late to act, who attack limpers that have come in before them. But raising isn't exciting either since a raise won't discourage anyone who thinks they have a hand from calling.

   Suited connectors like jack-ten are a good hand for playing cheaply from late position. That's true in tough games, and it's equally true, oddly enough, in weak games.

   Players who think they are the class of the table in weak games make one key mistake over and over. They play too many hands thinking they can bully players out of pots. Weak games are the worst possible venue for that approach since so many of the players pride themselves on their ability not to be pushed out of pots! Instead, stick to playing good cards and take what you're given.

Example No. 8

   You're playing at a 10¢-25¢ online table that is loose and aggressive, with players playing lots of cards and raising often. Your stack is $24, about where you started.

Action: Player A, under the gun, makes a mini-raise to 50¢. Player B, who has been playing a wide variety of hands, calls 50¢. Player C folds and it's on you in fourth position. You have 9♣9♠.

Question: *What do you do?*

   Answer: You have a good but not great hand, and it's not clear just how wild and wooly the action will get with this crew. You're hand is probably better than the two players in

front of you, but you should like to get a little more
information before trying to make a really big pot. Just call
and see what the players yet to act do.

Action: You call 50¢. Player E in fifth position calls 50¢. The
remaining players and the blinds fold. The pot is now $2.35.
   The flop is K♥9♥6♦. You hit a set of nines. Players A and B
check.

Question: *What do you do?*
   Answer: Things have clarified and you're in great shape with
   middle set. Someone could have a flush draw, and there are
   a couple of possible straight draws. With this crowd, the
   likelihood is that with three other players in the pot, at least
   one player is drawing to something.
       You need to start building the pot and charging any
   draws. Anyone with a king or a draw will almost certainly
   stick around for any reasonable bet, so you should bet
   something between half the pot and the whole pot.

Action: You bet $1.30. Player E calls. Player A folds. And Player
B calls. The pot is now $6.25. The turn is the 2♦. Player B, who
started with $15 and now has $13.20 left, checks. Player E started
with $24 and has $22.20 left, the same as you.

Question: *What do you do?*
   Answer: The deuce certainly didn't hurt you, and two players
   have shown an interest in the pot. Keep betting. The right bet
   range now is about $3 to $4. Both players could be on draws,
   so you need to get the money in the pot before the last card
   arrives.

Action: You bet $3.50. Player E folds and Player B calls. The pot
is now $13.25 and Player B has $9.70 left in his stack.

River: T♦

Action: Player B checks.

Question: *What do you do?*

    Answer: The ten probably didn't help Player B much because he checked. If he had hit a straight or a flush, he would have bet. (The only possible flush was a back door diamond flush, so the chance he was drawing to that flush was small.) If he paired the ten, he'll call a small bet on the end. You're almost certainly winning, so you need to make a bet that can be called. Bet $3 to $4 again and see what happens.

Action: You bet $3. Player B calls and shows Q♠6♠ for a pair of sixes.

He called you all the way down with bottom pair and no draws. Not an unusual result for these tables.

Example No. 9

    You're playing in a live $1-$2 game at a major Las Vegas casino. You bought in for $200 and your stack is now $160. You're on the button. A player new to the table, in second position with a stack of about $200, raises to $15. Everyone folds to you. You have the 3♦3♣.

Question: *What do you do?*

    Answer. Fold. Remember that with a small pair, your goal is to flop a set and then get a big payoff. Flopping a set is 7½-to-1 against. Getting a big payday after flopping a set is hard to determine, but if it happens one time in three you're doing extremely well. That's why you like to see at least a 20-to-1 ratio between the bet you're calling and the potential maximum payoff. Your stack is currently $160, so after you call the bet, the most you can win is another $145. That's less than ten times the bet you need to call, so let the hand go.

Simply changing the stack sizes would make this an easy call. If you have $400 and he has $400, then the ratio between stack size and bet is about 26-to-1, and you can call with confidence.

When you visit a casino for the first time, be sure to inquire about the rules regarding buyins. Some casinos only allow you to buy in for 100 big blinds. Others will permit much larger buyins, up to several hundred big blinds. Your buyin size, combined with the nature of the table, will have an effect on the starting hands you can play.

Example No. 10

A similar scenario to the last hand. You're again at a $1-$2 live table, your stack is $160, and once more you're on the button. A new player with $200 raises to $15 from early position. It folds to you on the button and this time you have T♦9♦.

Question: *What do you do now?*

Answer: Suited connectors have similar requirements to small pairs. You're playing for the small chance of making a big hand, but in order to justify your play you need to know that your implied odds are in place. As with small pairs, you want to see a 20-to-1 ratio in place between the size of the bet you need to call and the stack you could win if all goes right. In this example, the limit is your own stack which is a bit more than ten times bigger than the bet that's been made. Those implied odds aren't good enough, so fold.

Example No. 11

You're playing at a 10¢-25¢ online table. The table is mostly loose with a few weak-tight players mixed in. Your stack is $22.

Action: Under the gun, Player A (loose and very aggressive, with a stack of $50) limps for 25¢. The players in second and third position fold. In fourth position, Player D (also loose and aggressive, with a stack of $20) limps for 25¢. The table folds to you on the button with A♦K♣. According to your notes, both Players A and D have a history of limping and calling raises.

Question: *What do you do?*

    Answer. You should raise. You have what certainly rates to be the best hand at the table, and you have position as well, so increase the stakes on these two players. Based on what you know, there isn't any fold equity associated with this raise, but there doesn't need to be. At weak tables, creating big preflop pots with good starting hands will pay off in the long run.

Action: You raise to 60¢. The blinds fold. Players A and D both call. The pot is now $2.15.

    The flop comes K♦8♣4♠. You have top pair, top kicker. Players A and D both check.

Question: *What do you do?*

    Answer. The board is free of draws and your opponents haven't shown any strength. You could check and bet the turn no matter what comes, but since you're against two players, it might not hurt to bet right here. Make a normal bet of 60 percent of the pot and see what happens.

Action: You bet $1.20. Player A raises to $4. Player D folds. The pot is now $7.35.

Question: *What do you do?*

    Answer. Did your opponent hit a set of eights or fours? Did he call preflop with junk and now hit an improbable two pair? Weak games are treacherous. Players will make big moves with big hands or with nothing, and you won't know the difference. Your solid play will win in the long run, but meanwhile you'll be faced with a lot of hands that look like this.

    In tough games, we said that top pair, top kicker becomes a marginal hand when the betting gets serious. Opponents aren't usually willing to get a lot of chips involved in a pot unless they could beat that particular hand. In weak games, that's not true any longer. Often players are fooling around, enjoying the thrill of bluffing you out of a pot with nothing. Right now, you still have to call.

Action: You call $2.80. The pot is $10.15. Your stack is $17.40, and your opponent easily has you covered. The turn is the Q♥. Your opponent bets $20, putting you all-in.

Question: *What do you do?*

    Answer. Player A made the logical follow-up to his check-raise. You simply have to decide if your top pair, top kicker is good enough to call for the rest of your chips. In a tough game, I would certainly lean toward folding, especially if my opponent had no history of making all-in bluffs. In weak games, you have to call here unless you've seen him do this with real hands. His bets look more like he wants you to go away than that he wants you to call.

Action: You call. The river is the 5♥ and he shows T♦9♦. You win and double up.

    He moved all-in with nothing but an inside straight draw. Good call on your part. In these games, big bets will be made with hands that are very weak by the standards we laid out earlier in the book. The consequence is that you have to call these bets with solid hands, even if they are weaker than you'd like.

Example No. 12

You're playing at a 10¢-25¢ online table. The table mostly consists of weak-tight players. Your stack is $32.

Action: The under the gun player folds. Player B, in second position with a stack of $26, makes a mini-raise to 50¢. The players in third and fourth position fold. In fifth position, you hold the 3♣3♦ and call. Player F behind you, also tight and with a stack of $20, calls. The button and the blinds fold. The pot is $1.85.
The flop is K♠7♦6♥. Player B checks.

Question: *What do you do?*
Answer. Check. You have an underpair to the board. If you bet and someone has you beaten, they will call. If the hand is checked around, you can think about doing something on the turn.

Action: You check. Player F also checks. The turn is the 5♣. Player B checks again.

Question: *What do you do?*
Answer. Bet about two-thirds of the pot. Now that you've seen a round of checks, it's likely that you have the best hand. In addition, you've picked up an inside straight draw if you get called. Remember that in these games, actions are more likely to mean what they appear to mean, particularly if the players are tight. If no one seems to have an interest in the pot, they probably don't.

Action: You bet $1. Player F folds. Player B folds.

Example No. 13

You're playing at a $1-$2 live table. Your stack is $200. The casino just put the table together and it is a full 10 players. You have never seen any of them before, and you're in the cutoff seat for the fourth hand.

Action: The second player, Player B, raises to $6. You've played previously in this casino, and know that's an unusual raise for the $1-$2 tables where the standard opening raise is more like $10 to $15. But this guy might be an Internet player in his first live game, and he may not know the local customs. He gets called by the fourth and sixth players, Players D and F. You look at your cards and see Q♦T♠.

Question: *What do you do?*
    Answer: Call. You can assume that at these stakes the table is pretty loose. You're trying to see a cheap flop in position with a hand that could develop into something promising.

Action: You call for $6. The button folds. The small blind (with a stack of $200) calls, and the big blind folds. The pot is $32.
    The flop comes K♥ J♦ 4♠. The small blind bets $20. Player B folds. Player D calls. Player F folds.

Question: *What do you do?*
    Answer: Call. The other two players have probably each hit a pair. You have an open-ended straight draw, and the pot is offering you almost 3-to-1 expressed odds. If you hit your straight, it will be well concealed and there will be a bunch of high cards on board so you should have good implied odds. This is actually almost exactly the scenario you were hoping for when you picked up your hand.

Action: You call. Three players remain. The pot is $92. And you have position.

The turn is the K♣. The small blind checks. Player D checks.

Question: *What do you do?*

First, you're a little puzzled at the action. At least one of these two players was supposed to have a king, based on the action on the flop. But a second king appeared, and nobody bet. Did they both have a jack? Probably not. More likely, one of them had a king and is now slowplaying trip kings. Your position is making you some money as now you get to see the river card for free. You should just check.

Action: You check. The pot remains at $92. The river is the A♠. The small blind and Player D both check.

Question: *What do you do?*

Answer: You made your straight and it's well-concealed. You have to bet. Your stack still has $175, and the small blind and Player D seem to have roughly the same amount. If your analysis of the turn was right, one of the players may be sitting on three kings, in which case he'll at least call any reasonable bet you make. Bet $100 or so, and see what happens.

You bet $100. The small blind raises you all-in for another $75. Player D folds. The pot is $367 and it costs you $75 to call.

Question: *What do you do?*

Answer: Now you know who has the three kings. If he has an ace or a jack to go with his king, you're going to lose to his full house. But the pot is offering you 5-to-1, and you can't fold a straight in a low stakes game with those kind of odds. Call and see.

Action: You call and he turns over K♠7♦. Your straight beats his three kings. As often happens, a weak kicker cost him a big pot.

Example 14

You're playing at a 10¢-25¢ online table. The table is a mix of weak-tight and loose-aggressive players. Player D, sitting right behind you, has been loose and aggressive with many odd bets. His stack is about $18.

Action: The first two players fold. In the third seat with a $20 stack, you pick up K♥Q♥.

Question: *What do you do?*
> **Answer:** Nothing special here. This is a good hand for making a standard raise.

Action: You raise to 75¢. Player D raises you to $1.25. The other players all fold.

Question: *What do you do?*
> **Answer:** It's a strange bet which gives you excellent calling odds of more than 4-to-1. He might have a big hand, but it's just as possible he has nothing and simply wants to sweeten the pot. You should call.

Action: You call. The pot is now $2.85.
The flop comes K♠9♦4♥.

Question: *What do you do?*
> **Answer:** You act first. Your top pair, good kicker is a fine hand for betting, but it's a little optimistic for check-raising. Just make a good solid bet of $2.

Action: You actually check. Player D bets $1.50.

Question: *What do you do?*

    Answer: You showed weakness and you induced a bet from Player D. You still rate to have the best hand, so continue with the plan and raise to about $4.50.

Action: You raise to $4.50. Player D goes all-in with his last $15.25. The pot is now $24.10 and it costs you $10.75 to call.

Question: *What do you do?*

    Answer: When we discussed all-in moves earlier in this book, we tried to make a firm point. In normally tough games, such as you find in mid-stakes and high-stakes play, pushing or calling an all-in with a hand like top pair, top kicker is generally a losing play. In those games, your opponents won't call or move all-in unless, at a minimum, they can beat that hand.

    In small stakes game the dynamics are different. The stakes are relatively small even for the players involved, and many see an all-in as just another bet. Anyone who would call an all-in with middle pair might push all-in with much less than that. So your calling requirements have to change as well. As a rough guess, I'd say that if you called an all-in with top pair top kicker, you'd be ahead a minimum of 60 percent of the time in small stakes games.

Action: You call. The turn and river are the A♥ and the 2♦. Your opponent shows A♠4♦, and wins with his two pair.

    Your opponent pushed all-in with bottom pair plus an overcard, and hit one of his outs on the turn. Unlucky for you, but you had the best hand when the money went to the center, which is the best you can do.

Example 15

You're playing at a 10¢-25¢ online table. The table is a mix of various sorts of players. Player A limps about 40 percent of the time, but very rarely raises preflop. After the flop he will call with any sort of pair or draw. He currently has $26 in his stack after his third buy-in. Player D is a standard loose-aggressive player who gets involved in too many pots. He has $22 in his stack. You're on the button and have both of these players covered with $32 in your stack.

Action: Player A, under the gun, raises to 75¢. Players B and C fold. Player D calls 75¢. Players E and F folds. You're on the button with 7♥7♣.

Question: *What do you do?*
   Answer: A raise is unusual from Player A who usually limps in. Player D, who's loose and aggressive, doesn't raise, but just calls, so his hand is probably weaker than yours. If you hit a set, your implied odds are excellent against two calling stations. You also have position in the hand. Call.

Action: You call 75¢. The blinds fold. The pot is $2.60.
   The flop is 6♣4♥2♥. Player A bets $2. Player D folds.

Question: *What do you do?*
   Answer: Don't ignore your hard-won knowledge in the heat of the moment. When a normally passive calling station starts betting aggressively, it means only one thing — he has a big hand. Since he also raised pre-flop, he can only have a premium pair. Although you have an overpair, it's worthless. Fold.

   Remember that reads on players in weak games are more reliable than in other games because the players are very linear in their behavior. Let this knowledge work for you.

Example 16

You're playing at a 10¢-25¢ online table. The big blind is a weak-tight player. He has $22 in his stack. You've been having a good day and are up to $40.

Action: You pick up A♣A♦ in second position. Player A folds. You raise to 75¢. Everyone folds around to the big blind, who calls 50¢. The pot is $1.60.
  The flop is J♠8♠4♣. The big blind bets 30¢.

Question: *What do you do?*
  Answer: The tiny bet from a weak-tight player in low-stakes games usually means only one thing: "I have a draw, so let's play this flop cheap." (If you're against someone who has read this book it might mean something else.)

Question: *What should you do?*
  Answer: The proper response is "Let's not." Raise. Actually, you should make a pretty big raise because these raises tend to be called.

Action: You raise to $2. The big blind calls. The pot is now $5.60.
  The turn is the 2♦. The big blind bets 50¢.

Question: *What do you do?*
  Answer: The big blind probably has a spade flush draw. The only straight draw possible comes if the big blind had precisely ten-nine, but that's an unlikely call out of position from a weak-tight player. You're still in command, so make another raise and deny him proper calling odds.

Action: You raise to $5 and the big blind calls. The pot is now $15.60.

    The river is the A♠. The big blind pushes all-in for his last $14.25.

Question: *What do you do?*

    Answer: Trust your analysis. You were pretty sure he had a spade draw and another spade hit. Your trip aces are no good. Fold.

Action: You fold. The big blind flashes the K♠Q♠.

Last Example

A $1-$2 game at the Venetian in Las Vegas with 10 players. The players in first and second position limp, player three folds, players four and five limp, and player six folds. The player in seat seven is about 30 years old and has been playing for an hour or so. He's built his $200 buy-in up to $250 with fairly conservative play and no fancy moves. Now he raises to $100 and announces "Don't call me boys, I've got a big hand."

The button and small blind fold. The big blind, a white-haired gent who has been playing for a few hours and looks like a regular, starts to think.

After 15 seconds or so, the raiser comments "You don't want to call me, friend. I've really got a big hand."

"I know you do," says the older gent, and pushes all-in.

The limpers all fold. The original raiser begins to think, and starts to look a little green around the gills. After about 30 seconds he says "If I fold, will you show me your hand?"

The older gent pauses for a second and then says, "Sure, no problem."

The raiser folds and shows a pair of queens, saying "See, I wasn't kidding. Now let's see those aces."

The older gent shows his 6♦4♣ and scoops the pot.

Moral. If you clearly know what your opponent wants you to do, it usually pays to do the opposite.

Part Eleven

Bankroll
Management
and Other Topics

Bankroll
Management
and Other Topics

Introduction

Being a successful poker player isn't solely a matter of playing your cards well. Pitfalls abound even after you stand up from the table. Here's a brief guide to some issues that a successful player needs to handle well.

In addition, the last chapter in this section, "Transitioning to Live Games," is something that would not have been written a few years ago. That's because the Internet is, as far as poker is concerned, still very new. But it now dominates the poker scene.

However, for those of you who just play on the Internet, there is more to poker than just sitting in front of your computer screen. There's another whole world that's certainly worth visiting, and this chapter will get you started.

Bankrolls

The money a poker player uses to fund his playing activities is known as his *bankroll*. If your goal is to improve as a player and move gradually from low-stakes play to higher-stakes play, your bankroll needs to be viewed as your working capital, and be kept as a separate account from your day-to-day expenses. When you win, your bankroll grows. When you lose, the losses come from your bankroll and don't affect your ordinary standard of living.

Growing and nurturing a bankroll is a key skill for a cash game player, perhaps as important as knowing when to raise and fold. Handle your bankroll well, and you need never go broke. Handle it badly, and you can be out of action pretty quick.

Many well known poker players have gone broke several times during their careers. Listening to them talk or write about busting out makes it sound almost romantic, like a rite of passage on the road to being a successful gambler. Nonsense. Going broke is often a sign that greed and foolishness overcame your poker skills. It doesn't have to happen as often as it does, and if you understand the science of bankroll management, your chances of going broke can be kept to an acceptable minimum.

Who Needs a Bankroll?

If you're a casual player for whom the occasional poker game or tournament is just a form of entertainment, like going to a good restaurant, and the stakes are modest or even trivial compared to your income, then you don't need to worry about a bankroll. Just continue to play at stakes you're comfortable, and you'll be fine.

Another time you don't need to worry about your bankroll, when you are playing for more serious money, is if you're a losing player. If you don't have the skills to win, your bankroll won't last. This is true no matter what sort of "money management techniques," such as limiting your losses, quitting when you win a certain amount, or always playing an extra hour if you're losing, you may employ.

If, however, the game is your main hobby, and you have become a serious player, and you want to someday play for stakes that will not be trivial compared to your net worth, then bankroll management becomes important. Let's lay out a plan.

Start Small

Your first step should be to fund your bankroll with an amount of money you can afford to lose without impacting your day-to-day life. That might be a relatively small amount, but it's perfectly alright.

Let's say your starting bankroll is $100. I recommend that you divide that bankroll into 20 equal pieces. Each of those pieces represents a full buy-in for a cash game session. With your $100 bankroll, you can afford to buy into a game for $5, which means you're going to begin by playing 2¢-5¢ cash games (where $5 is 100 times the big blind of 5¢).

"What!" you scream. "I wouldn't play in those games! I'm way better than those guys. I want to take a crack at 25¢-50¢ games. It only costs $50 to buy into those games, so I've got enough for two buy-ins."

Calm down. If you're really good enough to play several levels above where you are, then you'll be there soon enough. While you may feel that you're good enough to move up right now, you don't have the money yet to play without a significant risk of ruin. So learn patience. It's a great virtue for a poker player in any event.

However, before we go on, there is one issue that needs to be addressed a little more clearly. Why did I say to divide your bankroll into 20 equal parts? Is there something magic about this number? The answer is no.

The reason I recommend "20 equal parts" is that it is a figure, based on my experience, which happens to work. Assuming you play well relative to the other players at the particular stakes, and you want an acceptable risk of going broke, often referred to as "risk of ruin," yet still want an acceptable win rate, this division by 20 is a good way to go. But if you're willing to assume a higher risk in exchange for a larger expected win rate, which means dividing your bankroll into a smaller number of equal parts and playing at higher stakes, that's a personal decision which only you can make.

Moving Up
and Moving Down

Once you're playing at a given level, at what point have you won enough to move up? And when should you drop down if your results have been negative? Well, again I'll draw on my experience, and while no means (close to) perfect, here are some guidelines you may want to follow.

1. Move up when your bankroll is 50 percent larger in terms of full buy-ins (than what you started with) at the next higher stake.

2. Move down when your bankroll has shrunk by half at your current stake.

Now before we move on, there are two important points to make. The first has to do with why you need more buy-ins at the higher level. In most cases, the answer is very simple. As you move up in limit, the players on average are better, meaning the games are tougher. The consequence of this is that losing streaks are more likely to occur, and they are also more likely to be more severe. Thus I like the comfort of additional buy-ins.

But there is also another side to this coin. Be willing to take a shot. If you see a very good game at a higher limit, and you don't, by these guidelines, have enough buy-ins to play, I see nothing wrong in playing anyway. Just be aware that if you are losing and start to put your remaining bankroll in jeopardy, you'll need to move back down. In fact, you may even need to move to a lower game than where you were before you entered the higher limit game.

Now let's return to our hypothetical player starting with a bankroll of $100 who has divided it into 20 equal pieces and is playing the 2¢-5¢ games on line. If he follows my advice, his rules look approximately like this:

1.   He can move up to the 5¢-10¢ games (the next highest games on most sites) when his bankroll grows to $300. A full buy-in (100 big blinds) at 5¢-10¢ is $10, so at that point he'll have 30 full buy-ins.

2.   He has to move down to the 1¢-2¢ games when he has only 10 buy-ins at the 2¢-5¢ level, which requires $50.

So he moves down when his bankroll shrinks to $50, and he moves up when his bankroll grows to $300. Of course, if a good opportunity comes along he might take a shot, and if he is willing to assume more risk he might move up with less than $300 and keep playing at his current level even if his bankroll is a little less than $50.

What These Guidelines Accomplish

The purpose of these guidelines is to keep you in action, playing consistently at levels you can beat, and only allowing you to move up when you've demonstrated, through a combination of skill and persistence, that you can soundly beat the level where you're playing (in which case you'll probably do fine at the next level as well). There's not an enormous difference between any one playing level and the next level up. So a player who can beat the 2¢-5¢ game well enough to move from $100 to $300 (representing an accumulated profit of 4,000 big blinds) should continue to win, although at a slower rate in the 5¢-10¢ games.

Remember too that it's no disgrace to move down a level. If you begin with a bankroll of $2,000, hop into the 50¢-$1 games, and lose half your stake, then don't feel ashamed to move down to the 25¢-50¢ games with the $1,000 you've got left. Moving down doesn't mean you failed, it just means you started with more money than skill (or ran exceptionally badly). Skill can be learned with some time and persistence. Using this approach, you can eventually find the level where you belong for the moment, then build from there.

Multi-Tabling

Multi-tabling is the practice of playing several tables at once at an online site. Most sites now allow you to size the table windows as you wish, so with a big screen monitor it's not hard to arrange your screen so that four tables are completely visible at one time. In addition, the software at most sites will push a table where you're required to make an action to the front, so even if your tables are layered, you won't miss a play when it's your turn.

Most players could manage two tables without much difficulty, particularly if they're full tables where the action moves relatively slowly. Stories are always circulating of this or that online specialist who can play 8, 10, or 12 tables at once while making a fortune; it might be possible, but a healthy dose of skepticism is always in order.

Multi-tabling has some advantages and disadvantages. The main disadvantage, of course, is that you're not able to concentrate on any one table. You will notice the most obvious patterns, like a player who is involved in most of the hands, but you'll miss the subtle betting patterns because your attention is usually distracted elsewhere.

Should you multi-table? My advice would be that while you're learning the game, or after you've moved up to a new, higher stake, the answer is "no." You shouldn't be in a hurry when you're in learning mode. You want to look at the other players, see what they're doing, and see if you can figure out what their bets mean and just what they might have. After you've been playing a long time and you're doing many good things automatically, you can consider trying to increase your expectation by judicious multi-tabling. But be cautious and don't be ashamed to stick to one table at a time if that's what feels comfortable.

Interestingly, your bankroll requirements aren't affected by multi-tabling assuming your win rate and level of fluctuations are approximately the same for each table. However, if you can't pay attention as well, expect your win rate per table to drop and your fluctuations to increase.

This translates into a higher required bankroll to assure the same probability of survival. In English, what this means is that if I'm playing four tables instead of one, I would like my bankroll to be 50 percent larger and perhaps more.

Tilt and Its Forms

What happens when your opponent hits a one-outer on the river to win your whole stack?

- Do you chuckle about the vagaries of existence, or muse about the absurd ups and downs that accompany our path through this vale of tears?

- Do you clench your fist, mutter 'nice hand' through gritted teeth, and proceed with a burning desire for revenge?

- Do you shrug it off and play the next hand as if nothing has happened?

- Do you start to play like a maniac and become a favorite to lose several more buy-ins?

If you chose the first or third answer, you have the inner fortitude to be a successful poker player. Skip the rest of this section.

If you chose the second or fourth answer, you're prone to going on tilt, which is a poker term for losing emotional control when things go wrong. (In other games it's called 'steaming.') Since everyone suffers bad beats from time to time, an inability to control tilt can ultimately destroy your game no matter how well you play otherwise.

Players who don't have problems with tilt are able to view bad beats as simply part of the game, and when they lose a tough hand they remember that they've had their share of unexpected wins as well. If you are prone to tilting, try to remind yourself that poker is, after all, only a game, and try to view bad beats as simply one challenge among many that you will have to train yourself to conquer.

If you don't have your tendency to tilt under control, there are some defenses you can put in place to minimize the damage. The simplest is to obey the following rule religiously:

> Anytime you feel that your emotional control has been affected by a bad loss, just quit for the day (or some reasonable length of time). If you're multi-tabling, shut down all tables. Take a walk, read a book, watch a movie, but don't play any poker until you're ready.

Will this cut into your poker action? It might. But in a tilting state of mind, "action" is the very last thing you need. Better to break even for a few hours than become a favorite to blow a few hundred big blinds punishing yourself. Sometimes you gotta know when to hold 'em and know when to fold 'em.

Other Times
for Sitting Down

Tilting isn't the only emotion that can get in the way of playing your best. Depending on your mindset, *euphoria* and *the accountant's syndrome* may play a role as well.

Euphoria occurs when you've been on an incredible hot streak and now feel you're invincible. You start playing hands you shouldn't, betting at flops out of position, and in general pushing the action without regard for your table image and the expected reaction of the other players. Since you're way ahead when euphoria sets in, the cost may not be so obvious; instead of a 250 big blind winning session, you end up "only" 175 blinds ahead. But that's a loss of 75 big blinds through careless play, and that's a big loss. The cure for euphoria is to pick up your chips and walk away if you notice that you've lost any sense of danger.

The accountant's syndrome isn't the worst problem to have, but it can interfere with good play nonetheless. The syndrome occurs when you view cash games as a job, and you feel you have a certain amount of money you're supposed to win every day. When you win your quota, you start to tighten up, trying to make sure you don't lose a big hand and dip below your quota again. If you're playing well and the table is very favorable, you may be blowing a terrific money-making opportunity just to hit an arbitrary target.

Here's a classic true story. Years ago I was playing in a cash game in Las Vegas. A fellow that I knew liked to quit when he won a couple of thousand, was at the table. After a few hours, he won a big pot, reached his quota, and started to gather his chips into a tray although he still had a few hands before the big blind would reach him.

I couldn't resist the opportunity and blurted out "You can't quit all those free hands! What if you get aces?" By this time he had his chips in the racks, all ready to go, but he got embarrassed and sat back down, waiting for the big blind to come around so he could quit with some dignity. The very next hand he picked up aces, lost a huge pot, and went negative for the day. When I left the game five hours later he was still there, chipping his way back. I later heard that he stayed until 5:00 am before he eventually got even!

Paying Taxes

When you win a lot of money in a tournament, the host casino is required to file a 1099 form with the I.R.S. But when you win money in a cash game, you receive cash. Since no one at the casino cage knows if the chips you're redeeming represent a net profit or a net loss, no 1099s will be filed.

To many players, this represents an opportunity. Why declare the money at all? Why not just stick it in a safety deposit box and pat yourself on the back for outsmarting the I.R.S.?

We won't go into the legal or ethical reasons for paying taxes here. That's not our bailiwick. Instead, we'll explain why it makes good (in fact overwhelming) sense to declare your winnings and pay taxes on them.

Let's imagine two professional poker players: Cagey Cal and Simple Sam. Both earn exactly $100,000 each year playing no-limit hold 'em in Las Vegas. We'll suppose that their variance is precisely zero, and neither their skill nor the available games change over time. Every year, regular as clockwork, they make their $100,000 each.

Cagey Cal doesn't pay taxes. From his $100,000, he takes out $30,000 each year for modest living expenses, and sticks the rest ($70,000) in a commodious safety deposit box at his local bank. Each year on December 31 he goes to his box and, Midas-like, chortles over his growing hoard. Here's a chart of what Cagey Cal has in his box as 30 years roll by.

Cagey Cal's Approach

End of Year	In Box	End of Year	In Box
1	$70,000	16	$1,120,000
2	$140,000	17	$1,190,000
3	$210,000	18	$1,260,000
4	$280,000	19	$1,330,000
5	$350,000	20	$1,400,000
6	$420,000	21	$1,470,000
7	$490,000	22	$1,540,000
8	$560,000	23	$1,610,000
9	$630,000	24	$1,680,000
10	$700,000	25	$1,750,000
11	$770,000	26	$1,820,000
12	$840,000	27	$1,890,000
13	$910,000	28	$1,960,000
14	$980,000	29	$2,030,000
15	$1,050,000	30	$2,100,000

Pretty impressive. After 30 years, his stash has grown to $2.1 million in cash.

Simple Sam takes another approach. Each year he takes $30,000 for living expenses, and pays $30,000 in taxes. Since he doesn't have to worry about concealing his money, he invests the remaining $40,000 in some good mutual funds, returning, on average, 10 percent per year.

The first year he only earns $2,000 on his investment, because he was depositing money each month over the course of the year. He had $0 to invest at the beginning of the year but $40,000 at the end, so he earned 10 percent on his average balance, which was $20,000. In the second year, he made $6,000 on his investment: $4,000 on the money he had invested from the start, and another $2,000 on the new money he put in during the year.

Over the course of the same 30 years, here's what Simple Sam's balance looked like.

Simple Sam's Approach

Year	Start of Year	Deposited	Investment Gains	End of Year
1	$0	$40,000	$2,000	$42,000
2	$42,000	$40,000	$6,200	$88,200
3	$88,200	$40,000	$10,820	$139,020
4	$139,020	$40,000	$15,902	$194,922
5	$194,922	$40,000	$21,492	$256,414
6	$256,414	$40,000	$27,641	$324,056
7	$324,056	$40,000	$34,406	$398,461
8	$398,461	$40,000	$41,846	$480,307
9	$480,307	$40,000	$50,031	$570,338
10	$570,338	$40,000	$59,034	$669,372
11	$669,372	$40,000	$68,937	$778,309

Year	Start of Year	Deposited	Investment Gains	End of Year
12	$778,309	$40,000	$79,831	$898,140
13	$898,140	$40,000	$91,814	$1,029,954
14	$1,029,954	$40,000	$104,995	$1,174,949
15	$1,174,949	$40,000	$119,495	$1,334,444
16	$1,334,444	$40,000	$135,444	$1,509,889
17	$1,509,889	$40,000	$152,989	$1,702,878
18	$1,702,878	$40,000	$172,288	$1,915,165
19	$1,915,165	$40,000	$193,517	$2,148,682
20	$2,148,682	$40,000	$216,868	$2,405,550
21	$2,405,550	$40,000	$242,555	$2,688,105
22	$2,688,105	$40,000	$270,810	$2,998,915
23	$2,998,915	$40,000	$301,892	$3,340,807
24	$3,340,807	$40,000	$336,081	$3,716,888
25	$3,716,888	$40,000	$373,689	$4,130,576
26	$4,130,576	$40,000	$415,058	$4,585,634
27	$4,585,634	$40,000	$460,563	$5,086,198
28	$5,086,198	$40,000	$510,620	$5,636,817
29	$5,636,817	$40,000	$565,682	$6,242,499
30	$6,242,499	$40,000	$626,250	$6,908,749

At the end of 30 years, Simple Sam has $6.9 million in his investment account, more than triple Cagey Cal's total.

If we look at the two tables closely, we can note a few interesting points. Cagey Cal starts out with a $28,000 lead after Year 1, and his lead keeps increasing for awhile, eventually reaching $96,000 after Year 6. But in Year 7, Simple Sam's investment earnings reach $34,000, so his total gain for the year tops Cagey Cal's for the first time.

By Year 11, Sam's investment earnings are almost equal to Cal's entire poker profit for the year, and Sam takes the lead for the first time, $778,000 to $770,000. After that things go downhill fast for Cal. By Year 14, Sam's total income is more than twice Cal's. By Year 30, Sam is making nine times as much from his investments alone as Cal is from poker.

Why does Sam's strategy win by so much? By paying his taxes, he leaves the remainder of his money free to be legally invested. Any reasonable investment strategy, whether based on equities or real estate, builds on the awesome power of compounded interest. Cal's money grows linearly; Sam's money grows geometrically. In a few years, Cal's early lead gets erased and Sam moves in front to stay.

These tables represent a very simplified analysis, but taking more factors into account causes Sam's advantage over Cal to grow even more. Inflation, for instance, even when held to a very low level, causes the value of dollars held as cash to diminish over time. Even an inflation level of 1 to 2 percent per year (historically very low for a 30-year period) would cause the true value of Cal's cash horde to decline dramatically. Because so many more investment options exist, money held legally is intrinsically far more valuable than money stashed away as cash.

Moral: You'll do far better financially by simply declaring your poker profits and investing what remains as wisely as you can than by trying to hold on to piles of cash.

Transitioning
to Live Games

Today, most players start out playing no-limit cash games online, then later transition to live games in casinos or card rooms. (Live games are also referred to as B&M, or brick and mortar rooms.) It's a sensible approach which allows you to gain a lot of experience very cheaply in games where a full buy-in might be only $10 or less. In Las Vegas casinos, the minimum no-limit game is usually the $1-$2, with a typical buy-in of $200. In other parts of the country, you'll occasionally find a live game for even less.

In online games, the site takes care of all the bookkeeping, and a good site will allow you to takes notes and get access to hand histories. The mechanics of live play are a bit different and will require some adjustments for the first-time player. Here's a quick guide to some of the features of live play that won't seem routine, and that may differ from casino to casino. When you go to a new casino or card room for the first time, it's worth taking a moment to talk to the floor manager and make sure you know just what their rules are.

1. **What is the rake?** Competition has forced online poker rooms to offer a pretty standard rake of 5 percent of the pot up to a maximum of $3. If no flop is seen, the pot isn't raked.

    In live rooms, the rakes can vary a bit more. A typical rake in a low-stakes game ($1-$2) might be 10 percent of the pot up to a maximum of $4. At cardrooms in Los Angeles, they often assess a rake of $1 before the flop, $3 on the flop, and $1 on the turn, but of the $5 collected, $1 goes in a bad-beat jackpot. Collecting a set fee rather than a percentage makes the dealer's work easier and quicker. In higher-stakes games, like $10-$20, the rooms typically charge a table fee of $8 to $10 per half hour. For poker rooms in out of the way places, the rakes may be even higher.

Apart from a simple desire to know what's going on, you need to be aware of the rake for two reasons. The first is that the structure of the rake affects the style of play you want to employ. A high rake that's assessed on a per-pot basis implies that tight play is favored over loose play since the entire rake falls on the winner of a pot. A player who makes his profit winning a few big pots is better off than a player who splashes around and wins lots of little pots. A rake that's assessed as a constant table fee on each player doesn't favor any style over any other style. All that matters is that you be able to average a profit that's bigger than the hourly fee.

The second reason for knowing what's going on is that a high enough rake can make a table unprofitable even if the players seem weak. I've heard of card rooms in outlying areas where the rake gets as high as 15 percent and the buy-ins are capped at 50 big blinds. In a game like that it's tough to win over time even if the general level of play seems poor.

2. **What is the maximum buy-in?** Online, the maximum buy-in is 100 big blinds across nearly all sites and stakes. In live play, this isn't the case. A few rooms restrict the buy-in to less than 100 big blinds, mostly in their lowest games. Some other rooms cap a buy-in at 100 big blinds. Others will permit buy-ins of much more, sometimes as much as 200 to 500 big blinds. You should inquire about the buy-in rules any time you play in a new room.

    In general, if you think you're going to be one of the best players at the table, you want to buy in for as much as you can. However, there's no particular advantage to having many more chips than anyone else since you can always buy back if you lose your stack. So if the maximum buy-in is 500 big blinds but you're sitting at the table where the biggest stack is 200 big blinds, that's probably what you want as well. Buying in for a stack that's clearly bigger than any other is conspicuous, and you're not usually looking to attract attention.

3. **Does cash play?** In live games, if you have a pile of chips in front of you as well as cash, the cash can be considered part of your stack. Although a few casino rooms don't permit this, and require you to play with chips only, about 90 percent allow cash to play. So you could, for instance, buy into a $1-$2 game for $200 worth of chips, and put the chips as well as $500 in cash in front of you, and have a total stack of $700. This approach makes cashing out much easier, but remember that your cash is in play as well as your chips.

For cash to be in play, it must be physically on the table. You can't (as Edward G Robinson did at the end of *The Cincinnati Kid*) pull some cash out of your pocket for a final raise when you have the nuts.

4. **Can you take money off the table?** No you can't, not while you're playing. This rule includes the cash you may have in front of you as well as your chips. The only way you can remove cash from the table is by standing up and cashing out. This is one of many situations that can't arise in online play, but which occasionally occurs in live games because players don't really understand the rules.

When should you cash out? This differs from player to player, but I would certainly cash out in the following situations:

● You realize you're getting tired and think your play will start to deteriorate.

- The table used to be very good, but now it's changed for the worse either because better players have sat down or your table image has deteriorated.

- You're naturally conservative and you've won a lot of money, which you think will make you play passively to protect your lead.

One could argue that in the case of the second and third reasons on the list, you should stay at the table and correct these tendencies in your game. While that's true, it's also not irrational to just walk away once in a while with a big win in your pocket. Life doesn't always need to be blood, sweat, and tears.

5. **Can you ask the dealer to count the pot?** Yes. In online games this is done automatically, but in live games you have a right to know what's in the pot before you make your play since you may not be able to estimate it accurately yourself. In that case you can ask the dealer to count the pot. Note that remembering the bets in live games and keeping track of the pot in your head is an excellent skill to develop.

6. **Do you have to reveal your hand at a showdown?** Rules may differ slightly from casino to casino, but in general the idea is that the winning hand needs to show, but a losing hand can muck its cards. This, by the way, is consistent with online play, where the only hand that's necessarily revealed is the winning hand.

   Confusion can arise when one player has his bluff called on the river. For example, Player A checks on the river, Player B makes a bet, Player A calls the bet, and Player B (who was trying to steal the pot with a bluff) now mucks his hand. Player A has won the pot no matter what cards he holds, but does he need to show his hand? Some casinos would rule that he does.

Note that in cash game play, the hole cards are not revealed when the players push all-in. Instead the cards remain face down and the board is dealt to the river. On the *High-Stakes Poker* television show, the hole cards are shown just as in a tournament, but that's only for dramatic effect and doesn't reflect the practice in real live games.

7. **Can you "run it twice" in a live game?** If you've watched the *High Stakes Poker* show, you've been introduced to the idea of running a hand twice. It's a clever idea which works like this. Let's say two players get all-in on the flop. They expose their hands, and one of the players will be the favorite. But he's by no means a lock, so he says, "Let's run it twice" meaning that two different sets of turn and river cards will be dealt. If one of the players wins both sets, he takes the whole pot; otherwise they split it.

Running it twice is a fair way of reducing the variance in the game. The expectations of the two players are unaffected by running the hands multiple times, but the swings are lessened because instead of a guaranteed result that one player will win the whole gigantic pot, there's now a significant chance that the pot will be split. The player who's ahead is happy because the chance that he'll actually lose the whole pot is greatly reduced. The player who's behind sees that he now has a significant chance to walk away even. If both players are feeling some money pressure, both might feel they are better off with this arrangement.

Running it twice is pretty much unknown in small stakes games, but most casinos will allow the practice in large stakes games to accommodate the players. Both players have to indicate they're interested in a deal, at which point the dealer turns the hole cards face-up and the players can then decide if they want to run the hand more than once, and if so, how many times.

If you have a small bankroll for the stakes you're playing, you may want to run hands multiple times to cut down on your variance. If you have a large bankroll, then you probably don't need to do it. In that case, it's usually to your advantage to put as much pressure on your less-well-bankrolled opponents by letting them know that if they call your all-in, the full fluctuations present in the game will apply.

Part Twelve

An Interview
with Bobby Hoff

**Bobby Hoff
with Sailor Roberts in the Background**

An Interview
with Bobby Hoff

Introduction

Bobby Hoff, known in the poker circles as "The Wizard," is one of the best and most respected no-limit hold 'em cash game players in the world. Hailing from Victoria, Texas, he learned his poker forty years ago playing in hold 'em games with the other great Texas road gamblers, men like Doyle Brunson, Sailor Roberts, and Jack Strauss. Today he is regularly found playing, and winning, in the toughest no-limit cash games around.

While he's long been a cash game specialist, Bobby has occasionally ventured into the tournament arena. His best result in the World Series of Poker was runner-up to Hal Fowler in 1979. Although on three different occasions he had Fowler all-in with the worse hand, each time Fowler was able to draw out and survive. In the end, after a marathon heads-up session, Fowler managed to crack Bobby's pocket aces by hitting an inside straight on the turn.

Today, among the poker cognoscenti, it's fair to say that Bobby Hoff is our Chuck Yeager. While others seek out the cameras and the limelight of the big tournaments, Bobby exercises his considerable skills quietly, mostly at the Commerce Club in Commerce, California.

Unlike many of the other poker players of his generation, Bobby is trim, fit, alert, and alive. While he rarely talks about the game, he joins us now for a discussion of the poker scene and big-stack cash game strategy.

The Interview

When did you start playing no-limit? How long ago, and who was involved?

Well, I started a really long time ago. I started playing in 1960, in my home town, Victoria, Texas, but didn't really learn much. I just learned to be a break-even player in a small local game.

After Ed Thorpe published his book, *Beat the Dealer*, I realized blackjack could be beaten, so I played a lot of blackjack in the 1960s. I eventually formed one of the early blackjack teams, and we did well for awhile. But I got barred, finally, from all the casinos, and by 1969 that game was pretty well burned up everywhere. So I started playing no-limit hold 'em again.

In Texas and Louisiana, there were only two games that were played for serious money. No-limit hold 'em and deuce-to-seven lowball, also no-limit. There was one place in Texas that played wheel lowball, and sometimes you'd find a game of pot-limit hold 'em. But no-limit hold 'em was always the big game.

Was there anyone special that taught you?

The biggest influence on my game was a man named James Roy. His nickname was 'Long Goody.' He played all over Texas and Louisiana, and eventually Las Vegas. He was one of the best players who ever lived. A super player. I really learned the game from watching him play and then playing against him in 1971 and 1972. He was a real nice guy, besides being a great player. He retired from playing in 1980.

Did they ever have any limit hold 'em in Texas?
> Very little. In Victoria they had all kinds of small games, and other places too. But very little limit.

> Limit really became popular in Vegas at the Golden Nugget. That's where they started playing, around 1970. And from there it spread across the town and to Reno and Tahoe, then eventually to California.

Who started spreading no-limit cash games in Vegas?
> They started at the Golden Nugget as well. Corky got the game going. His real name was Felton McCorquodale, but everyone knew him as Corky.

> I never played with him, never even met him, but he was a legend, a hell of a player. A complete master at no-limit hold 'em. In the South, no one could beat him. They even cheated him, and they still couldn't overcome him!

Scary. If you can't cheat a guy and beat him ...
> McCorquodale told a great story about playing 5-card stud — he was a fine stud player too — in southern Louisiana. After awhile, he suspected that he might get cheated. He thought they were setting him up for one big hand where he'd lose all his money.

> Right away the hand came up. With one card to come, he had a king in the hole and a king on board, and the other guy had garbage showing, no pair, no straight, no flush. All the money was in, and the only way he could lose was if the guy had an ace in the hole and hit an ace on the river.

> Now McCorquodale got a strong suspicion that the hand would play out exactly that way, so he said "I'd like to cut the cards." (In the places we played, where everybody dealt for themselves, it was common practice to be allowed to cut the cards off in the middle of the deal.)

> But they said, "No, we don't allow any cuts."

> Then he said, "Well, what about insurance?"

"No, we don't allow any insurance."

He said, "Well, can we split the pot?"

"No, we don't allow any split pots."

He said, "Well, what about cab fare home? Can I get cab fare?"

He got the cab fare.

So just how far back does no-limit hold 'em go? I've heard all kinds of guesses, as far back as the early 1900s.

In the South, the progression of the big no-limit games went like this — first 5-card stud, then lowball, then hold 'em, and finally pot-limit Omaha. Since 5-card stud was popular in the 1920s and 1930s, hold 'em probably appeared in the late 1940s, maybe the early 1950s. It was a great invention, really unbelievable, when you see how complex the game really is.

I'd like your impression of a couple of players from that era. First, Johnny Moss.

Johnny Moss, when I started playing with him, 1970, 1971, had the reputation of being the best player in the world. But I didn't see that. It might have been just age or fatigue, but he'd definitely lost a step. And everyone else felt this way too. He would have — maybe an hour at a time he would just play brilliantly. Then something would happen and he would start playing poorly again. But he had flashes of brilliance. Still he was fairly advanced in age when I started playing with him. He was still a good player, don't get me wrong, but he wasn't like he was. He wasn't like Doyle described, by far the best player. By far. At his peak, he was probably as good as they said he was. He could have played even with McCorquodale.

The other thing about Moss, at that time he was playing a lot of games where he really wasn't very good. Games like seven-stud and seven-stud hi-lo split and some other games where he was very bad. The other players built the games around him, they beat him out of millions. And he was not a good limit player at all. But Doyle said he was by far the best no-limit deuce-to-seven player in his day, by far the best player. Probably true.

How about Buck Buchanan?

Buck Buchanan was a good friend of mine and a great player. He played so well after the flop that he just didn't throw his hand away on the button. He felt that with position he could outplay anybody, so when he was on the button, he just made up his mind to play the hand.

He was a super-tight player, but he made his living stealing. I mean, there was just no way to call him. I remember one session in particular, we played for eight hours, and he showed just two hands. One was two aces, and the other was two kings, and you realized, the other eight hours, we never saw his hand. He won $2,800, and he showed his hand twice in eight hours. We didn't know what he had. But you couldn't call him.

And he'd do things like call twice to take the pot away at the river.

He was really tough to beat. His nickname was "Double-T." Here's how he got it. They charged this game we played in a lot — 5 percent commission on the chips. When you bought chips they charged 5 percent, that's where they got the rake. So if you bought $1,000, they gave you $950 in chips.

There was no cash in the game, so they had a record of all the chips everybody bought, and all the chips everybody cashed out. Buck won 5 percent of the chips out. They called him Double-T, double take-off. He was the other half of the rake.

That's an amazing win rate.

Now he had another gear, a looser gear where he'd play sometimes. Where he would raise the pot. But when he got into his tight mode, he'd only raise the pot with aces, kings, or ace-king, and even then only in the back.

He really thought a lot of position. He thought position was everything, and he didn't want anybody to know what he had. When he limped in he could have two queens, when he was up front he could have anything. He could have a lot of hands, a wide variety of hands. He just didn't raise the pot before the flop. So it was almost impossible to put him on a hand.

What about Stuey Ungar? Did you ever play with him?

Yes I did. He was the last guy in the world you wanted to play heads-up. But if you could book him in a cheap 9-handed game, or 10-handed, he would have no chance. He would literally be the worst player in the game. But playing really high and really short, he'd be fantastic.

The first time he played no-limit hold 'em, he played in my room at the Horseshoe in 1979 or thereabouts. He played Jack Strauss heads-up. They played a stack of hold 'em for $2,000, and then they played gin to 150 points for $2,000, and I think they played 5 or 10 of each. Jack won all 10 of the hold 'em sessions, and Stuey won about two-thirds of the gin. Jack, who was a good gin player, said when he was done that he had no chance against Stuey at gin, and coming from him that was quite an admission.

He was a terrific player shorthanded and high, but at a cheap full table he was hopeless. Just hopeless.

What was his big problem?

Just too loose. He'd overplay his cards, over and over again. I remember Stuey once, we were playing with me, Buck Buchanan, Jesse Alto, Mike Cox, and four or five guys like that, tough, tight, tight players, and Stuey would raise the pot, and it would come seven-five-five or something, and they'd check, and he'd bet, and they'd raise, and he put them on a bluff and call with ace-high or something. They had trips, you know?

Or it would come king-seven-seven, and he'd raise it with two eights. They'd check and he'd bet with the eights, and they'd move in on him. He would put them on a draw, and sometimes they'd be drawing, but often not. Just hopeless.

But if it was heads-up or three-handed, I wouldn't get in a game with him. There he was deadly.

Do you like playing no limit hold 'em better than any other form of poker?

I like pot limit hold 'em better. It's quite a bit better.

Why?

Well, if I were going to make a perfect game for myself, I'd play pot-limit before the flop and no-limit after the flop. What hurts no-limit hold 'em, even in deep-stack cash games, is the big reraise before the flop. You get a shutout. And often the first reraise, from the big blind, is a shutout raise. You just can't make that play in pot-limit. In pot-limit, if the chips get really deep, that second raise still leaves your opponents with big implied odds.

At no-limit, you can cut their implied odds way down. It takes away from a good player. But with that minor variation, it's the best. There's just more skill, more opportunities than in any other form of poker. So many situations come up where everybody misses their hand. I do well in those spots where everybody misses. If the cards will just stay ice-cold, I'll do fine.

So when did you feel that you were a good hold 'em player, you could pretty much sit in any game you wanted to?

By 1971. Up through 1969, I had played a lot of twenty-one. But that game dried up, so I took my twenty-one money, I had a goodly sum, and I lost it all, in the last part of 1969 and the first part of 1970. But I got to play with some good players. See, in Victoria there was only one good player, but when I started playing at the Horseshoe and the Nugget I got to play with Goody and Doyle and Sailor and Bill Smith, those guys, and I got to be a pretty good player by the time I got broke.

What was the usual limit in those days?

We played $5-$10 blinds, or $5-$10-$25 blinds, $5 on the button. That was a big game back in 1970. So Sailor started staking me in the $5-$10-$25 game. He had confidence in my play. And I remember one day, I was making plays in my head, and every play would have worked. And I said — you know what? I'm going to go in today, and every time I see a play, I'm going to make every play I see. I eventually won $80,000 over a period of a few months in that poker game. I just killed it. I went overboard. I literally made every play I saw and destroyed that game.

You played without fear.

I totally played without fear. Every time I saw a play, a chance to take the pot, I took it. And I took so many of them I couldn't believe it.

Of course, the cards have to hit you too. But if they do hit, oh my God.

When Santa Ana took the Alamo, the Mexican army blew a song called the Digueo. It's a mournful song, it means take no prisoners. So sometimes in my mind I play the Digueo, and I attack every pot. But only if I have a good image — only if the cards have been running my way.

Compared to the 1970s, how has your game evolved?

I'm playing tighter more often than before. Let me tell you what my main problem was. I would drive players right into the corner. And then I would just stay right on them. You take anybody, and you keep beating on them, and beating on them, they're going to go crazy and attack you. You take a little dog and beat on him and he's going to growl at you and bite you. So the art to poker is to beat on somebody until just before they play back at you, with the ten-five offsuit, and then you give them one.

Doyle encouraged that in his book and that's really the art of the game. How far can you push your guy before you're making him play back at you with nothing? Before, in effect, you've made him a better player. So you push him just as far as you can, and then you stop. I think I do that better now than I did. And also I think I'm more aware of my image now. But the rest of it's very much the same.

I do play a little differently now because I played in much tougher games then, in general. The games I played in Texas were really tough games. I'll give you an idea — you know I played Bill Smith. Bill was a very tight player. He was a really tight player and a really good tight player. We played 10-handed in Dallas and he's under the gun with ace-king offsuit and he discards it. "I'm not going to play it." No good for him. When he had the ace-king, they knew what he had. So if he got action, it was no good. It was just as good to be representing the ace-king when it came as to actually have it. Or better, maybe. So he just threw the ace-king away under the gun.

Dallas was one of those kind of games where around in back — I didn't like to have a weak hand because it was too obvious you had a weak hand. Against good players, I'd need to have a good hand. I'd probably have a hand you could easily raise with. That's against very good players.

But it's all different now. I mean, the game I play at the Commerce, if I'm in the middle of the pack, I don't hesitate to limp in with the ace-jack offsuit. In Dallas, I wouldn't consider it. At least I didn't play it. In Dallas, I might have to be in the cutoff or the button before I played that hand. I mean, I might raise with the five-four suited, even in Dallas, but around in back I didn't limp with it because the players were too good. There were too many good players who knew what a limp like that meant.

Do you play online at all? It sounds like your style is more ideally suited to live games.

I prefer to play online because of the sheer convenience, but I can't afford it. I feel like I have twice the advantage in a live game as I do online. I'm not totally sure why, but I can see some reasons. I've thought about this a lot. I played online for about 18 months. The main reason, I think is the depth of the chips. The ratio between the chips and the blinds. It's so much higher in the game I play at the Commerce Club than it is online. It's just ridiculously high. And that's a big help to a skilled player.

A second reason is that people don't play for as long as they do in a live game. Chips don't build up the same way. They didn't have to drive from Pomona to the Commerce Club to play. You wouldn't drive 30 miles to stay an hour and then drive home, so you stay. And the chips build up.

And also, of course, you get to read the players much better. For instance, you're playing live, you're playing a stranger, I'm going to have a really good idea of how he plays in just a few minutes. I can watch him handle his chips. I can see the way he's dressed. I can see his age. I'll have a good idea.

Online, I have no idea. He might be a great player. He might be a total donkey. It'll be a while figuring it out. You might be playing against a grandmother instead of some young hotshot kid. Or your opponent's drunk and you don't know it. You're playing with him every day and all of a sudden — I know there were people online that were drugged and doing drugs, I know there were. You can just tell. But in the casino you know instantly. As soon as they slur their first word you know they've been drinking. Online it may cost you a lot of money before you figure it out.

Do you like the structure of the online cash games?
The games are a little too conducive to playing tight. I'd like to see that changed. There's a structure I've been talking up, but I haven't gotten anyone to try it yet. A three-unit ante, and a one, two, and three-unit blind in front of that. It would be nothing but action, action, action. People would love this game, but so far I haven't gotten anyone to try it.

Since 2003, the number of people willing to play no-limit cash games, live or online, has exploded. Have you noticed the live cash game players at the Commerce Club getting better? They've certainly improved online.
I've thought about it a lot, but no, I don't think so. For awhile, I was alarmed because I thought — I've never seen so many good players in all my life, I've just never seen so many good players. They're everywhere. There are all these kids, they've got a million-dollar bankroll and they all play good! This is incredible.

But you know what? I've also never seen this many bad players before! That's what it is. I don't think the percentage of good players has changed.

There are more players of all kinds. There are a lot more good players now than there ever were. Than have ever lived, probably. There are more good players alive right now than have ever played the game. But, there are more bad players by far than there ever were. And more come every day to the Commerce Club. Incredible.

The $20-$40 blind game is really a pretty big poker game if you think about it. They take $200 an hour, that's to start. That's just for collections. Than there's tokes to everyone. Then there's winning players. You add all that up, you're talking millions. And the game goes around the clock for a couple of years. The money that's been lost in that poker game is incredible. And it's more active now than it was a couple of years ago. That means there's a tremendously big pool of players out there.

Obviously you see a lot of young players coming in the club, they want to be a pro. That's why they're there. This is their dream. If a guy like that came to you and said, "What are the most common mistakes that I'm likely to make here?" what would your answer be?

I would say the danger for these young players in the way they play their hands is the fact that most of them have never gone bad before. So what you're looking at when you see these young players, these young Internet guys, you're seeing people who don't know what it's like to lose for a month. It's never happened to them. You're looking at hundreds or thousands of players who started and this is a handful that the cards ran over. Now they may have talent — some of them have a lot of talent, they're very good players, but they don't have any experience on the downside. You don't really get to improve your game until you go bad. It changes you.

Right. As far as you know, this is just the way it's supposed to be. You play, you win, you play, you win.

What can you do when you just go win, win, win, win? You don't know how to change it. You don't start thinking about it until you're losing. Ray Zee made a famous statement. Right on that point. "You show me a guy that's been lucky at poker for a year, and I'll show you someone that can't be playing well." There's a lot of truth to that. A lot of truth.

The biggest mistake they make. Is that what you want?

Yes. Could be more than one. But do they come in with any characteristic thing that, if you were a mentor to these guys, you'd say, "Look, this is what you have to work on?"

My good-playing opponents, my good-playing young opponents, the mistake that I see them make most? They call the reraise too much. I see it over and over and over again.

You learn by watching somebody who did it. I mean, if I raise with ace-king and I get reraised, I think the reraise is legitimate, I don't even think about it. When I say I don't think about it, I mean seriously I don't even think if I'm throwing a good hand away. I just put it right in the muck, like this. That's how fast I put it in there.

Now I'm talking about somebody who has a big stack. If they have a short stack, I may reraise and race with them. But if we're playing $20-$40 blinds and I've opened for $200, I get two callers, and then someone in late position calls the $200 and raises $1,100, and we've both got $12,000 or $15,000 left, I don't even consider it. I mean, you have to hope they're bluffing before you touch that call. I mean, do they have ace-queen? Maybe, maybe, but not likely. You've got an ace in your hand, they probably don't.

What do you hope they have? Two queens? They probably have something like two queens. So, it's 2-to-1 against you that you catch the ace or the king after you call the reraise, and even then you don't get action unless you're buried. So — I just muck it. Now if I've got seven-five suited, I can think about it, especially if I'm in position. But ace-king? And ace-queen offsuit? That's really a bad hand to call a reraise.

I think another mistake they make is not paying enough attention to the trouble hands before the flop. Hands we're talking about like ace-queen, king-queen, ace-jack. Two big unsuited cards. They're very troublesome hands. I really like limping with these hands or making very small raises.

The mini-raise?
That's the Internet play. I see a lot of good Internet players making that play, and that's fine.

How about the buy-in? If you were playing in a cash game and there was no limit on the buy-in, let's say it's a $20-$40 game and most people were buying in for $4,000, but some people were buying in for $12,000 to $15,000, would you want to buy in for the biggest stack that you could?
Not necessarily. There's a couple of considerations. One is a bankroll consideration. And the other one is — I like to be able to draw. So sometimes, even with a $6,000, $7,000, or $8,000 stack, you'll have a short stack against two big stacks. You've got the advantage. Because I can move in, drawing to my flush. And they can't. Because the other guy's got them for $15,000.

Sometimes you get in a situation where a big stack, but not a huge stack, may be some kind of advantage. On the other hand, if you're a really good player, and you're playing guys who make lots of mistakes, you may get to win the whole $15,000. I suppose if bankroll were no consideration, I would probably prefer the $15,000 to $20,000 stack to the $7,000 to $8,000 stack.

So when you go to play at the Commerce Club in the afternoon, do you sort of look at the table and say — this table, these players, I'd like to buy in for this much. Or do you have a constant figure that works pretty well?
Usually I'll just sit down and buy-in for $10,000. That's 250 big blinds (in the $20-$40 game). Somewhere in that

neighborhood. It's all right to buy 500 big blinds too. I'd be comfortable either way.

What about 100 big blinds, you don't feel like that's enough to work with?

Yeah, barely. Now sometimes I'd rather have it. Sometimes it's clearly better to not have a big stack. For instance, when you have someone that's raising way too many pots. You know you're going to have to play with him, and you want to reraise him before the flop and then get comfortably in on the flop.

So, in other words, you've got ace-king, and you can limp in, have him raise the pot, get several callers, and reraise, and have enough to move all-in on the flop. Whereas if you have $20,000 in front of you, reraising here is not such a good idea because you're not going to be able to move that huge stack in on the flop comfortably.

Another example. Say you're playing $20-$40 no-limit and you've bought in for $15,000, a nice deep stack. Now what do you do against a player like me? I raise the pot, you've got two nines, it comes seven-five-deuce, I bet, you call, the turn is a deuce, I bet and you call, and now you have to think — this crazy SOB might bet me all three times. You're talking about putting your whole stack into this pot to defend your nines. It's not just call $600 on the flop and raise $1,200 all-in. You'd like to do that with your nines, you'd love it. But you can't!

A short stack would have a big edge here because their downside is so limited. You can't move the short stacks out in that situation. It's difficult to bluff a short stack. So as the stacks get really deep, the bluffs get really strong.

Would you characterize your play as more aggressive than most people, or just selectively aggressive in particular spots that you see and you like?

I'm sort of aggressive, absolutely. But, there are certainly players that play more aggressively than I do.

I play two ways. I have two games. I play one game when my image is really good and the chips are really deep. And then I have another game I play when my image is not good and the chips are not deep. You're forced to play a different game when the ratio between the stacks and the money in the pot before the flop changes; the higher the stacks, the more aggressive you can be.

Now where's the cutoff? When do you see a game change from tight/aggressive to loose/aggressive? Do you want it to be 100 times the big blind or —

That's very good. That's exactly right. Put it this way. I don't think it's right to start raising with smaller cards, smaller hands, until almost everyone at the table has 100 times the big blind or more. Now you can get by with just one player with a short stack. Maybe you can get by with two short stacks. But you're spotting them an edge — if they're good players, you're going to lose to those guys. That may be okay because you'll more than make up for it against some of the others. For instance, I can think of a couple of players at the Commerce who, if they were sitting on my right, would limp in almost every pot, and call the raise 80 to 90 percent of the time. Those guys, if I have a king and a queen, I love my hand.

Now I got two guys sitting over here on my left with short stacks, they're going to kill me. I'm giving them money when I raise with king-queen, but I'll more than make up for it because the guy that limps in front of me, he'll be limping with a queen and an eight, and he'll call the raise. I'm going to have him in terrible shape. So the short stacks behind make money from me in the long run in this spot. But I make up for it because of this guy that limps and calls the raise.

If the chips are really deep, and you have a good image, I don't see anything wrong with raising in the dark. Sometimes I've had players tell me they knew what I had and I hadn't looked at my hand yet!

Talk a little bit about table image. What changes your image from good to bad and back again? It would seem to a lot of players that if you play a lot of poker, and you must see a lot of the same players day after day, your image would be a pretty constant thing.

Your bluffs just work more often when you show over the best hand. And if you show over enough of them, it's really, really hard for them to call you. Even in limit poker, when a bluffing situation comes up, if you have a good image, you should bluff. If you have a bad image, they're going to study and study and study and call you. If you have a good image, they're going to study and study and throw their hand away. It's just that simple. Even at limit poker, you can really see the difference. At no-limit, it's a very, very big difference.

So just remembering all the cards you've had to show down since the session started is a huge edge.

It comes down to a simple question — did you show the winning hand? That's what counts. Did you win the pot?

If you take an ace-king and beat two aces, that counts. If you take the seven-four offsuit and beat the two aces, that's great for your image. They're scared of you because you showed only the best hand at the end. If you keep showing the best hand, if every time you show your hand you take the pot, it's just hell to call you.

I remember the time, it was on TV, when Tommy Franklin had a pair of eights and I had ace-nine and had made a big raise on him, and he just studied and studied and said "You know, I know you're making a move in this situation, and I saw you make the move before, and you hit the hand, I ain't going to go for it anymore," and he threw the hand away.

There you are. That's it exactly. He was right. Your image is just what you showed over. And it can even carryover when you're playing with the same people a lot. It carries over. So when you've been on a run, it still counts, although your image in general doesn't really last too long. It's the next hand or two that either maintains it or destroys it.

That switch can happen very quickly, can't it? You've been running well at the table, pushing people around, and then a couple of bad beats or whatever and you suddenly have to say "Okay, my image has changed. They're looking at me differently, I now have to play differently."

You bluffed, you got caught, and that changes everything. I play tighter after that.

That puts you in contrast to some of the younger players that you see at the table. When they get caught bluffing, they figure they'd better step up the bluffs now. It becomes a point of pride.

Well, you know, against a particular opponent, it depends what he's thinking. But in general, I don't like that. Your image is created by winning pots and showing the best hand. Or by winning a lot of pots.

How do you feel about raise sizes? There's a trend these days towards the mini-raise in early position, just raising to twice the big blind.

Well, I don't like that play. If I have aces, I'll raise — generally, I always raise the size of the pot. If I'm first in the pot, that means a raise to three and one-half big blinds. I'll do that with two aces, or with a five-four type hand, either one. What you hope for, with two aces, is to get in the third bet before the flop. With the deep stacks now, the second raise isn't that big. You really want to make the third raise. That's why, with the deep stacks, I want to make the third raise with the two aces.

You raise in early position, you get reraised by somebody behind you, and you want to make the third raise.

Right, and see if they can get away from their hand. See if they can get away from two kings.

How do you go about sizing up new players? Guy sits down at your table in the Commerce Club, you've never seen him before, what are the first couple of things you look at? What do you start to pick up first?

I look at his age, the way he handles his chips, the way he's dressed —

What's his age likely to tell you about him? How is a young player different from an older player, typically?

He's not likely to be an old player and be a very good player. Odds are. A young player, you don't know. Could be a really good Internet player. Could be a big donkey. But if it's an older guy, and he's well dressed, and he doesn't know how to cut his chips, he's a turkey. You can lay 10-to-1 on it. He's just not going to be a good player.

So you know he's not good, but you don't know exactly yet how he's not good. That you're going to have to see a few hands.

Sure, absolutely. But in general, you know what bad players do. They check their good hands. They trap with good hands. They lead off and bet their mediocre hands to find out "where they're at." Boy, I love that. You want to bet to find out where you're at? Okay, I'll tell you, you're in big trouble.

Question about Doyle. Do you think Doyle's game has changed over the years? It seems like no matter how far the game has come, Doyle's stayed near the top. And he's perfectly comfortable playing tournaments or cash or whatever. Do you think he's a player who's sort of steadily progressed in his approach? I don't get the sense watching him that he plays the way he described in Super/System years ago.

There's two things about that. First, he doesn't play no-limit hold 'em in the big cash games. That just isn't played anymore in the Big Game at the Bellagio which is where he mostly plays now. I can tell you for sure how he played in the 1970s, but how he plays now, well, I wouldn't think it has changed very much. I'm sure it has not. But Super System was a pretty accurate description of how he played at the time.

Observing his play, it looks like he plays tighter than he did then.

It was probably because the game he described in *Super/System* is really a big stack game. He didn't emphasize stack sizes in the book because all the games at the time were deep stack games, with people buying in for 400 big blinds.

Now, when they do play a little no-limit at the Bellagio, it's a capped game. It has $1,000 and $2,000 blinds and a $75,000 cap on the pot because they've got huge stacks on the table, and they don't want to get a million in the pot on one hand. And most of the players there don't play the game. They're not comfortable playing no-limit hold 'em.

Now seven-six is no good! You can't play the seven-six in that game. Except perhaps every great once in a while to show you don't always have big cards, I don't know. Probably you don't ever bother to play two little cards in that game. It's just too much like a limit game.

But Doyle's got a good thing going in the *High Stakes Poker* show. He said it was the best game he ever played in. It does look like a very good game.

I know you object to the way a lot of the players on that show handle the trouble hands. What are your thoughts on playing these ace-queen or king-jack type hands?

I remember one play that was so bad it was just beyond belief, at least for me. Daniel Negreanu raises a pot with the ace-queen offsuit. Okay, we'll put a question mark there. In my mind, put a question mark by that play. Maybe it's okay. That's a three-way hand for me. I don't mind raising with it. I don't mind calling with it. I don't mind throwing it away. How do you like that? It's just okay. Now Todd Brunson reraises and Daniel calls!

Now if my choice was to call with the ace-queen, or to take two cards, not out of the deck, but out of the muck, that the other players had mucked, give me the two out of the muck. Now I hope I catch a seven and a four, you know. And at least I don't have an ace in my hand.

The way this hand made TV, it came queen-high, and Daniel won a nice pot. And Todd did have ace-king. But not Gabe or anyone mentioned what a horrible play that was, the call of that reraise.

They're calling decent raises from early position with king-jack in late position.

That's another example. I'd rather throw the king-jack away and pick two cards from the discards. If I get 6♥3♥, that's fine.

So if you're playing against a guy raising from early position, and for whatever reason you think he doesn't have a pair, your main goal is to make sure you're not dominated.
Well, let's say one of your main goals is to stay out of a bind. If I have a six and a trey, it's hard to get in a real bind. If I have a king and a jack, and I make a pair, it's really hard to play, it's a really tough spot to be in. What do you want to do with the king-jack? You want to make a straight, or trips, or two pair. You don't want to make one pair because it's hard to make one pair and make any money. It's a terrible spot to be in. It's a trouble hand. You want to stay out of it. Stay out of trouble. That's why they call them trouble hands. Good players have trouble playing them, and bad players will lose a fortune.

So with the 6♥3♥, you want the hearts to come, or two pair or a straight to come.
For me, it's okay if a good flop for the king-jack comes. It's just as good. It's just as good to have a six-high as to have two kings with a jack kicker, almost. There's not a lot of difference in the two hands. I know I'll make some money with the 6-high. With the other hand, I might make some or lose a lot, but over time I'll show a little profit as well. That's the thing.

Elaborate on what you just said because I'm sure a lot of readers will be surprised by that comment.
Okay, look at it this way. Think of a couple of hands where you make a raise in early position and you get a caller. In the first hand you have six-trey offsuit and in the second hand you have king-jack. Now in both hands the flop comes king-seven-deuce, three suits. You bet out on the flop.
Now look at the six-trey hand first. When they fold you take the pot. When they call, you know you're beat. You're

done with the hand. They fold more than they call, so you make a little money.

Now look what happens when you hold king-jack. When they fold, you win the pot like before. But when they call, what did they call you with? Maybe it was AK, KQ, 77, or 22. Those hands are bad news. You're hoping they called you with KT, K-9, or K-8, but most guys who can play a lick don't call with those hands before the flop. Maybe they called you with nine-eight suited and they don't want to throw away middle pair just yet.

The point is, you don't know. You're out of position, and you don't know what's going on, and that's a bad way to try and make some money. I don't know that you show much of a profit with king-jack once you get called here. I don't think you do. That's why I'm pretty much just as happy with six-trey as king-jack when that flop hits.

So the problems you see with the guys on High Stakes Poker are not so much that they're playing middling cards or even low cards that are suited, as that they're playing higher cards that could be easily dominated by still better combinations.

That's part of it. I also see them limp in with weak hands. I don't like that.

You'd rather raise or fold with those hands?

Either. I might call. But I just don't call with a weak hand. Not out front. And if I was playing in Dallas, in the games I used to play in, where there were so many good players in the game, I don't even like limping around back with a weak hand. Because they know what you've got when you limp. If you've got a weak hand and they put you on a weak hand, what are you going to do?

Do you ever fold kings pre-flop?

Well, I can tell you what Sailor Roberts said. If your opponent raises, and you reraise, and your opponent puts in the third raise, and you have two kings, you're a huge underdog to most everyone. You'd probably rather have two queens against a lot of players than have two kings, or you might want to have two queens, putting it better, because if that third raise is either aces, kings, or ace-king, your two queens might be the best hand. But if you've got two kings, and they're only reraising with those three hands, you're obviously close to a 4-to-1 underdog, whatever it works out to be.

But for the third significant raise, and it's against the same person, and you've got two kings, they are big trouble. The most difficult hand in no-limit hold 'em, without doubt, is two kings. I have no idea what to do.

And it's not just a question of being all-in before the flop. What happens in this case? You've got $20-$40 blinds, you're playing a really good, aggressive player. Make it — make it anyone, make it Antonio Esfandiari. Several players will limp in the pot, and he makes a raise, and you're in the little blind. And it's — let's say it's $300 or $400 to you, and he's got $20,000. You've got two kings. What's your play?

I don't have a clue what to do. I mean, I just don't have any idea what to do. Nothing feels good to me. I can make a case for making a mini-raise, I can make a case for calling, I can make a case for making a big raise. I don't like any of them.

But you're not making a case for folding!

No, see that's the problem. You can't fold. You cannot fold. You probably have the best hand. In fact, you're a big favorite to have the best hand. But that's not the problem.

If we just run five cards from here after calling the raise, we're in great shape, but that's not what's going to happen.

You're going to reraise. And now we have all this money left over. Now what flop do you want that doesn't have a king on it? Can't have a king. If you don't catch a king, what do you want? There's nothing that looks good. Suppose it's jack-seven-deuce, three suits. You bet. They call. Now what? That's a nightmare flop. I'd rather have just about anything there. I'd rather have two queens for sure. Much rather have two queens. Maybe that's sick, but that's how I feel. Because it's going to be easier to let go of two queens later on in the hand than it is the kings.

But I hate two kings. I've thrown them away many times before the flop. Against certain players, it's easy. They've got aces, and that's all they've got. I've thrown them away against Bob Brooks. I raised. He reraised. I threw my hand away because I knew he didn't reraise with queens. He would never reraise with two queens.

So he either had two kings, two aces, or a bluff. And he very seldom bluffed. He showed me the two aces. But not many players play as tight as Bob did.

Buck Buchanan was another player like that. You couldn't call Buck in that situation. Buck had a tight game where he never raised before the flop — except with aces, kings, or ace-king, in position. Otherwise, he didn't raise the pot before the flop. He called. Steve Lott plays something like that. He doesn't raise before the flop. He just calls. So you don't know what he's got when he calls. He could have two connectors or he could have a big pair, you don't know. Buck was like that. I think a legitimate way to play preflop.

I remember once with Junior B. I bet. He raised. I looked down at ace-king and said to myself, "You know what, he has queens, I'm going to make him lay them down," I came over the top, and he looked at me for awhile, showed me the kings, and then threw them away!

But a short stack game is a different story.

Oh Lord yes. Two kings are a beautiful hand in a short stack spot, almost the nuts.

But in a deep stack game, it's very different. Now two kings are a hand you can't fall in love with. If you told me I had two kings, but for some reason I couldn't make three kings, I would say, "Just give the kings to someone else." It wouldn't surprise me if in those deep stack situations I was talking about, if you were only a small winner in the pots where you started with two kings but didn't make three kings. The problem is, you lose the big pots, and when you win, you win a small pot. That's why the possibility of making a set is so important. Take the other two kings out of the deck, and let's see how a pocket pair of kings really stand in a situation where each side started with several hundred big blinds. The pots you lose are pretty big. The ones you win are small.

Now back in the 70s, did you run into any trouble playing in fixed games? Did you have any trouble avoiding them? Or were they generally well known among the players?

The way you got cheated in those days was in the country clubs. I didn't get to play in the country clubs. Games I played in, there were a lot of tough players. They were very hard to cheat. Very hard to cheat. Plus, you knew all the players. It's very difficult for a stranger to come through and be a cheat. And especially hard to do it for any length of time. He just stood out. Especially if he couldn't play. Cheats just never lasted very long.

They told me about one guy that came through Dallas in the old days. He was one of these lowball cheats. He never played no-limit hold 'em. He was a hold out guy. He had a machine. You know, the machine?

One of those things up your sleeve?

  He had a machine. Bob Brooks, who was in the game, said that he played so bad that they let this guy play even though they knew he cheated. After a couple of days, they had him stuck about $8,000. That was a lot of money in those days. Finally, one of the suckers in the game wanted to count the cards down. The deck felt light to him. So Bob picked up the cards and he said he counted to about 48 and he said "Oh, that's close enough," and he threw the cards in the trash can! But they asked the guy not to play anymore after that.

  Lowball players in general didn't play hold 'em well. They had a tendency to think that two aces was like a wheel. They'd get a few hundred dollars in before the flop and $3,200 afterwards. But when that happens, a lot of time two aces are no good, especially when folks know what you have.

Present company excepted, give us a list of your 10 or 12 top no-limit cash game players.

  Here goes. These are guys I'd hate to see sit down in my game. In no particular order: Doyle Brunson, TJ Cloutier, Gabe Thaler, Barry Greenstein, Carl McKelvie, Steve Lott, Ben Roberts, Bobby Baldwin, Eric Seidel, Scott Lungren, Prahlad Friedman, and Kenny Tran.

  I'll add something about one name on that list. Bobby Baldwin was the best player I ever played with in my life, by far.

That's high praise.

  He was the best no-limit hold 'em player I ever saw. He was frightening. When I looked at my hand, I was afraid he knew what I had. As soon as I looked at my cards, I thought he knew somehow. He was a wonderful player. A fine nine-handed player, and a great two-handed player. You don't often see that combination together. Even Doyle said so.

I would sit next to him and he would call people's hands. He was 26 years old, and it just made me sick he was so much better than I was. That's the only person I ever felt that way about.

Let's talk about some specific tactical situations. How do you feel about bluffing out of the small blind against some limpers?
I think bluffing out of the small blind before the flop is a good place to bluff. It's a feel thing. It depends on how often the back players limp in and how likely players are to call the raise no matter what. But if they're trying to win and playing fairly tight, a big raise out of the small blind before the flop, when you had some back limpers, can be very effective.

Now, in a really tough game, everybody knows that play. So it's just a question of — they know and you know that they know that you know. So we're into multi-level thinking here. And then it's a question of — do they have the courage to do anything about it?

On High Stakes Poker they call that the Barry Greenstein play. He does that all the time. And give Ted Forrest full credit. Barry Greenstein did it the first time, and then the next time around he raised again from the small blind, and Ted said "No way, he's got something this time," and he did have something.
Well, a strong play is like what Bobby Baldwin showed me years ago. He bluffed me, and a few deals later, he bluffs me again, and he shows me, and says "The second bluff against a good player is the good one." He bluffed me twice in a row.

What do you think about playing very low cards in late position — hands like three-two or four-two?
I would always limp on the button with those sorts of hands if the stacks were deep.

I saw you win a huge pot in the $25-$50 game online with trey-deuce. Flop came ace-five-four, and you hit someone with three aces.

That's exactly what that hand is designed for. It's the wheel. The wheel's got the record pots at hold-em.

Your thoughts on playing the flop after you hit a little piece of it.

When I was so much more aggressive, in the early 1970s, I just didn't bet the flop when I caught a piece because I had people playing back at me. So in that spot, when I had something, I took a card. Because, whoopee, I've got something. But if I didn't have anything, and they played back at me, so what? But if you've got something, and they play back at you, you might have to throw away the best hand.

But I overdid it. I had them playing back at me quite often. It's a great way to learn how to play, however. If I was going to recommend a way of learning how to play, it would be a great way to learn.

You've got a little reputation for jabbing at pots on the river with very small bets. What's your thinking there?

I'll do it in a lot of different situations. If the minimum bet is $10, I might make a $10 value bet on the end, or a stone bluff. You have to be careful because they might take it away from you. But after you bet $10 a bunch of times, they might not take it away from you. I might call them when they raise me.

That's another one of those plays where they're thinking about what you're thinking about what they're thinking. But I've won those pots a lot where I make those little bets at the river and sometimes call a big reraise.

But if you do it very much — I'm one of the few players who does it — you also have to do it occasionally, when you play all the same players all the time, with the cold nuts.

Absolutely.

You're really giving someone with nothing a chance to bluff his money off twice! Say you've got a board where a jack is the nuts, filling an inside straight. And you've got a jack. Now your opponent bets, and he's bluffing at you. The right play in that spot is to make the minimum raise. Make the $10 raise or whatever it is. You can't lose, and you give them a chance to bluff again, if they're bluffing.

I remember once Bob Ciaffone said in that situation, "I would be in favor of making the minimum bet, $5 or whatever, except that I don't know when to do it." So I told him when.

But in my life, I have stolen a number of pots for one chip. Completely stolen. I have done that several times. The thing is, they get sick of paying you off. They just get sick of it. So they let you have a pot for one chip. Sounds incredible, but it happens.

We're seeing a lot more people at the tables who are willing to go beyond a single continuation bet on the flop. If they get called, they'll fire a second barrel on the turn. How do you defend against that?

The question is, how to play against strangers? If you're playing against strangers, I like to get a feel for the situation. Does he just fire one barrel or does he continue with his continuation bets?

How about — such a rare person, the three-barrel guy? He just fires and keeps coming!

Scratch those off the list. I don't like the three-barrel guys unless they're completely crazy.

Exactly. How do you defend against them?

I'm a three-barrel guy, so I know it's hard to play against me. My friend Carl [McKelvie], he's been in with me a lot, he hates it when I fire three barrels. But I would bet my life I'm winner on the third barrel.

And, I know it does good things for your game. Now it makes that first bet on the flop much harder to call.

Let's say you sit down at a table where you know most of the players, and you have a choice of seats. What do you look for in picking your seat?

One thing I really like is to have a limper on my right. That's so important for a lot of different hands. When I pick up that ace-x suited, I want the player on my right to limp. Then you can get a whole cascade of limpers.

That's why position is so important. If you get a limper on your right, it's just huge for all kinds of things like that. Small pairs, ace-x suited, those kinds of hands, it's so much easier to get the shape of the pot that you want before the flop.

The other thing I like to see are players that are really easy to read. There are some players that are just incredible. Every time they make a little bet, they have a little hand. Every time they make a bigger bet, they have a bigger hand. They just tell you exactly what they have. It's like cheating!

Bobby, thanks for your time.

A pleasure. Hey, let's find a game!

Conclusion

Now that you've finished the two volumes of *Harrington on Cash Games*, you should have a pretty good idea on how cash games should be handled. Let's summarize the key ideas we have covered.

- **Deep stack cash games are the most challenging, but also the most rewarding, form of no-limit hold 'em.** All forms of no-limit hold 'em are challenging, but the particular challenge of deep stack cash games is that no decisions are trivial. Although in tournaments moves can be forced by the dwindling stack sizes, in deep stack games each play must be carefully considered because your entire stack is at risk at all times.

- **Always be aware of your stack size, your opponent's stack size, and the size of the pot.** As more of your money goes into the pot, you're increasingly likely to become pot-committed. Unless you have a very strong hand, you don't want to marry yourself to the pot. Remember that even a very deep stack actually contains relatively few bets, so use them carefully.

- **Remember that you must play more than premium hands to be successful.** If you restrict yourself to a limited range of quality hands, your opponents will know that many flops cannot help you. In order to win your opponent's whole stack, you must have a hand which is unexpected given what your opponent knows. The difference between tight and loose players is only that loose players play even more deceptive hands than tight players. Big stacks imply better implied odds, which implies you should play more hands.

367

Index

NOTES

NOTES

NOTES

Books from Two Plus Two

MASON MALMUTH
Blackjack Essays

Includes:
- Card Domination
- Theoretical Concepts
- Blackjack Biasis
- Mistaken Ideas
- Current Blackjack
- Casino Play
- Obsolete Techniques
- Front Loading
- Supplemental Strategies

US $24.95

For T...

GAMBLING THEORY and Other Topics
by **Mason Malmuth**

Includes...
- Gambling Theor...
- Pseudo T...
- Poker Tour...
- New Games ...

Absolutely
for All Ser...

$19.95

THE PROFESSIONAL Poker Dealer's *HANDBOOK*

Dan Paymar • Donna Harris • Mason Malmuth

MASON MALMUTH
Poker Essays

Includes:
- General Concepts
- Technical Ideas
- Structure
- Strategic Ideas
- Image

In...
Pok...

Absol...
For All ...

For Both Hold 'e...

WINNING CONCEPTS IN DRAW AND LOWBALL
by Mason Malmuth

$24.95

INCLUDES
- Reasons
- Advanced Strategy
- ...Mistakes
- High Draw Math
- ...Strategy
- Psychology
- ...ical Plays
- Killing the Pot
- ...nced Plays
- Game Theory
- ...ot Games
- Poker Engine Results

...ADING FOR ALL SERIOUS PLAYE...

MASON MALMUTH
Poker Essays
Volume III

$24.95

Includes:
- General Concepts
- Technical Ideas
- Strategic Ideas
- In the Cardrooms
- Hands to Talk About
- The Ciaffone Quiz
- Two More Quizzes

For Both Hold 'em and Stud Players

MASON MALMUTH
Poker Essays
Volume II

$24.95

Includes:
- General Concepts
- Technical Ideas
- Structure
- Strategic Ideas
- In the Cardrooms
- Poker Quizzes
- Erroneous Concepts
- Something Silly

For Both Hold 'em and Stud Players

Books from Two Plus Two

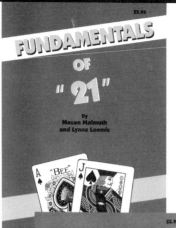